T0385897

high note 2

Workbook

Pearson
KAO TWO
KAO Park
Hockham Way
Harlow, Essex
CM17 9SR
England
and Associated Companies throughout the world

www.english.com/highnote

© Pearson Education Limited 2020

The right of Rod Fricker to be identified as author of this work has been asserted by him in accordance with the Copyright, Designs and Patents Act, 1988.

All rights reserved. No part of this publication may be reproduced, stored in a retrieval system, or transmitted in any form or by any means, electronic, mechanical, photocopying, recording or otherwise without the prior written permission of the Publishers.

First published in 2020
Sixth impression 2023
ISBN: 978-1-292-20949-4
Set in Akko Pro
Printed in Slovakia by Neografia

Image Credit(s)

The publisher would like to thank the following for their kind permisson to reproduce their photographs:

123RF.com: Antonio Guillem 65, Boris Divizinuk 30, choreograph 53, Dima Sobko 42, dolgachov 102, fffranz 30, Georg Henrik Lehnerer 80, Heinz Leitner 40, jedimaster 114, José Alfonso de Tomas Gargantilla 32, lopolo 73, rangga173 21, Richard Semik 29, satina 45, Sergey Novikov 80, sorax 89, Wavebreak Media Ltd 17; **Alamy Stock Photo**: Bill Cheyrou 93, Cultura Creative (RF) 83, Francisco Gonzalez Sanchez 102, Juliet Brauner 52; **Getty Images**: Corbis / Fuse 4, DigitalVision / David Sacks 46, DigitalVision / PictureNet Corporation 47, E+ / Pavliha 29, E+ / Stigur Már Karlsson / Heimsmyndir 67, Icon Sportswire / Jason Mowry 21, iStock / contrastaddict 8, iStock / mediaphotos 103, iStock / monkeybusinessimages 90, iStock / SolStock 70, Photolibrary / Hans-Peter Merten 83, Photolibrary / Scott Montgomery 78, Photos. com / Jupiterimages 116, Sebastian Meyer 34, 35, The Image Bank / Terry Williams 88, Westend61 100; **Shutterstock.com**: 41, Adrian Niederhaeuser 41, antoniodiaz 59, 107, Artazum 55, Bardocz Peter 35, beats1 43, 59, Bika Ambon 85, Daniel M Ernst 11, EPA / Ferdy Damman 105, George Rudy 81, gevision 36, Gorodenkoff 80, 91, happysmiling 99, hxdyl 45, ITV 113, Jaromir Chalabala 29, KateChe 30, KC2525 123, Kiselev Andrey Valerevich 102, Kletr 80, Kobal / Universal Tv 112, Kryuchka Yaroslav 30, kudia 6, LifeCollectionPhotography 36, Markus Gann 117, mentatdgt 9, metamorworks 109, Monkey Business Images 7, 85, Moviestore Collection 119, Mtsaride 21, newyear 30, ollyy 25, Pixel-Shot 101, Rawpixel.com 94, SpeedKingz 54, Syda Productions 5, 58

Cover Image: *Front:* **Getty Images:** skynesher

All other images © Pearson Education

Illustration Acknowledgements

Illustrated by Kavel Rafferty (Illustration) p19, p23, p51, p57, p69, p71, p97; Stefanie Clemen (Illustration) p106, p120-121; Ivan Gillet (NB Illustration) p33, p41, p43, p44, p49, p56, p63, p68 (l), p76-77, p95.

Every effort has been made to trace the copyright holders and we apologise in advance for any unintentional omissions. We would be pleased to insert the appropriate acknowledgement in any subsequent edition of this publication.

CONTENTS

01 Close to you

1A GRAMMAR AND VOCABULARY

Present Simple and Present Continuous

1 ⭐ **Match the two parts of the sentences.**

1 ☐ Joe is
2 ☐ What are you
3 ☐ Where do they usually
4 ☐ Amelia often
5 ☐ Jack and Sam never
6 ☐ My dad
7 ☐ Ian's parents usually
8 ☐ How many guests are they
9 ☐ How do you

a usually listen to music?
b eats lunch in the park next to the school.
c agree about anything.
d carrying in your bag? It's really heavy.
e get home at 4 p.m., but today they're late.
f meet their grandparents?
g inviting to their wedding?
h loves watching old films in his bed.
i looking for a summer job in a café.

2 ⭐ **Choose the correct forms to complete the sentences.**

1 What language ___ at the moment?
   a does Elizabeth speak
   b Elizabeth is speaking
   c is Elizabeth speaking

2 Peter and Helen ___ to school on time.
   a hardly ever come
   b come hardly ever
   c are hardly ever coming

3 My brother isn't very sporty, but he ___ a lot of football this summer.
   a plays
   b play
   c is playing

4 I usually ___ my dad's car on Saturday.
   a am washing
   b wash
   c washing

5 ___ letters to your friends?
   a Do you sometimes write
   b Are you sometimes writing
   c Do you write sometimes

6 They ___ their piano lesson today because their teacher is ill.
   a are having
   b don't have
   c aren't having

3 ⭐⭐ **Choose the correct forms to complete the conversation.**

Eliza Hello, James. Come in. Cathy **1**_has / is having_ a shower at the moment. She **2**_always gets up / is always getting up_ late on a Saturday. Come into the kitchen. I **3**_have / 'm having_ breakfast. Are you hungry?

James No. I'm fine, thanks.

Eliza Do you want some coffee?

James No, thanks. I **4**_don't often drink / 'm not often drinking_ coffee.

Eliza How **5**_do you get on / are you getting on_ at school this year?

James Quite well, thanks. I **6**_study / 'm studying_ a lot at the moment because I want to do medicine at university. I enjoy the challenge though, so I **7**_don't mind / am not minding_.

Eliza Cathy **8**_works / is working_ hard at the moment, too. Well, actually, she **9**_always works / is always working_ hard. She ...

Cathy **10**_Do you talk / Are you talking_ about me, Mum? Hi, James. I'm ready. Let's go. Bye, Mum. See you later!

4 ⭐⭐ **Complete the sentences with the correct forms of the verbs in brackets.**

Steve **1**_usually wears_ (usually/wear) jeans and a T-shirt, but today he **2**_____ (go) to a party so he **3**_____ (wear) a smart shirt and trousers.

Matt and Jenny **4**_____ (often/argue) about money. At the moment, they **5**_____ (shop) and they **6**_____ (argue) about a wedding gift that Matt wants to buy for his brother.

John **7**_____ (not often/meet) his cousin because she **8**_____ (live) in the USA, but this week, she **9**_____ (stay) in the UK with John's family.

5 ★★ Read the answers and use the prompts from the box to write questions.

What language / they / speak?
What languages / Max / speak?
What / you / do?
~~What / your dad / do?~~
Where / you / go?
Where / your parents / go / every Thursday?

1 *What does your dad do?*
He's an engineer.

2 _____
I think they're speaking Chinese, but I'm not sure.

3 _____
To the supermarket. We need some milk.

4 _____
He speaks French, Italian and a little Spanish.

5 _____
To the Save the Cats home – they do voluntary work there once a week.

6 _____
We're making a cake. Do you want to help us?

6 ★★ Look at the underlined words and choose *S* for state verbs and *A* for action verbs.

1 I don't <u>know</u> anyone here.   S / A
2 Do you <u>understand</u> this question?   S / A
3 I <u>have</u> breakfast every morning at seven o'clock. S / A
4 Nick <u>agrees</u> with our idea.   S / A
5 Lucy <u>makes</u> cakes for her friends every Sunday.   S / A
6 Tom <u>thinks</u> this book is very interesting.   S / A
7 Why don't you <u>go</u> to the cinema more often?   S / A
8 This ice cream <u>tastes</u> great. What flavour is it? S / A
9 I <u>hate</u> films which don't have a happy ending.   S / A

7 ★★ Use the prompts to write sentences in the Present Simple and Present Continuous.

1 This is a great party. you / enjoy / it?
Are you enjoying it?

2 Wait a minute. I / talk / to Steve / on the phone
_____

3 Vicky and Stella / learn / French / this year
_____

4 you / know / who that boy / be?
_____

5 This cake / taste / strange
_____

6 you / agree / with me?
_____

7 The best man / give / a speech. It's really funny!
_____

8 We / not believe / you / tell the truth / at the moment
_____

8 ★★★ Complete the conversation with the correct Present Simple or Present Continuous forms of the verbs from the box.

do (x2) not understand organise try usually/hate
watch you/like you/want

Agata Hello?
Maria Hi, Agata. It's Maria. What **¹***are you doing*?
Agata I **²**_____ a film on my computer right now.
         ³_____ Hugh Jackman? It's one of his films.
Maria Yes, of course. He's one of my favourite actors. Is it a musical?
Agata Yes, it is. I **⁴**_____ musicals, but this one is quite good. How about you?
Maria I **⁵**_____ my homework – well, I **⁶**_____ to do it, but it's hard. I **⁷**_____ some of the exercises.
Agata **⁸**_____ to meet up this evening? We can go to a café and I can help you with your homework.
Maria Sorry, I can't. My parents **⁹**_____ a big family dinner, but thanks for the offer. Oh, Mum's calling me. Talk to you later. Bye!
Agata Bye!

9 ON A HIGH NOTE Write a short paragraph about yourself. What is your normal daily routine on a school day? How is it different from today?

1B READING AND VOCABULARY

1 Read the first two paragraphs of the text quickly. Write the names of the people in the photos.

a *Martin*   e _____   i _____
b _____   f _____   j _____
c _____   g _____   k _____
d _____   h _____   l _____

2 Read the text and match headings A–I with paragraphs 1–8. There is one extra heading.

A Entertaining discussions
B Advantages and disadvantages
C Disorganised but happy
D Thoughts about the future
E Enjoying the differences
F A family of nine
G No brothers or sisters
H Taking an interest
I A difficult question to answer

3 Read the text again and complete the notes with 1–3 words in each gap.

1 Emma and Alec have got *two young children*.
2 All of Jeff's family enjoy _____.
3 In the photo, Rebecca and her parents are on _____.
4 The topic that Rebecca and her parents don't always agree about is _____.
5 One thing that Jeff appreciates about Rebecca's home is the _____.
6 Jeff's parents couldn't afford to send their children on _____.

Vocabulary extension

4 Match the highlighted words and phrases from the text with the definitions.

1 Not having any brothers or sisters.
   only child
2 Brothers and sisters.
   _____
3 When a couple plan to marry.
   _____
4 Look after a son or daughter and help them grow.
   _____
5 The husband of your sister or your husband or wife's brother.
   _____
6 The care of children by trained people while parents are at work.
   _____

ACTIVE VOCABULARY | Suffixes -ful, -ic, -able

We can add the suffixes -ful, -ic and -able to some verbs and nouns to create adjectives.

---

5 Look at these three adjectives from the text and the words which they were formed from. Then complete the table with the correct adjective forms of the words from the box.

- **joyful** (adjective) – very happy
  joy (noun)
- **chaotic** (adjective) – very disorganised
  chaos (noun)
- **enjoyable** (adjective) – very happy
  enjoy (verb)

agree athlete hero ~~peace~~ poet predict remark
skill wonder

-ful	-ic	-able
peaceful		

6 Complete the sentences with the adjectives from Exercise 5.

1 Emily is very *skillful* at drawing. She's got real talent.
2 Matt is a(n) _____ young man – he's kind and gentle.
3 Jumping into the sea to save that young girl was a _____ thing to do.
4 Harry uses beautiful words and phrases in his writing – it's very _____.
5 What a(n) _____ meal! I want to come to this restaurant again.
6 The park is such a(n) _____ place; there are no cars or motorbikes – only the sound of the birds.
7 This film is a bit _____; you always know what's going to happen next.
8 Ashley is very _____ and is good at all the sports she tries.
9 My aunt is a(n) _____ woman. She is raising three children and is also the director of a successful business.

7 ON A HIGH NOTE Compare your family with a friend's family. Write a short paragraph about the size of each family and some of each family's routines.

Is there a perfect family size?

1 ☐ Jeff is a twenty-two year old student. He's celebrating his birthday today. That's him on the right, close to the camera. He's next to his mum, Betty. We can also see his brother-in-law, Alec, and Alec's wife, Emma. She's standing up. At the end of the table is Jeff's dad, Nigel with Emma's two young children, Hamish and Alice. The other two people are Jeff's sisters, Melissa and Meghan – Meghan is the one with darker hair. They love spending time together as a family.

2 ☐ Rebecca, the young woman in the other photo, is an only child. She's with her mum and dad, Rose and Martin, having a cup of coffee on holiday. They get on very well with each other.

3 ☐ Life at home is very different for Jeff and Rebecca. Jeff's house is always a bit chaotic, but full of joyful laughter. Emma's children often come to visit as they live very close to their grandparents. Jeff and Melissa are at university and sometimes they stay up late to study or go out with friends. Jeff's mum and dad never know who they can expect for dinner or when, except on Sundays when Emma and her family always join them for a long, relaxed lunch.

4 ☐ At Rebecca's house, meal times are quieter, but also enjoyable. Rebecca and her parents chat about work and friends and all three enjoy discussing politics. Their opinions aren't always the same but they are happy to 'agree to disagree' with each other.

5 ☐ Jeff and Rebecca are engaged to be married. Their wedding is in four months. But what kind of family would they like to have – a big family like Jeff's or a small family like Rebecca's?

6 ☐ Jeff and Rebecca's homes are very different, but they often visit each other. Jeff enjoys the quiet atmosphere at Rebecca's house and she likes the fact that, at Jeff's house, you never know what might happen next. 'It's funny,' says Rebecca, 'We sometimes talk about our future family. Jeff thinks a small family like mine is a great idea, but I sometimes look at his family and think that I'd like to have lots of children one day.'

7 ☐ 'There is a problem with that plan though,' says Rebecca. 'I read that to raise a child from birth to the age of twenty-one in the UK, you need about £230,000!' she says. 'So maybe a big family isn't such a good idea. It might be more sensible to stick to having just one or two children. I know that a lot of my friends struggle to pay for childcare and education.' However, Jeff is quick to add, 'you say that, but in a big family like mine, children often share clothes and toys, so the financial side isn't as difficult as you might think. And having plenty of money isn't the most important thing about family anyway. Maybe my siblings and I didn't go on expensive holidays, but on the other hand, we learned a lot from each other about love, sharing and responsibility.'

8 ☐ So, is there a perfect family size? The answer depends on so many different things that it really isn't possible to say, and parents often change their mind. A couple with one child may later want more kids while a couple who want a large family might finally decide that one child is enough. What about Jeff and Rebecca? 'It's a difficult question,' says Rebecca. 'We can tell you, but not now. Maybe in twenty years!'

1C **VOCABULARY** | Family, personality

1 ★ **Complete the descriptions with the words from the box.**

adopted   divorced   half-sister   single mother
stepfather   twins   ~~widower~~

1 Charlie is seventy-five. His wife, Betty, died last year. He's a _widower_.

2 Howard and my mother are married now. I really like him. He's my _____.

3 Debbie and Simon were married but now they aren't. They're _____.

4 Millie has the same mum as me but a different father. She's my _____.

5 Vicky has two children. Their father doesn't live with them now and Vicky looks after them alone. She's a _____.

6 Amber gets on very well with her mum and dad although they aren't her birth parents. She's_____.

7 Aaron and Tim are brothers. They were born on the same day, but Aaron is half an hour older than Tim. They're _____.

2 ★★ **Complete the sentences with one personality adjective in each gap.**

1 Amy is very g_enerous_ – she often buys me presents.

2 Don't be r_____ – say 'hello' and 'thank you'.

3 My little cousin is always very g_____ with his pet mouse because he doesn't want to hurt it.

4 Why are you always so s_____? You only ever think about yourself!

5 My grandfather is very k_____ – he always gives food to stray cats in the neighbourhood.

6 I find it difficult to relax. I'm n_____ and I panic easily.

7 Kelly is so s_____ that she finds it difficult to talk to people or to make new friends.

8 My Physics teacher is very s_____ and nobody is allowed to talk in class.

9 Carl is so v_____ that he always stops to look at himself in every shop window he passes!

10 Our new neighbours were really h_____ when we moved in – they even carried some boxes for us.

3 ★★ **Choose the correct words to complete the sentences.**

1 The cat is cleaning _it / itself_. Look at _it / itself_ – it's so sweet!

2 Don't worry about _me / myself_ – I can carry these bags by _me / myself_.

3 Do you want me to go with _you / yourself_ or will you talk to the director by _you / yourself_?

4 My parents haven't got time to cook and clean the house _them / themselves_, so I always help _them / themselves_ when I haven't got much homework.

5 That's Vicky. She loves taking photos of _her / herself_ and posting them online. She's very popular. Everyone in her class likes _her / herself_.

6 Our grandmother made this cake for _us / ourselves_. Now we want to make a cake _us / ourselves_.

4 ★★ **Complete the sentences with reflexive pronouns.**

1 Our dad is working late today, so we're making dinner by _ourselves_.

2 The computer will switch _____ off after about ten minutes.

3 That funny noise is my brother singing to _____ in the shower!

4 There are three of you. You can tidy the house by _____.

5 I don't like being in the house at night by _____.

6 Peter bought _____ a new suit for the wedding.

7 This is a great game. You can see that the children are enjoying _____!

8 My grandmother lives by _____, but she's got lots of friends so she isn't lonely.

5 ★★★ **Complete the second text with one word in each gap so that it has the same meaning as the original text.**

> Kelly's got a brother who is the same age as her. They look similar, but they have different personalities. Kelly tells other people what to do all the time. Her brother, Tom, is very nice and friendly and always thinks about other people more than he thinks about what he wants or needs. Tom likes meeting new people, but Kelly prefers to spend time on her own.

> Kelly and her brother are [1]_twins_. They look similar, but have very different personalities. Kelly is very [2]_____. Her brother, Tom, is very [3]_____ and thinks about other people more than he thinks about [4]_____. Tom isn't [5]_____ – he likes meeting new people, but Kelly prefers to spend time by [6]_____.

6 ON A HIGH NOTE **Write a short paragraph about two friends or members of your family. Describe their personality and give examples of their behaviour which show this personality.**

UNIT VOCABULARY PRACTICE > page 13

Indefinite pronouns

1 ⭐ **Choose the correct words to complete the sentences.**

1 I haven't got ___ to say to you.
  a nothing **b** something **c** anything

2 Is there ___ else you'd like to visit while you are here?
  a anywhere **b** everywhere **c** nowhere

3 We're bored. There's ___ to do here.
  a anything **b** something **c** nothing

4 I want to go ___ exciting next year, like India.
  a anywhere **b** somewhere **c** everywhere

5 Do you know ___ here?
  a somebody **b** nobody **c** anybody

6 Listen, ___. I have something important to tell you.
  a everyone **b** someone **c** anyone

2 ⭐ **Replace the underlined parts in the sentences below with indefinite pronouns with the same meaning.**

1 I want to go <u>to all the countries</u> on this list.
  I want to go *everywhere* on this list.

2 I know <u>nothing</u>.
  I don't know _____.

3 Let's meet at a different <u>place</u>.
  Let's meet _____ different.

4 I know <u>all the people</u> in my school.
  I know _____ in my school.

5 My brother doesn't do <u>anything</u> to help in the house.
  My brother does _____ to help in the house.

6 He has <u>no place</u> to sleep tonight.
  He has _____ to sleep tonight.

7 Let's call <u>another person</u> to help us.
  Let's call _____ to help us.

8 I don't want <u>any people</u> to see my new haircut – it's terrible!
  I don't want _____ to see my new haircut – it's terrible!

3 ⭐⭐ **Complete the mini-conversations with indefinite pronouns formed from the words in bold.**

THING

Mum Hi, Ed. It's Mum. I'm sorry. I'm still at work and there's **1**<u>*nothing*</u> for you to eat.

Ed Don't worry, Mum. I'll cook **2**_____ for us both. See you later.

WHERE

Rosy I want to go **3**_____ warm this summer.

Harry **4**_____ on this website is very expensive. There isn't **5**_____ under £1000 a week.

BODY

Rachel Is there **6**_____ here?

Dean Yes. I can hear **7**_____. They're coming down the stairs.

4 ⭐⭐⭐ **Complete the mini-conversations with the correct forms of the words from the box.**

everyone/like   everyone/wait   everywhere/look
nobody/know   nobody/make   nothing/be right
something/happen   ~~something/smell~~

Niall Mmm. **1**<u>*something smells*</u> nice. What is it?

Cathy Freshly-baked bread. Would you like some?

Niall Yes, please. Yummy! **2**_____ better bread than you!

Chris Do you want to see the new Ryan Gosling film?

Max No, I don't really like him.

Chris What? **3**_____ Ryan Gosling! He's so cool.

Jane Where are we?

Lisa I don't know. It's too dark. **4**_____ the same at night.

Bella Hi, come in. **5**_____ for you.

Fay I'm sorry I'm late. **6**_____ in the town centre today and all the buses are late.

Mr Green This is a terrible wedding reception. **7**_____ – the band is late, the cake tastes awful and it's really cold in here!

Mrs Green Never mind. Let's go and talk to the newlyweds.

Mr Green I'm afraid we can't. **8**_____ where they are!

5 ON A HIGH NOTE **Look at the quotes which include indefinite pronouns. Write a short paragraph explaining whether you agree with them or not and why.**

- 'Everything has beauty, but not everyone sees it.' *Confucius*

- 'Logic will get you from A to B. Imagination will take you everywhere.' *Albert Einstein*

1E LISTENING AND VOCABULARY

1 🔊 *2* You are going to listen to an interview about learning languages. Before you listen, write information for each of the questions 1–5. Then listen and choose the correct answers.

6.30 a.m.   ~~autumn~~   cousin   Dijon   father
half past five   Italian   Lyon   Spanish   ~~summer~~

1 When does Mike go to France every year? in the *autumn* / *summer*

2 Where does the family live? near _____ / _____

3 What time does the family get up? _____ / _____

4 Who doesn't speak any English? Marie's _____ / _____

5 What other language does Marie speak? _____ / _____

2 🔊 *2* Listen again and choose the correct answers.

1 Mike stays with his stepfather's family once a
   a month.   **b** year.   **c** school term.

2 Mike's French family lives
   a in the middle of a city.
   b close to an airport.
   c away from the city.

3 When he's in France, Mike
   a only speaks English to Marie.
   b speaks English to Marie's mum.
   c never speaks English.

4 How many foreign languages does Marie's father speak?
   a none   **b** one   **c** two

5 At the market, people know Mike is
   a foreign.   **b** French.   **c** English.

Vocabulary extension

3 Match the words from the box, which you heard in the interview in Exercise 1, with the definitions.

accent   communicative   exchange visit   false friend
~~to correct~~

1 Tell someone they have made a mistake and tell them the right thing to say. *to correct*

2 The way of pronouncing a language. _____

3 A word in one language which looks similar to a word in a different language, but which has a different meaning. _____

4 Able to talk to people easily. _____

5 When you go to stay in a different country with a family, usually to learn the language. _____

4 ON A HIGH NOTE Write a short paragraph about the foreign languages you can speak. How often do you use them and what for? Which skills (reading, writing, listening, speaking) are you good at?

Pronunciation

5 🔊 *3* Look at these words from the interview in Exercise 1. How is *u* pronounced in each word? Listen and repeat.

/juː/ comm<u>u</u>nicative
/w/ lang<u>u</u>age
/aʊ/ ho<u>u</u>se
/ʌ/ pron<u>u</u>nciation

ACTIVE PRONUNCIATION | The letter *u*

The letter *u* appears in many different words in English and there are different ways to pronounce it depending on the word in which it appears.

6 🔊 *4* Match the words from the box with the correct phonetic symbols. Listen and check.

biling<u>u</u>al   co<u>u</u>sins   ~~opportunity~~   so<u>u</u>nds

/juː/   *opportunity*
/w/   _____
/aʊ/   _____
/ʌ/   _____

7 🔊 *5* Listen and repeat the words.

8 🔊 *6* It can be difficult to hear the difference between /ʌ/ and /æ/. Listen to these pairs of words. Tick the word you hear first.

1 ☑ b<u>u</u>t   ☐ bat
2 ☐ h<u>u</u>t   ☐ hat
3 ☐ s<u>u</u>nk   ☐ sank
4 ☐ r<u>u</u>ng   ☐ rang
5 ☐ c<u>u</u>t   ☐ cat
6 ☐ s<u>u</u>ng   ☐ sang
7 ☐ r<u>u</u>n   ☐ ran

9 🔊 *6* Listen again and repeat the words from Exercise 8.

10 🔊 *7* Is *ou* in these words pronounced /aʊ/ or /ʌ/? Choose the correct phonetic symbol. Listen, check and repeat.

1 ab<u>ou</u>t   /aʊ/ or /ʌ/
2 c<u>ou</u>nt   /aʊ/ or /ʌ/
3 c<u>ou</u>ntry   /aʊ/ or /ʌ/
4 d<u>ou</u>ble   /aʊ/ or /ʌ/
5 en<u>ou</u>gh   /aʊ/ or /ʌ/
6 s<u>ou</u>nds   /aʊ/ or /ʌ/
7 tr<u>ou</u>ble   /aʊ/ or /ʌ/
8 c<u>ou</u>ple   /aʊ/ or /ʌ/

11 🔊 *8* Practise saying this sentence. Listen and check.

It sounds to me as if the country's favourite couple are about to get into trouble.

1 🔊 *9* **Listen and repeat the phrases. How do you say them in your language?**

SPEAKING | Expressing Interest

ECHO QUESTIONS

'He loves animals.' 'Does he?'

'My sister's really into music.' 'Is she?'

'We've got a band.' 'Have you?'

OTHER EXPRESSIONS

Awesome!

Cool!

Wow!

Really?

Amazing!

That's (really) interesting!

---

2 **Choose the correct echo questions to complete the mini-conversations.**

1

Frank   My mum's Russian.

Jane   ___

a Are they?   **b** Does she?   **c** Is she?

2

Jane   Bob and I come here every year.

Ahmed   ___

a Do we?   **b** Do you?   **c** Is it?

3

Paul   I'm interested in History.

Steve   ___

a Are you?   **b** Do you?   **c** Have you?

4

Molly   My brother's got a beautiful voice.

Sue   ___

a Is he?   **b** Does he?   **c** Has he?

5

Phil   It rains a lot where I live.

Luis   ___

a Is it?   **b** Do you?   **c** Does it?

3 **Match sentences 1–8 with echo questions a–h.**

1 ☐ My cousins are staying with us this weekend.

2 ☐ I'm a big fan of American sports.

3 ☐ Oliver looks good in his new suit.

4 ☐ This is my new photo blog.

5 ☐ Tom and Julie have got a lot in common.

6 ☐ The bride's very late.

7 ☐ This photo always makes me smile.

8 ☐ I keep in touch with my friends from primary school.

a Have they?

b Do you?

c Does it?

d Are they?

e Is it?

f Are you?

g Does he?

h Is she?

4 🔊 *10* **Complete gaps 1–5 in the conversation with echo questions. Then listen to the conversation and complete gaps a–e with other words expressing interest.**

Jesse   Hi, my name's Jesse. I'm here on holiday.

Angie   Hi, me too. I'm Angie. We're staying in a villa.

Jesse   ¹*Are you*? ᵃ*Wow*! Are you here with your family?

Angie   Yes, my mum and dad and my sister.

Jesse   I'm staying at my cousin's house. He lives here.

Angie   ² _____? ᵇ _____! Is he Spanish?

Jesse   He's half Spanish. His mum's English. He's teaching me Spanish.

Angie   ³ _____? ᶜ _____! I don't know any Spanish.

Jesse   Really?

Angie   Well, a few words. I use a smartphone app.

Jesse   ⁴ _____? That's ᵈ _____!

Angie   Here, look. There are useful phrases, games and other activities, and it's completely free.

Jesse   ⁵ _____? ᵉ _____! What topic are you learning at the moment?

Angie   Food and drink. You know, bread, milk, fruit, ice cream …

Jesse   Ice cream! Hey! Let's get an ice cream! It's so hot.

Angie   OK, good idea.

Jesse   er … dos … er …

Angie   Dos helados de chocolate, por favour.

Jesse   Wow! What's the name of that app?

1G WRITING AND VOCABULARY | An informal email of introduction

Greet your friend and thank for the email.

Introduce yourself and give some information about yourself, e.g. your school, hobbies, plans for the future, etc.

Describe your family and where you live.

Mention any other important information for a visitor, e.g. about food, the weather, clothes to bring, etc.

End your email with an informal expression.

Hi Pia,

Thanks for your email. I ¹wish / hope you're well. I'm really happy you're coming to Georgia to visit me.

I'm eighteen years old and I'm a big ²fan / like of sports and outdoor activities. My ³best / favourite activities are walking and climbing in the mountains – Georgia has beautiful mountains. I love spending time there in the summer ⁴because / so I can meet people from lots of different countries and practise my English with them. I'd ⁵want / like to study economics next year at the university here in Tbilisi.

I live with my parents, Giorgi and Mariam, and my sister, Ana. She's fifteen. We live in a house in the city ⁶middle / centre near my grandparents and my uncles and aunts. I've got seven cousins so we're quite a big family!

There are lots of things to do in Georgia. You can swim in the Black Sea, visit beautiful old towns and walk in the mountains. The weather is hot and dry in the summer, but in the mountains it can be cold and wet. So ⁷carry / bring a coat and warm clothes.

I'm looking forward to ⁸meet / meeting you in the summer.

All the ⁹best / love,

Davit

1 Read the email and answer the questions.

1 Why is Davit writing to Pia? *to tell about himself and his family*

2 Who does Davit live with? _____

3 What can you do in Georgia? _____

4 What's the weather like in the mountains?

_____

2 Read the email again and choose the correct words to complete it.

3 Here are other things Davit could write in his email. Match sentences 1–5 with headings a–e.

1 ☐ People say I'm helpful and kind.

2 ☐ It's a great place for sightseeing.

3 ☐ How are you?

4 ☐ I can't wait to meet you.

5 ☐ My parents are great cooks.

a Greetings

b Introduce yourself

c Mention your family and where you live

d Any other important information

e Final greetings

4 Choose the correct words to complete the sentences.

1 The weather is cold so / because bring a coat.

2 It's a popular town so / because it's next to the sea.

3 I go there every summer so / because it's my favourite place.

4 I speak some English so / because I can talk to people who come here.

5 The trains are slow so / because they're very old.

5 WRITING TASK Imagine that you are Brad or Emily. Use the information in the fact file and your imagination to write an email of introduction to a student from a different country who is planning to visit you on a school exchange.

Name:	Brad / Emily
From:	Miami, Florida
Interests:	sailing, dancing
Family:	one brother (Kyle – aged 24, works at a car factory, Orlando); father from Cuba; mother from USA

ACTIVE WRITING | An informal email of introduction

1 Plan your email.

• Thank the person for their email.

• Make brief notes about personal information.

• Make brief notes about your family and where you live.

• Think about anything the person needs to know.

• Choose a final greeting.

2 Write the email.

• Start and finish your email appropriately.

• Use paragraphs to organise your email.

• Use phrases from the Writing box in the Student's Book.

3 Check that ...

• you have included all the relevant information.

• there are no spelling or grammr mistakes.

• you have used interesting and relevant topic vocabulary.

UNIT VOCABULARY PRACTICE > page 13

Wedding
PLANNING

There's a lot to organise before you get [1]m_arried_. The first thing to do is to decide on a day and find a place where you can have the [2]w_____ r_____ – a hotel, a restaurant or even a castle! Your choice depends on how many [3]g_____ you want to [4]i_____ – all the people you know or just your family and close friends.

Next you have to think about your clothes. A smart suit for the [5]g_____ and an elegant, white [6]w_____d_____ for the [7]b_____. This day is once in a lifetime and you want to look as good as you can! And, of course, you need to choose [8]r_____ – most people usually choose gold ones.

Another important thing is the [9]i_____ – you can design them yourselves or ask somebody for help. Don't forget to include all the important information about the wedding – the date, the place and the time. If you want, you can write what kind of [10]g_____ you'd like to receive.

Even if you prepare everything, the wedding day is usually a stressful time for the [11]n_____. So, how can you make it fun and perfect? Read on for our top tips …

1 **1A GRAMMAR AND VOCABULARY** **Complete the article with one word in each gap.**

2 **1B READING AND VOCABULARY** **Choose the correct words to complete the sentences.**

1 Alex is very *open / close* with people and *spends / makes* friends easily.

2 I've got lots of *contacts / companions* on social media, but I don't know many of them personally.

3 My brother doesn't usually *get / keep* on well with other people, so he doesn't have a lot of friends.

4 Jane doesn't *keep / spend* in touch with her friends from Wales. She's at university in Scotland now and *gets / spends* a lot of time with her friends there.

5 I've got *a companion / an acquaintance* in New York – she's a friend of my parents, but I don't know her well.

6 Carl lives in a different city now. He's independent and doesn't *rely / share* on his parents anymore.

3 **1C VOCABULARY** **Choose the correct words to complete the sentences.**

1 'Do this! Don't do that!' Why are you so ___?
a selfish   **b** bossy   **c** nervous

2 My mum is married to Tom now – he's my ___.
a groom   **b** widower   **c** stepfather

3 Wait! It's ___ to start eating before everyone is at the table.
a rude   **b** vain   **c** strict

4 What an amazing present! You're so ___!
a helpful   **b** generous   **c** gentle

5 Sara's not ___, she just likes to wear nice clothes and look smart.
a sweet   **b** vain   **c** shy

6 Don't be so ___! Let your friends play your computer game, too.
a selfish   **b** strict   **c** generous

7 Myra is a ___. Her husband died two years ago.
a widow   **b** half-sister   **c** single mother

8 My father was married before and has a daughter who is my ___.
a twin   **b** half-sister   **c** stepdaughter

4 **1E LISTENING AND VOCABULARY** **Match the two parts of the sentences.**

1 ☐ Peter isn't
2 ☐ Sarah isn't studying
3 ☐ I always mix up
4 ☐ Sometimes I can't find
5 ☐ Most people usually make
6 ☐ Aleksy and Klaudia speak

a a lot of mistakes when they start learning a language.
b the right word when I speak Spanish.
c bilingual, but his Russian is very good.
d German and English. But why? They sound so different!
e Polish, English and French – they're trilingual.
f French at university – she's learning it at home.

5 **1G WRITING AND VOCABULARY** **Complete the text with the verbs from the box. There are two extra verbs.**

arrange   give   introduce   ~~invite~~   offer   pay   ring
say   show   talk

ADVICE FOR HOSTS AND GUESTS

Hosts: When you [1]_invite_ someone to dinner, [2]_____ the visit in advance so that you are ready on the day. It's important to make your guests feel welcome. [3]_____ them to your family and [4]_____ them a drink. You can [5]_____ them around your house too if they have never visited you before.

Guests: Remember that in some countries it is important not to be late. In others, it is important not to be early! When you arrive, [6]_____ the doorbell and, when the hosts open the door, [7]_____ hello in a friendly manner. It's a nice idea to [8]_____ your hosts a gift or some flowers too.

6 ON A HIGH NOTE **Write a short paragraph about yourself. Think about your character, interests and skills.**

1 **For each learning objective, write 1–5 to assess your ability.**

1 = I don't feel confident. 5 = I feel confident.

	Learning objective	Course material	How confident I am (1–5)
1A	I can use present tenses to talk about routines and temporary situations.	Student's Book pp. 4–5	
1B	I can understand the main topic in an article and talk about friends.	Student's Book pp. 6–7	
1C	I can describe my family using personality adjectives and reflexive pronouns.	Student's Book p. 8	
1D	I can use indefinite pronouns with prefixes *some-*, *any-*, *every-* and *no-*.	Student's Book p. 9	
1E	I can find specific information in an interview and talk about language learning.	Student's Book p. 10	
1F	I can use echo questions and other expressions to show interest in a conversation.	Student's Book p. 11	
1G	I can write an email to introduce my family and myself.	Student's Book pp. 12–13	

2 **Which of the skills above would you like to improve in? How?**

Skill I want to improve in	How I can improve

3 **What can you remember from this unit?**

New words I learned and most want to remember	Expressions and phrases I liked	English I heard or read outside class

GRAMMAR AND VOCABULARY

1 Complete the text with one word in each gap.

Carol Ladies and gentlemen. The **¹**g<u>room</u> will now **²**g_____ a speech.

Andy Thank you, everyone! Thank you all for coming to our **³**w_____. It's lovely to see so many people here. Not just our families, but our **⁴**c_____ friends, too. It means a lot to us both that you're here. Thank you for all the wonderful **⁵**g_____. It was very kind and **⁶**g_____ of you and we appreciate them all very much. I'd also like to thank my beautiful **⁷**b_____ for agreeing to marry me, and her parents for helping us to organise this amazing **⁸**r_____ today. I won't talk too long. I know you all want to enjoy **⁹**y_____ on the dance floor but let me tell you how Marie and I first met …

/ 4

2 Choose the correct words to complete the sentences.

1 Promise to __ in touch when you leave.
  a keep   **b** spend   **c** share

2 My best friend would never let me __ if I needed help.
  a out   **b** off   **c** down

3 It's important to have a friend you can rely __.
  a in   **b** on   **c** to

4 It must be very difficult for a(n) __ mother to work and look after her children.
  a single   **b** half   **c** adopted

5 Don't forget to __ your aunt and uncle a drink when they arrive.
  a share   **b** offer   **c** arrange

6 Her English is very good, but she still __ some mistakes with tenses.
  a gets   **b** does   **c** makes

/ 6

3 Complete the sentences with the correct Present Simple or Present Continuous forms of the verbs in brackets.

1 *Do you speak* (you/speak) more than one language?

2 Oh good, it _____ (not rain) this morning, so I can walk to school.

3 Why _____ (you/cry), Helen? What's the problem?

4 Everybody _____ (know) that it isn't easy to be a single mother.

5 Jim _____ (hardly ever/share) his thoughts and feelings – even with his closest friends.

6 What _____ (this word/mean)? Let's check in a dictionary.

7 _____ (you/design) your invitation? Isn't it too late? You're getting married next week!

/ 6

4 Choose the correct indefinite pronouns to complete the sentences.

1 There isn't *nowhere / anywhere* interesting to go and I'm really bored!

2 Listen! *Everyone / Someone* is ringing the doorbell.

3 Excuse me. Is *anybody / nobody* sitting in this seat?

4 Maria isn't shy and gets on well with *everybody / somebody*.

5 There's *anything / nothing* to eat – let's eat out.

6 Who? Where? When? Tell me *everything / nothing*.

/ 6

USE OF ENGLISH

5 Choose the correct words a–c to complete the texts.

1
> *John & Alison* have the pleasure of inviting you to their ___ reception on Saturday, 12th July.

  a newlywed   **b** married   **c** wedding

2
> **DO YOU WANT TO IMPROVE YOUR ENGLISH?**
> Do you sometimes have problems to ____ the right word? Join First English classes.

  a find   **b** make   **c** keep

3
> **TAUNTON TOWN FESTIVAL**
> Family fun, food, music and much, much more! There's something for ___ at Taunton town festival.

  a anyone   **b** everyone   **c** someone

4
> **Student EXCHANGE programme**
> Spend two weeks in France. Meet local people who will ___ you around the town and help you to improve your French.

  a invite   **b** turn   **c** show

/ 4

6 Complete the second sentence using the word in bold so that it means the same as the first one. Use no more than three words including the word in bold.

1 Mum isn't dressing my sister Mia today. **HERSELF**
My sister Mia is *dressing herself* today.

2 Let's stand at the bar – there's nowhere to sit. **ANYWHERE**
I'm not staying here – there _____ to sit.

3 I don't need your help, but thank you anyway. **MYSELF**
I can do _____, but thank you anyway.

4 My English isn't always correct when I speak. **MISTAKES**
I sometimes _____ I try to speak English.

5 I hope the students are having a good time on the school trip. **ENJOYING**
I hope the students _____ on the school trip.

/ 4

/ 30

02 Learn to play

2A GRAMMAR AND VOCABULARY

Past Simple

1 ★ Complete the sentences with the Past Simple form of *to be*.

1 Is he embarrassed because he fell on the floor?

Was he embarrassed because he fell on the floor?

2 Today it's cold and we're hungry.

Last Monday it _____ cold and we _____ hungry.

3 I'm late for school this morning and my teacher is angry.

I _____ late for school yesterday morning and my teacher _____ angry.

4 Is Elaine selfish these days?

_____ Elaine selfish when she was younger?

5 The students aren't quiet today.

The students _____ quiet in their last lesson.

6 Are you in the laboratory for Physics today?

_____ you in the laboratory for Physics last week?

2 ★ Which verbs are regular and which are irregular? Find the odd one out in each group.

1 go   do   have   (laugh)
2 tell   take   happen   make
3 stand   sit   put   watch
4 speak   listen   look   try
5 fill   observe forget   fail
6 hit   pay   ride   see

3 ★ Complete the blog post with the words and phrases from the box. There are two extra words/phrases.

did   didn't get   didn't play   played   read   sat   took wasn't   was   watched   went   were

PRIMARY SCHOOL: WHAT DID YOU LIKE? WHAT DO YOU MISS?

We **¹**_didn't get_ homework! Every evening, I **²**_____ TV or **³**_____ computer games. There's no time for those things now. _Mia, 17_

We **⁴**_____ on the floor and **⁵**_____ things like drawing or singing. Sometimes we **⁶**_____ on school trips to the zoo or the cinema. They **⁷**_____ great! _Josh, 18_

I liked reading lessons. We **⁸**_____ a book from the library and **⁹**_____ quietly for half an hour. That **¹⁰**_____ a great way to spend time. _Brenda, 16_

4 ★★ Put the words in order to make questions about your primary school. Then write short answers which are true for you.

1 like / did / you / all your teachers / ?

Did you like all your teachers?
Yes, I did. / No, I didn't.

2 were / bright / the classrooms / ?

_____

_____

3 the same person / with / every day / did / sit / you / ?

_____

_____

4 big / was / the school / very / ?

_____

_____

5 your teachers / did / you / give / homework / ?

_____

_____

5 ★★ Complete the text with the correct forms of the verbs from the box.

have learn listen ~~move~~ not be not have not wear sit stay take work wear

Last year, I **¹**_moved_ to England with my family. Now I go to school here and things are a little different to school in my country.

In my old school, I **²**_____ a uniform. We all **³**_____ our own clothes – jeans, trainers and sweatshirts. I like my new uniform though – I guess that's because it's something new for me.

I **⁴**_____ very hard at my old school. I **⁵**_____ about four hours of homework every day and I often **⁶**_____ at home on Saturdays and Sundays to study too.

We **⁷**_____ modern classrooms. There **⁸**_____ any laptops or computers. We **⁹**_____ behind desks, **¹⁰**_____ to the teacher and **¹¹**_____ notes. In England we do more project work and group work.

So, it's easy here and interesting but I think I **¹²**_____ more in my country.

6 ⭐⭐ Choose *S* for subject questions or *O* for object questions. Then complete the sentences with the correct forms of the verbs in brackets.

1 Who usually *organises* (organise) trips at your school? S / O
2 Whose parents _____ (help) to organise the last school trip? S / O
3 Where _____ (you/go) on that trip? S / O
4 How many students _____ (go) on the trip? S / O
5 Who _____ (you/sit) next to on the bus? S / O
6 Which teachers _____ (go) with you? S / O
7 What _____ (you/see)? S / O
8 What _____ (happen) on the way back? S / O
9 What _____ (you/eat) for lunch? S / O
10 Where _____ (you/want) to go on the next school trip? S / O

7 ⭐⭐ Use the words in brackets to complete the questions in the Past Simple.

1 *What did you do* (what/you/do) at school yesterday?
2 _____ (you/pass) the exam last week?
3 _____ (who/help/you) with this homework?
4 _____ (how many students/put up) their hands?
5 _____ (you/have) English last week?
6 _____ (who/put) the poster on the wall?
7 _____ (the students/work) in pairs for the project?
8 _____ (how many students/be) at school yesterday?

8 ⭐ Match answers a–h with questions 1–8 from Exercise 7.

a ☐ Nobody – I did it by myself.
b ☐ Miss Smith put it there.
c ☐ Yes, I did. The questions were easy.
d ☐ Not many because it was the day of the school trip.
e ☐ No, they didn't. They worked in groups.
f ☐ We had a Geography test.
g ☐ No, our English teacher was ill.
h ☐ Only two – nobody else knew the answer.

9 ⭐⭐⭐ Read the answers and complete the questions.

1 Which *school did you go to last year*?
I went to Park Manor School last year.
2 Who _____?
Yesterday, I sat next to Leo.
3 Where _____?
After school yesterday, I went to my mum's office.
4 Why _____?
I arrived late this morning because my bus was late.
5 How _____?
I knew about the test because I listened to the teacher!
6 When _____?
I decided to study Spanish after we went to Cordoba on holiday.
7 What _____?
Last summer, I worked for three weeks, I went camping with friends and I relaxed at home.
8 How long _____?
Not long. I think it took me five days to finish it. It was a really good book.

10 ⭐⭐⭐ Look at the notes and write sentences.

At my old school …
1 the teachers / friendly (✔)
2 have after-school activities (✔)
3 learn a foreign language (✗)
4 finish early on Fridays (✗)

At your old school …
1 which teacher / you like / best?
2 who / be / always / late?
3 which teachers / give / you homework?
4 where / you / eat lunch?

At my old school …
1 *the teachers were friendly.*
2 _____
3 _____
4 _____

At your old school …
1 _____
2 _____
3 _____
4 _____

11 ON A HIGH NOTE Write a short paragraph about a time at school when you felt nervous. Describe what happened, how you felt and why. Use the Past Simple of regular and irregular verbs.

2B VOCABULARY | Education

1 ⭐ **Rewrite the sentences to make them more polite. Use *very* and the words from the box.**

big   clean   clever   fit   good   interesting   kind
~~polite~~   quick   young

1. She's rude.   *She isn't very polite.*
2. I'm unfit.   _____
3. He's slow.   _____
4. Their house is small.   _____
5. My parents are old.   _____
6. You're bad at Maths.   _____
7. This book is boring.   _____
8. Your car is dirty.   _____
9. They're stupid.   _____
10. Helena is selfish.   _____

2 ⭐ **Complete the questions with one preposition in each gap.**

1. Which exams do you always get good marks *in*?
2. Do you find it easy to learn lists of vocabulary items _____ heart?
3. Which university would you like to study _____?
4. How long did you revise _____ your last Maths exam?
5. What sports were you good _____ as a child?
6. When did you last go _____ a History class?
7. What subject would you like to get a degree _____?
8. How do you prepare _____ difficult exams?

3 ⭐⭐ **Match the two parts of the sentences.**

1. ☐ Stewart was bad
2. ☐ I think I failed the
3. ☐ My dad has a degree
4. ☐ My brother is studying
5. ☐ Alexander goes to
6. ☐ I never get top
7. ☐ We have to learn
8. ☐ I can't come – I'm revising

a. Chemistry at university.
b. piano classes on Saturdays.
c. for end-of-year exams.
d. in Physics from York University.
e. at sport at college.
f. a poem by heart.
g. History test yesterday.
h. marks in English tests.

4 ⭐⭐ **Complete the conversations with the words from the box.**

attended   brainy   degree   ~~fail~~   good   marks
preparing   revised   skipped   study

Jermaine Why did your brother ¹*fail* the Maths exam? He's usually really ²_____ at Maths.
Anthony Well, he ³_____ a lot of classes last term.
Jermaine Really?
Anthony Yes, he only ⁴_____ about half of them and he ⁵_____ very little for his exams. The problem is he really wants to become a footballer and he spends all his time training.

Abigail What did your sister ⁶_____ at university?
Nicola Well, she got a ⁷_____ in Chemistry but I don't know how much studying she did!
Abigail I'm sure she did a lot. She's really ⁸_____ and didn't get any bad ⁹_____ when she was at school. She probably started ¹⁰_____ for her final exams while she was still in her first year at university!

5 ⭐⭐⭐ **USE OF ENGLISH Complete the text with one word in each gap.**

STEVEN SPIELBERG

From an early age, Steven Spielberg was good ¹*at* making films. When he was thirteen years old, he won a school prize for a film he made with a group of friends. He wanted to study film ²_____ the University of Southern California, but he didn't get very good ³_____ in his final exams. In the end, he went ⁴_____ a different university – California State. While he was there, Universal Studios offered him a contract. It was difficult to prepare ⁵_____ exams and work at the same time, so Spielberg left university to concentrate on his work.

Spielberg became a successful film director, famous for films such as *Jaws*, *E.T.* and *Jurassic Park*, but he always wanted to finish his degree. In 2002, he went back ⁶_____ university to complete his education. All the students on Spielberg's course had to ⁷_____ an exam in practical film making. For his project, Spielberg presented his Oscar winning film *Schindler's List*! Not surprisingly, he ⁸_____ the exam and ⁹_____ his degree – thirty-six years after he first went to university!

6 ON A HIGH NOTE **Write a short paragraph about how you are doing at school. Use words and phrases from the box.**

attend   bad at   bad marks   fail   good at   good marks
pass   revise   skip   study

2C GRAMMAR

Used to

1 ⭐ **Look at the pictures and complete the text with the phrases from the box.**

didn't use to have   didn't use to listen
didn't use to play   didn't use to ride   used to have
used to listen   used to play   used to ride   used to wear

aged twelve

aged eighteen

When Dan was twelve years old he **¹**_didn't use to have_
long hair. He **²**_____ short hair. He
³_____ smart clothes. He **⁴**_____
basketball, he **⁵**_____ tennis.
He **⁶**_____ a motorbike, he **⁷**_____
a bicycle.
He **⁸**_____ to pop music, he **⁹**_____
to heavy metal music.

2 ⭐⭐ **What did you use to do when you were ten years old? Write questions with *used to*.**

1 What / do / at the weekend?
What did you use to do at the weekend?

2 Where / go / in the summer holidays?
_____

3 use / pay attention in class?
_____

4 What / eat / for lunch?
_____

5 What computer games / play?
_____

6 use / social media?
_____

3 ⭐⭐ **Read the questions in Exercise 2 and write answers which are true for you.**

1 _____
2 _____
3 _____
4 _____
5 _____
6 _____

4 ⭐⭐ **In which sentences can the Past Simple be replaced with *used to*? Tick or cross. Then rewrite the sentences where possible.**

1 ☒ Caroline got her degree in 2010.
_____

2 ☐ I revised for months before all my school exams.
_____

3 ☐ Gareth was nervous before he took exams.
_____

4 ☐ In her final year at school, Kate failed her English exam.
_____

5 ☐ I think my teachers liked me.
_____

6 ☐ Andreas won an award for his project.
_____

5 ⭐⭐⭐ **Complete the texts with the correct forms of *used to* and the verbs in brackets. If *used to* is not possible, use the Past Simple.**

HUGH JACKMAN

Did you know that Hugh Jackman **¹**_used to be_ (be)
a PE teacher before he **²**_____ (become)
an actor? It's true. He **³**_____ (work) in
a secondary school in England. When he was young,
he **⁴**_____ (spend) a lot of time looking at
atlases. He **⁵**_____ (not dream) of being an
actor. He **⁶**_____ (want) to become a chef on
a plane. He **⁷**_____ (think) that, because you
get food on a plane, there was a chef cooking it!

Megan Fox

When Megan Fox was about fifteen years old, she
⁸_____ (live) in Florida. She **⁹**_____
(get) a job in a smoothie bar but she hated it. She
¹⁰_____ (not wear) normal clothes to work.
She got a banana costume and she **¹¹**_____
(dance) in it in the street to promote the bar. Her
friends from school **¹²**_____ (laugh) at her. It
¹³_____ (be) the worst job in her life.

6 ON A HIGH NOTE **Write a short paragraph about how you were different five years ago using *used to*. Think about your appearance, hobbies and habits.**

2D READING AND VOCABULARY

1 Look at the photo and read the first paragraph of the article. Then choose the best answer.

What is the main purpose of the text?
a To present the most successful American college football teams.
b To briefly introduce American college football.
c To compare American football to soccer.

2 Read the text and match headings A–F with paragraphs 1–5. There is one extra heading.

A The early years
B More than just a sport
C Why it is popular
D College football rules explained
E Amazingly large crowds
F The influence of the crowd

3 Read the text again and answer the questions.

1 How many people attended the match between Michigan State and Notre Dame in 2013?
over 115,000

2 What year did the first college football match happen?
_____

3 How did players in early American football matches score points?
_____

4 Which two sports influenced the rules of American football?
_____

5 What do students make to support their team?
_____

6 Whose fans wore white clothes in the match between Penn State and Ohio State?
_____

7 What two things helped Ohio State win the match against Penn State?
_____

8 According to Keith Jackson, what three groups does college football unite?
_____

Vocabulary extension

4 Complete the sentences with the highlighted words from the text.

1 At the match, my favourite b*anners* said, 'Your players make money. Our players make history!'
2 Oh no! My o_____ in next week's tennis competition is the school champion!
3 The coach and the team captain discussed t_____ before the second half of the game.
4 The f_____ wore black and yellow scarves.
5 If my team wins this match, we will be in the first l_____!
6 The s_____ waved flags during the match.
7 The match ended in d_____ for my team when they lost 0–1.

ACTIVE VOCABULARY | Suffixes *-ation*, *-ion*, *-tion*

We can add the suffixes *-ation*, *-ion* and *-tion* to some verbs to create nouns.

5 Scan the text to find the noun forms of these verbs.

1 attract (para. 1)   *attraction*
2 opt (para. 2)   _____
3 concentrate (para. 4)   _____
4 reflect (para. 5)   _____

6 Complete the sentences with the correct nouns formed from the verbs in bold.

1 She made an interesting *observation* about American sporting tradition. **OBSERVE**
2 Mo Farah is an _____ to athletes around the world! **INSPIRE**
3 They started an _____ to help athletes with disabilities. **ORGANISE**
4 Are you taking part in tomorrow's sports _____? **COMPETE**
5 I'd like some _____ about the tennis championship, please. **INFORM**
6 Teachers should do more to improve health and fitness _____ in schools. **EDUCATE**
7 You're not paying _____ to the game – be quiet and watch! **ATTEND**
8 There must be good _____ between members of the team if we want to win. **COMMUNICATE**

7 ON A HIGH NOTE Write a short paragraph about a team that you or some of your friends support. What league do they play in? Who are their rivals? How many fans watch their matches?

UNIT VOCABULARY PRACTICE > page 25

COLLEGE FOOTBALL IN THE USA

1 ☐ On September 7, 2013, an American football match between Michigan State and Notre Dame attracted a crowd of over 115,000 people. This may not seem surprising – after all, American football is extremely popular. However, you may be surprised to learn that this wasn't a match between two professional teams. Michigan State and Notre Dame are universities and college football regularly attracts crowds of 80,000 fans or more. So why is college football such a huge attraction for Americans?

2 ☐ One of the main reasons is that many cities don't have a professional team. Because there is no second league of teams in the USA, people who want to support their local team have only one option – the college team. The players themselves are often local and compete for the pride of the team rather than for financial success. Attending matches became a tradition passed down through the generations.

3 ☐ The first college football match took place in 1869 between Rutgers and Princeton universities. At that time, the game was similar to soccer as the teams used to kick the ball into their opponent's goal. The rules slowly changed over time and became more influenced by rugby, in which players can pick up the ball and run with it. Towards the end of the nineteenth century, the game developed into what we know today as American football.

4 ☐ Before the big day, students create banners, flags and even songs to sing during the match. They want to break the other team's concentration. College footballers are young and easily affected by the crowd, so these tactics sometimes work. In one match between Penn State and Ohio State, the Pennsylvania fans organised a 'white-out' where everyone in the crowd wore white clothes. This made it difficult for the Ohio players to concentrate and they lost the game. When the two teams played in Ohio, the home crowd all wore red. This 'sea of red', together with the noise of the crowd, caused one of the players to make a mistake and the game ended in defeat for the Penn State team.

5 ☐ College football isn't just about sporting achievements. Keith Jackson, a sports journalist, once said that it's a reflection of Middle America because it brings together three generations of a family. He claimed that not only the university but also the community and the families focus their attention on college football. And that's why it continues to attract huge crowds of passionate supporters.

2E LISTENING AND VOCABULARY

1 Choose the correct words to complete the definitions.

1 A *commentator* / *presenter* introduces a TV or radio programme and talks to guests.

2 A *commentator* / *presenter* tells viewers or listeners of a sports event what is happening.

2 🔊 **11 Listen to Part 1 of a radio programme and decide if statements 1–3 are true or false.**

1 ☐ Zinedine Zidane was a player and a manager at the same football club.

2 ☐ Zidane didn't want to leave Real Madrid.

3 ☐ Sports stars usually choose a TV career because they can't find work in sports management.

3 🔊 **12 Listen to Part 2 of the programme and choose the correct answers.**

1 Gary Neville won the English Premier League
a twice.   **b** five times.   **c** eight times.

2 His only experience of club management was in
a Manchester.   **b** Munich.   **c** Valencia.

3 Paula Radcliffe
a won an Olympic gold medal.
b is the women's marathon world record holder.
c never won a marathon outside the UK.

4 She enjoys being a commentator on TV
a but she misses her athletic career.
b but she doesn't have enough time for her family.
c because she can focus more on her personal life.

5 Richie Benaud took a presenter training course
a in Australia.   **b** for the BBC.   **c** after he retired

6 He commentated on cricket in
a England only.   **b** Australia only.
c England and Australia.

Vocabulary extension

4 🔊 **13 Match the two parts of the phrases from the radio programme in Exercises 2 and 3. Listen and check.**

1 ☐ achieve   **a** the record
2 ☐ appear   **b** on a game
3 ☐ hold   **c** from sport
4 ☐ retire   **d** a title
5 ☐ win   **e** on TV
6 ☐ commentate   **f** success

5 Complete the sentences with the correct forms of the verbs from Exercise 4.

1 In 2017, Roger Federer *won* the Wimbledon Gentlemen's Singles title for the eighth time!

2 Who _____ the world record for the 100 m race?

3 Jimmy Magee _____ on sports on TV and radio for more than fifty years. He died in 2017.

4 The winner of the marathon will _____ on TV to talk about her new record.

5 Most professional tennis players _____ from the sport before they are thirty.

6 Not all professional athletes _____ success.

Pronunciation

6 🔊 **14 Look at these words from the radio programme in Exercises 2 and 3. Which two words have a different *c* sound to the others? Listen, check and repeat.**

a<u>c</u>tive athleti<u>c</u>s <u>c</u>areer <u>c</u>learly <u>c</u>olleagues
<u>c</u>ommentators Olympi<u>c</u> on<u>c</u>e re<u>c</u>ord respe<u>c</u>ted
unlu<u>c</u>ky voi<u>c</u>e

ACTIVE PRONUNCIATION | Hard and soft *c*

The letter *c* can be pronounced as /k/ or /s/.

- It is pronounced /k/ when it is followed by *a*, *o*, *u* or a consonant (e.g. **c**ar, **c**rash).
- It is pronounced /s/ when it is followed by *e*, *i* or *y* (e.g. **c**ity).
- It is also pronounced /k/ when it appears at the end of a word (e.g. athleti**c**, Olympi**c**).

---

7 🔊 **15 These words all contain two letters *c*. Which sound is each *c*? Choose the correct answers. Listen and check. Then practise saying the words.**

1 ta<u>c</u>ti<u>c</u>s
a /k/ and /s/   **b** both /s/   **c** both /k/

2 su<u>cc</u>ess
a /s/ and /k/   **b** /k/ and /s/   **c** both /s/

3 <u>c</u>ir<u>c</u>le
a both /k/   **b** both /s/   **c** /s/ and /k/

4 <u>c</u>riti<u>c</u>ise
a /k/ and /s/   **b** /s/ and /k/   **c** both /k/

5 <u>c</u>ri<u>c</u>ket
a both /k/   **b** /k/ and /s/   **c** both /s/

8 🔊 **16 Study Active Pronunciation again and decide what sound the letter *c* represents in these place names. Write /k/ or /s/. Listen, check and repeat.**

Cities: Valen<u>c</u>ia */s/*, Bar<u>c</u>elona ___, Au<u>c</u>kland ___
Rivers: <u>C</u>olorado ___, Orino<u>c</u>o ___, <u>C</u>imarron ___
Mountains: A<u>c</u>on<u>c</u>agua ___ ___, <u>C</u>inder <u>C</u>one ___ ___, <u>C</u>ederberg ___
Islands: <u>C</u>uba ___, I<u>c</u>eland ___, <u>C</u>yprus ___

9 🔊 **17 Listen to some words. How many times does the letter *c* appear in each word? Write *once*, *twice* or *not at all*?**

1 *not at all*   **5** _____
2 _____   **6** _____
3 _____   **7** _____
4 _____   **8** _____

10 🔊 **18 Listen and check your answers to Exercise 9.**

UNIT VOCABULARY PRACTICE > page 25

1 🔊 *19* **Listen and repeat the phrases. How do you say them in your language?**

SPEAKING | Apologising

SAYING SORRY

Sorry!

I'm really sorry.

I'm sorry that I misbehaved in class yesterday.

I'm sorry that I didn't do the project on time.

Sorry about that.

It was my fault.

EXPLAINING

It was stupid/wrong of me.

I (completely) forgot.

I didn't realise (that) it was so late.

I did it by mistake.

It was an accident.

ACCEPTING AN APOLOGY

Never mind.

That's OK/alright.

Don't worry about it.

It can happen to anyone.
---

2 **Match the two parts of the sentences for apologising.**

1 ☐ Sorry about		**a**	by mistake.
2 ☐ It was my		**b**	fault.
3 ☐ It was wrong		**c**	to anyone.
4 ☐ I didn't		**d**	mind.
5 ☐ I did it		**e**	of me.
6 ☐ It was		**f**	that.
7 ☐ Never		**g**	an accident.
8 ☐ It can happen		**h**	realise that I was late.

3 **Complete the sentences with the words and phrases from the box.**

about that   an accident   completely forgot   ~~fault~~
mistake   realise   really   sorry that   stupid

1 Sorry, everyone. It was my *fault*. It was _____ of me to kick the other player.

2 I'm_____ sorry. It was _____. I kicked the ball towards the wall, but it hit the window.

3 Oh no! I _____ that it was your birthday!

4 Are you OK? Sorry _____. I didn't _____ you were standing there.

5 Sorry! I wrote 5.30 instead of 3.30 by _____ and you missed the match because of me!

6 I'm _____ I didn't come to see you. I was very busy.

4 **Match responses a–f with apologies 1–6 from Exercise 3.**

a ☐ Don't worry about it. I forgot your birthday too, remember?

b ☐ That's OK. They didn't play anyway because it started to rain.

c ☐ Don't worry about it. I can fix it.

d ☐ Never mind. It doesn't hurt.

e ☐ That's OK. It can happen to anyone. Luckily, we won the match.

f ☐ That's alright – I know you've got a lot of work to do.

5 **Choose the correct responses to complete the mini-conversations.**

1

Melanie Hi everyone. I'm really sorry I'm late. I didn't realise the meeting was this morning.

Harvey ___ We started without you.

a Never mind.

b It was your fault.

c I completely forgot.

2

Joyce Hey! That's my sandwich!

Brian Oh. ___

Joyce That's alright. I'm not really hungry.

a Really? That's interesting!

b Don't worry about it.

c Sorry about that.

3

Mum Hey, the door isn't locked.

Fiona ___ I forgot to lock it when I went out.

Mum I hope nothing's missing.

a Awesome!

b It's my fault.

c I didn't realise it was locked.

4

Kate I'm sorry, Dad. ___ to leave your umbrella on the bus.

Dad Don't worry about it. It can happen to anyone. I left it on the bus once myself.

a I completely forgot

b It was stupid of me

c I don't think it's bad

I'M SORRY

2G WRITING | A biography

An inspiration to everyone

Mention why you chose this person; say why he/she is famous/important/inspiring.

Talk about his/her early life and talents.

Talk about his/her achievements and what he/she did.

Talk about what the person did later (or does today).

Sum up the person's life in a few words; perhaps mention his/her personality.

The 2012 London Olympics were a chance for the whole country to celebrate Britain's multicultural society. The person I am **¹**_writing_ about is my inspiration because he represented modern Britain better than any other athlete.

Mo Farah was born in Somalia, East Africa, in 1983. His father had British citizenship, **²**_____ Mo moved to Britain when he was eight years old. He arrived in a foreign country and, what's **³**_____ , he spoke almost no English. His P.E. teacher soon noticed that he was good at running and Mo joined a local athletics club.

He won five school championships and, **⁴**_____ that, he started winning medals in adult competitions, but he achieved widespread popularity only after the Olympics, when he won two gold medals, in the 10,000 metre and the 5,000 metre races. **⁵**_____ of his success and a happy, smiling face, he became the symbol of Britain's Olympic team.

Mo Farah's success continued after the Olympics and, four years **⁶**_____ in Rio, he won two more gold medals for the same distances. In the 10,000 metres, he fell at one point after another runner bumped into him, but got up and still won the race! **⁷**_____ , in 2017, he received a knighthood from Queen Elizabeth and became Sir Mo Farah.

Mo's success and popularity **⁸**_____ that anyone can achieve their dreams. That's **⁹**_____ he is a great role model and inspiration to everyone, whatever their background.

---

1 Read the short biography and answer the questions.

1 Who is the biography about? _Mo Farah_

2 Why is he famous? _____

3 Where and when was he born? _____

4 When did he start to become really popular?
_____

5 What happened to him in 2017? _____

2 Read the biography again and complete it with the words from the box.

after   because   finally   later   more   show   so
why   ~~writing~~

3 Complete the sentences with linking words.

1 After training hard for a long time, she f_inally_ got into her college team.

2 Ten years l_____ she won her second gold medal at the age of twenty-nine.

3 She a_____ won two silver medals.

4 What's m_____, she does a lot for charity.

5 She's a great role model – that's w_____ I have chosen her.

4 Match the two parts of the sentences.

1 ☐ The person I am writing about is
2 ☐ She was born
3 ☐ She studied
4 ☐ She was good
5 ☐ At the age of thirty
6 ☐ Ten years later, she
7 ☐ She is a positive

a at explaining difficult ideas clearly.
b Physics and Maths.
c she became a teacher.
d an inspiration to many.
e started a political party.
f role model for all of us.
g in London in 1985.

5 WRITING TASK Use the Internet to research the life of an inspirational sportsperson or teacher. Write a biography of his/her life.

ACTIVE WRITING | A biography

1 Plan your biography.

Include the following information:
- Why the person is important/inspiring.
- Details of his/her early life.
- Key achievements and the main events in his/her life.
- His/her later life.
- A summing up.

2 Write the biography.
- Use 4–5 paragraphs to organise your writing.
- Explain when things happened: ten years later, next, after that, then, finally.
- Add information: and, also, what's more.
- Give reasons: because, so, that's why.

3 Check that ...
- your biography starts in an interesting way.
- your biography is organised into paragraphs.
- there are no spelling or grammar mistakes.
- you have a good range of vocabulary and structures.
- your biography finishes with a short summary.

UNIT VOCABULARY PRACTICE

1 2A GRAMMAR AND VOCABULARY **Complete the sentences with the verbs from the box.**

check   compare   ~~do~~   hand out   took   pay   put up(x2)

1 I want you to _do_ this exercise for homework.

2 I'd like you to _____ your answers with a partner before you tell the class.

3 Can you _____ these worksheets for me, please?

4 Please _____ attention to what I'm saying.

5 We _____ our posters on the classroom wall.

6 Our teacher told us about Napoleon and we _____ some notes.

7 Please don't shout – _____ your hand if you know the answer.

8 Don't forget to _____ your answers before you return your test papers.

2 2B VOCABULARY **Choose the correct words to complete the sentences.**

1 My dad gets upset when I don't *fail / pass* my exams.

2 I love Art but I'm not very good *at / in* it.

3 Which exam are you *revising / taking* for today?

4 I don't *cheat / skip* classes. I want to do well at school.

5 I need to get good marks *in / on* Maths this year.

6 Even very *brainy / selfish* students need to study hard.

7 I don't like tests where we need to learn about lots of new words *by / from* heart.

8 You can get a degree *on / in* Viking Studies at University College London. That sounds cool!

9 The students are *taking / reading* their Physics exam.

10 You need very good marks to study *in / at* Oxford University.

3 2D READING AND VOCABULARY **Choose the correct words to complete the sentences. Sometimes more than one answer is correct.**

1 We beat ___.
  a the other team   **b** the championship   **c** a medal

2 Did you win ___?
  a a medal   **b** the match   **c** a prize

3 The team played ___.
  a a competition   **b** a match   **c** a race

4 Our school organised ___.
  a a race   **b** a competition   **c** a medal

5 How many ___ did they score?
  a points   **b** draws   **c** goals

6 The two teams ___ the match 2–2.
  a beat   **b** won   **c** drew

7 We'd like to take part in the ___.
  a race   **b** competition   **c** team

8 My friends and I competed in different ___.
  a races   **b** matches   **c** games

9 You need a ball to play ___.
  a chess   **b** squash   **c** tennis

4 2E LISTENING AND VOCABULARY **Complete the sports report with one word in each gap.**

SPORTS
NEWS

And now for our report on the match between the English and French [1]champions: Paris Saint-Germain and Manchester City. There were four goals in the first [2]h_____ and the teams went off the pitch with the score at 2–2. After the break, the [3]r_____ gave Manchester City's goalkeeper a red [4]c_____ for a bad foul. The Manchester City [5]f_____ weren't happy, but most people agreed with the decision. At this point, the Manchester City [6]m_____ decided to change two players and surprised everyone when he took off the team's [7]c_____ .

With no leader on the pitch, the Manchester City players didn't know what to do and PSG scored three times in ten minutes.

Manchester City got a goal in the ninetieth minute but the final [8]s_____ was 5–3 to PSG. They will now play Barcelona in the quarter- [9]f_____ .

In athletics, there was joy for the Nigerian 400 metres runner, Amina Edoro. She won the gold [10]m_____ and also broke the world [11]r_____ with a time of 45.08 seconds.

5 ON A HIGH NOTE **Write a short report about a sports event that you watched recently. Mention the sport, who the teams or competitors were, what happened and how you felt about the result.**

1 **For each learning objective, write 1–5 to assess your ability.**

1 = I don't feel confident. 5 = I feel confident.

	Learning objective	Course material	How confident I am (1–5)
2A	I can use the Past Simple to talk about finished actions or states in the past.	Student's Book pp. 18–19	
2B	I can talk about learning and studying.	Student's Book p. 20	
2C	I can use *used to* to talk about regular habits or states in the past.	Student's Book p. 21	
2D	I can predict what a text is going to be about and talk about sports.	Student's Book pp. 22–23	
2E	I can identify key details in an interview about famous sportspeople.	Student's Book p. 24	
2F	I can apologise, give explanations and accept a simple apology.	Student's Book p. 25	
2G	I can write a short biography.	Student's Book pp. 26–27	

2 **Which of the skills above would you like to improve in? How?**

Skill I want to improve in	How I can improve

3 **What can you remember from this unit?**

New words I learned and most want to remember	Expressions and phrases I liked	English I heard or read outside class

GRAMMAR AND VOCABULARY

1 Complete the conversations with one word in each gap.

Amir What subjects are you ¹_good_ at, Terry?

Terry When I ²r_____ for exams, I usually ³p_____ every subject, but I always get very good ⁴m_____ in History.

Amir Do you learn all the dates by ⁵h_____?

Terry Yes. That's the best way to ⁶s_____ this subject. Some day I'd like to get a ⁷d_____ in History.

Miss D ⁸O_____ your books at page fifty-eight, please. You ⁹d_____ exercises 1 and 2 for homework?

James Yes, Miss Dodd.

Miss D Good, let's ¹⁰c_____ your answers now. Question 1.

James 'Went'!

Miss D Don't shout, James! Please ¹¹p_____ your hand up to answer. Now ... Question 2?

/ 5

2 Complete the sentences with the words from the box. There are two extra words.

athlete beat break champions cheat draw fans ~~manager~~ match prize referee score versus win

1 You're the _manager_ of the team – it's your decision who plays in the _____.

2 I don't know how we _____ them. We were lucky!

3 I think he might _____ the world record today – he's in excellent shape!

4 When the _____ makes a decision, you should accept it. Don't argue.

5 Our _____ make more noise than any others in the league.

6 I don't believe it. We're the world _____. No-one can beat us!

7 The match was a _____. It finished 2–2.

8 I want to win this competition – the _____ is a new tennis racket!

9 We're going to have a boys _____ girls chess competition.

10 I hate it when players _____ by pretending to be hurt.

/ 5

3 Complete the conversation with the correct forms of the verbs in brackets.

Josh We had an interesting lesson today.

Holly Really? What ¹_happened_ (happen)?

Josh A woman ²_____ (come) to watch Mr Granger. She was a school inspector.

Holly ³_____ (she/say) anything?

Josh No, she just ⁴_____ (sit) quietly and watched. Anyway, Mr Granger planned the whole lesson using the computer, but it ⁵_____ (not work)! Then he handed out some worksheets, but they all ⁶_____ (fall) on the floor!

Holly Oh dear. Poor Mr Granger!

/ 5

4 Choose the correct forms to complete the sentences. Sometimes more than one answer is correct.

1 When I was younger, I ___ to enjoy going to school.
   a didn't used   **b** didn't use

2 I didn't ___ school dinners at primary school.
   a like   **b** use to like

3 Did you ___ all your exams last month?
   a pass   **b** use to pass

4 Which sports did you ___ when you were younger?
   a play   **b** use to play

5 My parents always ___ me to school.
   a drove   **b** used to drive

/ 5

USE OF ENGLISH

5 Choose the correct words a-d to complete the text.

AN ALL-ROUND EDUCATION

The West London Free School aims to be one of the best schools in the country. Its pupils certainly get good marks ¹___ their exams. In some ways, the school is similar to how schools ²___ to be fifty years ago. There are strict rules: no-one is ever late for school and everyone ³___ attention to their teachers.

However, the students don't just ⁴___ exercises all day. They sit and ⁵___ notes and use the Internet for research. They often work ⁶___ groups to solve problems together and do project work. The students I saw seemed to enjoy their time at school.

1 a in	**b** at	**c** for	**d** from
2 a were	**b** did	**c** used	**d** use
3 a makes	**b** gives	**c** pays	**d** keeps
4 a make	**b** work	**c** do	**d** give
5 a carry	**b** do	**c** put	**d** take
6 a on	**b** with	**c** for	**d** in

/ 6

6 Complete the second sentence so that it means the same as the first one. Use no more than three words in each gap.

1 Al came first in the 200 m swimming race.
   Al won a _gold medal_ in the 200 m swimming race.

2 Dad always bought us a hot dog at half-time.
   Dad always used _____ us a hot dog at half-time.

3 Caroline is a good swimmer.
   Caroline is _____ swimming.

4 Did Richard play football when he was younger?
   _____ to play football when he was younger?

5 My dog is ugly!
   My dog _____ very beautiful.

/ 4

/ 30

3A GRAMMAR AND VOCABULARY

Past Continuous and Past Simple

1 ⭐ **Put the words in order to make sentences.**

1 4 a.m. / everyone / it / sleeping / was / was / and
It was 4 a.m. and everyone was sleeping.

2 was / Alison / six o'clock / at / eating breakfast
_____

3 for the rain / to stop / waiting / we / were
_____

4 coming up / the sun / was / behind the mountains
_____

5 my bag / I / at eleven o'clock / packing / still / was
_____

6 for the last time / my parents / checking / the documents / were
_____

7 were / a high mountain / climbing / the boys
_____

8 dad / driving / through town / was / the car
_____

2 ⭐ **Read Tom's notes. Complete the questions with the correct forms of the words in brackets. Use the Past Continuous.**

First day of the holidays!

6 a.m. – 6.30 a.m.	we – pack our bags
8 a.m. – 9 a.m.	we – drive to airport
11 a.m. – 3 p.m.	we – fly to Greece
4 p.m. – 4.30 p.m.	I – shower at hotel
5 p.m. – 5.30 p.m.	my parents – walk into local town, I – go for a swim!
6.30 p.m. – 7.30 p.m.	Mum – buy souvenirs
8 p.m. – 9.30 p.m.	we – eat dinner at hotel bar

1 What *were Tom's parents doing* (Tom's parents/do) at 6.15 a.m.?
2 _____ (they/drive) to the airport at 10 a.m.?
3 What _____ (they/do) at 2 p.m.?
4 _____ (Tom's dad/have) a shower at 4.15 p.m.?
5 Who _____ (walk) into town at 5.15 p.m.?
6 _____ (Tom/swim) at 5.15 p.m.?
7 What _____ (Tom's mum/do) at 7 p.m.?
8 _____ (they all/eat) dinner at 9 p.m.?

3 ⭐ **Match answers a–h with questions 1–8 from Exercise 2.**

a ☐ No, he wasn't.
b ☐ Yes, they were.
c ☐ They were packing their bags.
d ☐ Tom's parents.
e ☐ Yes, he was.
f ☐ No, they weren't.
g ☐ She was buying souvenirs.
h ☐ They were flying to Greece.

4 ⭐ **Match questions 1–8 with short answers a–h.**

1 ☐ Were you staying in a hotel?
2 ☐ Was Lena going camping?
3 ☐ Was I talking in my sleep?
4 ☐ Were the children visiting their aunt?
5 ☐ Was the booking system working?
6 ☐ Was Connor waiting at the bus stop?
7 ☐ Were your parents driving to Paris?
8 ☐ Were you and your friend sunbathing?

a Yes, he was. He wanted to catch the bus.
b No, we weren't. We were camping.
c Yes, we were. It was really hot!
d No, they weren't. They were visiting their grandma.
e Yes, it was. We booked our flights.
f No, they weren't. They were flying there.
g No, she wasn't. She was going skiing.
h Yes, you were. You were funny!

5 ⭐⭐ **Choose the correct forms to complete the sentences.**

1 I *chose / was choosing* a glass model of the Eiffel Tower when I *broke / was breaking* it!
2 I *answered / was answering* the phone while I *sat / was sitting* in the cinema.
3 We *saw / were seeing* a bear while we *drove / were driving* along the mountain road!
4 We *flew / were flying* to the USA when we *saw / were seeing* another plane fly past us!
5 We *waited / were waiting* for our plane when the police *told / were telling* everyone to leave the airport.
6 As we *sailed / were sailing* to the island, a dolphin *appeared / was appearing* in the water!
7 Amber and Johnny *ate / were eating* dinner when the waiter *dropped / was dropping* a bottle of water.
8 I *fell / was falling* and hurt myself as I *ran / was running* to catch the bus.

6 ★★ Complete the blog posts with the correct Past Simple or Past Continuous forms of the verbs in brackets.

TELL US YOUR HOLIDAY EXPERIENCES!

We **1** _were staying_ (stay) in the south of Morocco. One day, we decided to walk into the desert to watch the sun go down. At six o'clock, we **2**_____ (walk) towards the sand dunes. It was a beautiful evening. We **3**_____ (sit) on the sand when, suddenly, the wind **4**_____ (start) blowing really hard. It was impossible to see anything. It was scary!
Sand storm in Morocco –
Alex, 15

We **5**_____ (drive) in France last summer. I **6**_____ (look) at a map in the back of the car when Dad suddenly **7**_____ (open) the window. I **8**_____ (not hold) the map very tightly and it **9**_____ (fly) out of my hands and out of the window! Luckily there was no-one behind us.
Flying map! – Sarah, 14

7 ★★ Use the prompts to write sentences in the Past Simple and Past Continuous.

1 I / buy / souvenirs / when / someone / steal / my wallet
I was buying souvenirs when someone stole my wallet.

2 We / fly / home from Iceland / when / we / see / the Northern Lights

3 They / have / an accident / while / they / drive to the beach

4 My parents / meet / an old friend / while / they / sightsee / in Istanbul

5 Ben nearly / drown / while / he / swim / in the pool

6 I / eat / dinner / when / I / suddenly / feel / ill

7 As / the children / swim / it / start / to rain

8 While/ Callum / ride / his bike / he / see / a wild horse

8 ★★★ Use the prompts to write the questions to the answers.

1 What / you / do / at ten o'clock last night?
What were you doing at ten o'clock last night?
I was packing my bag for the holiday.

2 Arthur / look / at his holiday photos / when / you / see him?

_____
No, he wasn't. He was watching a travel programme on TV.

3 your parents / sleep / when / you / get home?

_____
No, they weren't. They were waiting for me.

4 it / rain / when / you / arrive?

_____
Yes, it was.

5 Where / you / go / when my dad / see / you?

_____
I was going to the library.

9 ★★★ Complete the sentences with the correct forms of the verbs from the box.

chat drive drop eat fall hit read ride run
sail shine sing tell ~~travel~~ wait

1 While we _were travelling_ by bus to our hotel, I _____ three chapters of my new book!

2 Dad nearly _____ asleep while he _____ along the motorway!

3 We _____ our bikes along a mountain road when I _____ a rock and fell off.

4 The sun _____ and the birds _____ as we began to climb the mountain.

5 As my mum _____ to catch the bus, she _____ her shopping bag.

6 My parents _____ at a bus stop when someone _____ them there were no buses on Sundays.

7 While the lorry driver _____ from England to France on the ferry, he _____ lunch in the ferry's restaurant.

8 At nine o'clock, the students on the summer camp _____ in their rooms.

10 ON A HIGH NOTE Write a short paragraph about two unusual, funny or unpleasant things that happened while you were doing something else. Say what happened afterwards.

3B VOCABULARY | Travelling

1 ⭐ **Match the kinds of holiday from the box with the definitions.**

> adventure holiday   city break   cruise   excursion
> expedition   journey   package holiday   ~~school trip~~

1 You go on this with your school friends.   *school trip*
2 This is a holiday on a boat.   _____
3 Explorers go on this to dangerous places.   _____
4 You can go canoeing, skiing or climbing.   _____
5 This is a short trip, maybe just for one day.   _____
6 You spend one or two days in a big city.   _____
7 This includes your flights, hotel and food.   _____
8 This is when you travel from one place
to another.   _____

2 ⭐ **What kinds of holidays are they? Match adverts a–h with the holidays from Exercise 1.**

a ☐

THREE NIGHTS IN LISBON
Shopping, culture and sightseeing.

b ☐

Year 10 students
spend three days in Wales with your History and Geography teachers.

c ☐

> ···· **TWO WEEKS IN SPAIN** ····
> **Flight, hotel and all meals included
> in the price.** ····

d ☐

SIX WEEKS SAILING
IN THE MEDITERRANEAN
ON A FANTASTIC SHIP.

e ☐

COACH FROM LONDON TO PRAGUE
**TWENTY-TWO HOURS.
CHEAP AND COMFORTABLE.**

3 ⭐ **Choose the correct words to complete the sentences.**

1 We arrived *at / in* the airport late in the evening.
2 We're going to leave *for / to* Paris at five in the morning!
3 Our plane *took off / landed* an hour late – we were really bored waiting at the airport.
4 What time are we arriving *at / in* Venice?
5 We're travelling *on / by* bus from the airport to our hotel.
6 Did you stay *to / in* a nice hotel in Prague?
7 The pilot said that we are going to *take off / land* at the airport in twenty minutes.
8 Suzie checked *in /on* the hotel immediately after she landed in Rome.

4 ⭐⭐ **Complete the mini-conversations with one word in each gap.**

Paula   Hurry up! We don't want to ¹m*iss* our train.
Jack   Don't worry. We can ²g_____ a taxi to the station.

Mother   How was the journey?
Adrian   Tiring. We ³b_____ the plane at 6.30 but we didn't ⁴t_____ off until eight o'clock. We ⁵l_____ in Croatia at half past eleven and got to the hotel after midnight.

Tom   Taxis from the airport are expensive. Let's ⁶t_____ the train into the centre of Madrid.
Scott   OK, but what about when we ⁷a_____ at the station? Can we walk from there to the hotel?

5 ON A HIGH NOTE **Choose one kind of holiday from Exercise 1 and write a short review for a website. Say how you got there, where you stayed, what you did and give your 'verdict' (if you liked it or not).**

f ☐

Spend **two weeks** in **Slovenia**.
Rock climbing, kayaking, hiking and swimming.

g ☐

Tomorrow: trip to the local market and castle with English speaking guide.
Please sign up at reception.

h ☐

WE ARE LOOKING FOR BIOLOGISTS TO STUDY ANIMAL HABITS IN INDONESIA.

1 🔊 *20* **Listen and repeat the phrases. How do you say them in your language?**

> ## SPEAKING | Asking for information
>
> **Excuse me, what time is the next train to** Glasgow?
> **Which platform does the train leave from?**
> **Where 's the nearest tube station/bus stop/taxi rank?**
> **Is there a bus/tram we can catch to** the Brunswick Centre?
> **Is there a restaurant/bank/travel centre near here?**
> **How far is it to** the bus station?
> **Pardon me, I didn't hear that.**
> **I'm sorry, I didn't catch that.**

2 **Put the words in order to make sentences.**

1 tube station / nearest / the / where's / ?
Where's the nearest tube station?

2 me / catch / didn't / that / pardon / I
_____

3 the restaurant / time / open / does / what / ?
_____

4 far / how / the railway station / to / it / is / ?
_____

5 does / from / platform / leave / the Paris train / which / ?
_____

6 here / there / near / is / a travel centre / ?
_____

7 Hereford / time / is / to / what / the next train / ?
_____

8 into the village / there / I / a bus / catch / is / can / ?
_____

3 **Complete the questions with the words from the box.**

Are   Is   How   What   ~~Where~~   Which

1 *Where* is the museum?
2 _____ time is the first train to Dover today?
3 _____ platform does it leave from?
4 _____ there a shopping centre near here?
5 _____ far is it to the park?
6 _____ there any trains to London in the evening?

4 **Match answers a–f with questions 1–6 from Exercise 3.**

a ☐ I think it leaves from Platform Six.
b ☐ Yes, the last one leaves at 21.08.
c ☐ Yes, there is. It's on Liverpool Road.
d ☐ It's on Baker Street, just opposite the taxi rank.
e ☐ It's three kilometres. You can get a bus from here.
f ☐ There's one at 6.15. It arrives at 7.42.

5 **Complete the questions with one word in each gap.**

1 Is there a map *of* the city centre?
2 Which platform does the Glasgow train leave _____ ?
3 What time is the next coach _____ Birmingham?
4 Is there a bus stop _____ here?
5 How far is it _____ the museum?
6 Is there a train we can catch _____ the city centre?

6 **Choose the correct words to complete the sentences.**

1 Where's the nearest bus *rank / park / stop*?
2 *There is / Is there / What is* a bus I can catch to the airport?
3 Sorry, I didn't *catch / find / keep* that.
4 What *stop / line / platform* do Blue Line trains leave from?
5 Is there a taxi *centre / rank / stop* near here?
6 Excuse me. *Where / How / What* far is it to Park View Hotel?

7 **Put the sentences in order to make conversations.**

1

a ☐ It's about 200 metres from here, outside the railway station.

b ☐ Where's the nearest bus stop?

c ☐ No, 200. Outside the railway station.

d ☑ Excuse me. Is there a bus I can catch to the airport?

e ☐ I'm sorry, I didn't catch that. Did you say 300 metres?

f ☐ Yes, the A1.

2

a ☐ What platform do Blue Line trains leave from?

b ☐ Oh, that's a long way. Is there a taxi rank near here?

c ☐ They don't have a number. Just look for the Blue Line and get off at the second stop.

d ☐ It's about two kilometres from here.

e ☐ No, but there's an underground station here. You need a Blue Line train to Mark's Square.

f ☑ Excuse me. How far is it to Park View Hotel?

Relative pronouns

1 ⭐ **Choose the correct relative pronouns to complete the sentences about people, places and things in Britain.**

1 It's a sport *who / which / where* is popular all over the world.

2 She's the person *whose / who / which* was Britain's first female Prime Minister.

3 It's the town *where / who / whose* the Beatles come from.

4 He was the first person *which / that / whose* played James Bond.

5 He's the boy *which / whose / who* could be king one day.

6 She's a woman *who / whose / where* home is a castle.

7 It's the thing *which / where / who* British people love to talk about.

8 It's a food *that / who / where* is famous in England.

2 ⭐ **Tick the sentences in which the relative pronoun can be left out. Put a cross if it cannot be left out.**

1 ☒ This is the café in which we had that delicious cake.

2 ☐ Our Maths teacher is the person who we love going on school trips with.

3 ☐ Where's the market where we bought our souvenirs?

4 ☐ These are the ruins that we visited on our second day.

5 ☐ Do you want to see a photo of the waiter who dropped my soup?

6 ☐ I'd love to meet the person who painted this.

7 ☐ Is there a shop near hear which sells water?

8 ☐ We met a Chinese couple whose daughter is a famous blogger.

3 ⭐⭐ **Complete the blog with relative pronouns.**

4 ⭐ **In which sentences in Exercise 3 can you leave out the relative pronoun?**

☐ ☐

5 ⭐⭐⭐ **Join the two sentences using a relative pronoun. Make any other necessary changes. Write the relative pronoun in brackets if it is not needed.**

1 This is the girl. I told you about her.
This is the girl (who/that) I told you about.

2 This is the taxi driver. He drove us from the airport to the hotel.

_____

3 This is the market. I bought your present there.

_____

4 This is the room. I shared it with my brother.

_____

5 This was the woman. Her dogs were really noisy.

_____

6 This was the local boy. He taught me a few useful phrases.

_____

7 This is the hotel. We stayed here on holiday.

_____

8 He is the chef. I love his food.

_____

6 ON A HIGH NOTE **Write a short paragraph about three of the things from the box. Use relative pronouns.**

a place which you love
food which you often eat
someone who you admire
an activity that you enjoy
someone who is important for people in your country
a famous person whose opinions are interesting

CANADA QUIZ

Not many people know much about my country so here's a small quiz for you (answers below!)

CAN YOU NAME ...

1 a delicious sauce *which/that* you put on your pancakes?

2 the province that includes Montreal _____ French is the first language?

3 the leaf _____ you can see on our flag?

4 the film director _____ famous films include *Avatar* and *Titanic*?

5 the tower _____ is over 550 metres tall?

6 the Canadian actor _____ starred in *La-la Land*?

7 the sport _____ is played by the team _____ name is the Blue Jays?

8 the name of the island _____ got its name from an English Queen?

Answers
1 maple syrup 2 Quebec 3 maple leaf 4 James Cameron 5 CN Tower, Toronto 6 Ryan Gosling 7 Baseball 8 Victoria Island, British Columbia

3E LISTENING AND VOCABULARY

1 Look at the picture and the questions in Exercise 2. Choose the best answer.

What do you think the recording will be about?

a a flight which couldn't take off

b landing at the wrong airport

c lost luggage because of security problems

2 🔊 *21* Listen and check your answer to Exercise 1. Then choose the correct answers.

1 What did the speaker arrive with at the airport?

a phone batteries **b** tablet **c** boarding pass

2 What did he NOT do in the departure lounge?

a buy a newspaper

b eat a meal

c argue with security

3 At the gate, he

a waited impatiently in the queue.

b made sure he was the first to board.

c relaxed while other people boarded.

4 When he got on the coach he was shocked by

a something the attendant told him.

b the bad condition it was in.

c the number of people on board.

5 He was upset because

a of the departure time of his flight home.

b the price of the return coach was very high.

c he didn't have any time to see Tromso.

Vocabulary extension

3 Match the words and phrases from the box with the definitions.

aisle seat   baggage claim   duty-free
recharge (my) batteries   ~~runway~~

1 The place where planes take off and land. *runway*

2 To relax and get (my) energy back. _____

3 Things you buy in special shops at the airport. _____

4 A place to sit next to the passage between the rows of seats. _____

5 The place where you get your luggage back after a flight. _____

4 🔊 *22* Complete the extracts from the recording in Exercise 2 with the words and phrases from Exercise 3. Listen and check.

1 'You won't see much in two days,' my colleagues told me, but it was enough time for me to *recharge my batteries*.

2 I bought some _____ – my favourite aftershave – and made my way to the gate.

3 I sat in an _____ and we took off on time.

4 At Bergen, we left the plane, took our luggage from the _____ area and found our coach.

5 We could see that the _____ was covered in snow.

Pronunciation

5 🔊 *23* Look at these sentences from the recording in Exercise 2. Find one word in each sentence which includes silent letters. Listen and check.

1 After a busy period at work, I needed to relax so I booked a cheap return <u>flight</u> to Tromso in the far north of Norway.

2 'You won't see much in two days,' my colleagues told me.

3 I sat in an aisle seat and we took off on time.

4 I bought some duty free – my favourite aftershave – and made my way to the gate.

5 The airline paid for food and drink, which is important in a country like Norway.

ACTIVE PRONUNCIATION | Silent letters

Silent letters appear in words, but are not heard when those words are spoken. This can be confusing because we can see the letter in the spelling of the word, but we don't actually say it.

6 Which of these words have silent letters? Put them in the correct column. There are three extra words.

~~guest~~   island   than   tonight   visa   wheel
wonderful

silent *gh*	silent *u*	silent *s*	silent *h*
	guest		

7 🔊 *24* Listen and write some more words with silent letters. What are the silent letters in each word?

1 *half*   *l*   **4** _____ __

2 _____ __   **5** _____ __

3 _____ __   **6** _____ __

8 🔊 *25* Listen to a foreign student trying to pronounce some difficult words which include silent letters. During the pauses, say the mispronounced words correctly.

9 🔊 *26* Now listen and repeat the correct pronunciation.

3F READING AND VOCABULARY

1 Look at the pictures and read the first paragraph of the article. Choose the best answer.

What was unusual about Jason's journey?

a He made the journey alone.

b He used only his own body power.

c He visited every country in the world.

2 Read the text and choose the correct answers.

1 According to their plan, Jason and Steve were not allowed to

  a go cycling.

  b travel on foot.

  c use a kayak.

  d travel in a car.

2 Jason and Steve

  a reached Miami 111 days after setting off on their round-the-world trip.

  b needed a rest from each other after crossing the Atlantic.

  c travelled by pedal boat to Portugal.

  d were travelling together when Jason had an accident.

3 After visiting Hawaii, Jason

  a didn't want to continue the journey.

  b continued alone, but often travelled with other people.

  c travelled back to the UK with some Australians.

  d travelled alone for the rest of the journey.

4 Jason was worried when travelling in Tibet because

  a he couldn't see very well in the dark.

  b he didn't have a visa to travel.

  c he thought he might get lost.

  d he thought the police would stop him.

5 How long did Jason spend in Jordan and Syria?

  a the whole of August

  b some months

  c some weeks

  d thirteen years

6 The article is about a man who

  a travelled the world alone.

  b found a new route around the world.

  c refused to give up his dream.

  d wasn't a good athlete.

Vocabulary extension

3 Find the words in the text that match these definitions.

1 The motor part of a car, boat, etc. (para. 1) e*ngine*

2 People travelling in a car, bus, etc. (para. 1) p_____

3 A kind of boat which you push with your feet. (para. 2) p_____ b_____

4 A journey by boat across a sea. (para. 2) c_____

5 Things you need for a journey. (para. 3) s_____

4 Match the travel-related phrasal verbs from the box with their definitions.

drop off   get away   get on/off   ~~pick up~~   see off   set out

1 To collect someone in your car. *pick up*

2 To take someone by car and leave them at a place. _____

3 To enter or leave a bus or train. _____

4 To say goodbye to someone as they leave on a journey. _____

5 To go on holiday to have a rest. _____

6 To begin a journey. _____

5 Complete the sentences with the phrasal verbs from Exercise 4.

1 I can *drop* you *off* at the railway station on my way to work.

2 When Columbus _____ for India, he travelled west and landed in the Caribbean.

3 I'll come with you to the train station and _____ you _____.

4 Jeremy's tired and stressed and would love to _____ for a few days.

5 Can you _____ me _____ from work at five o'clock, please?

6 The train is leaving in two minutes. _____ quickly!

6 **ON A HIGH NOTE** Write a short paragraph about an exciting/dangerous/difficult journey you went on. Describe what happened and how you felt.

JASON LEWIS
achieving the impossible

In 1994, Jason Lewis and Steve Smith set out from London on an incredible round-the-world adventure. Their plan was to use only forms of transport that they could power themselves – kayaks, bicycles, skates, even a pedal boat! They didn't want to use anything with an engine. They couldn't drive or be passengers in a vehicle – so even hitchhiking wasn't allowed!

They travelled across the English Channel to France in a pedal boat and then cycled across France to Portugal. That's where things began to get difficult. Most people use pedal boats to have fun with at the beach, but Jason and Steve wanted to use one to cross the Atlantic Ocean! The crossing took 111 days and when they finally arrived in Miami, they were hungry and exhausted. Not surprisingly, they were also tired of each other's company. So they decided to cross the USA separately. Steve cycled and Jason skated. While he was skating to a town called Pueblo, a car hit him. It was more than three months before he was fit enough to continue his journey.

Steve and Jason reunited in California, but there were more problems when they tried to cross the Pacific Ocean. Their pedal boat sank and it took them another year to replace it and to collect new supplies. They finally set out once more. In Hawaii, Steve decided to leave the expedition, but Jason was determined to complete the journey and carried on solo. In fact, he wasn't alone for long. In Australia, teachers and their teenage students cycled with Jason for a while and later on he met other friendly, hospitable people who wanted to share his adventures.

In Tibet, Jason cycled at night. He had a visa to enter the country but foreigners can't travel independently in the country and the police have checks on the roads. Luckily, nobody saw him but Jason still felt very happy when he crossed the border into Nepal. He wasn't so lucky in Egypt. The police there thought he was a spy and put him in prison. Finally, they found out what he was doing and let him go. Jason spent the next few weeks travelling through Jordan and Syria and finally entered Europe from Turkey in early August. When he reached Belgium, his old pedal boat was waiting for him for the final sea crossing back to the UK. After all the problems, adventures and changes to his original plans, Jason finally arrived back in the UK after thirteen years, two months and twenty-four days!

When they started on their journey, Jason and Steve had two aims: the first was to push themselves to the limit. The second was to make people think about the pollution caused by cars, buses and planes. Today Jason visits schools – more than 900 in thirty-seven countries so far – and talks to students about the environment and making the right choices in life. Jason's trip changed his life and he is now helping to change other people's lives too.

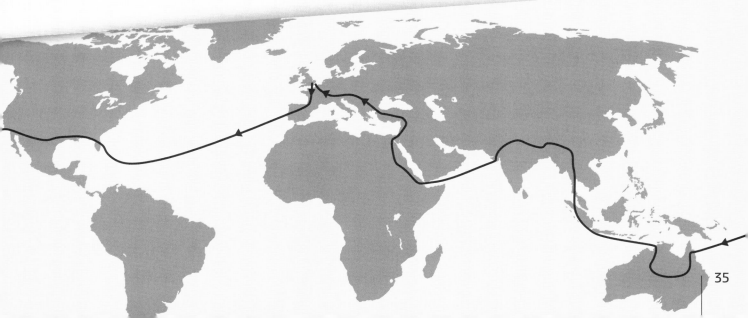

3G WRITING AND VOCABULARY | A blog post

AN AMAZING PLACE

Mention where you went.

I recently visited Vietnam with my parents. We spent a week in a town called Sapa. It's a tourist centre in the north of the country.

Say how you got there and describe the journey.

We flew to Hanoi. It took twelve hours but the journey was very comfortable. We flew with Vietnam Airlines so we had our first taste of Vietnamese food on the plane. It was delicious.

Talk about how you spent your time.

On the first day, we went sightseeing in Hanoi and then caught a night train to Sapa. It was an amazing journey with very scenic views. We booked a room at a local family's home and they were waiting for us at the station and drove us to their house. The next day, we went for a walk in the rice fields. It was a magical place. On the third day, we went to a market and tried different kinds of street food. Every day was special and I had a magical time. After Sapa, we had a week on Cat Ba Island. It was spectacular.

Sum up your overall experience.

Vietnam made a really positive impression on me. The people were all incredibly friendly and welcoming. Overall, it was a wonderful trip and I'd love to go back one day.

1 Read the blog post and complete the information.

Country: ¹*Vietnam*
Airline: ² _____
City they flew to: ³ _____
Two places they visited: ⁴ _____ ⁵ _____

2 Read the blog post again and complete the sentences with one word in each gap.

1 Sapa is a *tourist* centre.
2 They _____ to Hanoi.
3 They caught a _____ to Sapa.
4 They stayed with a local _____.
5 On the _____ day they went sightseeing.
6 On the _____ day they visited a market.
7 The writer had a _____ time in Sapa.
8 Cat Ba is an _____.
9 Vietnam made a positive _____ on the writer.
10 The people were friendly and _____.

3 WRITING TASK Look at these two adverts for holidays. Choose one and write a blog post about it. Research the place you choose online to help with ideas for activities.

COME TO THE JULIAN ALPS IN SLOVENIA
- Great mountain walks for beginners and experts.
- Beautiful Lake Bled with its castle on an island.
- Take a day trip to Italy or Austria.
- Swim in the magical Soca River.
- Excellent food, friendly people and spectacular views.
- Flights to Ljubljana. Then a bus or rent a car.
- 7 nights in a small guest house in the village of Bovec.

CITY BREAKS IN SYRACUSE, SICILY
- Scenic city streets.
- Amazing Italian food.
- Fresh fruit and seafood at the market.
- Greek and Roman ruins.
- Flights to Catania. Then bus or train.
- Visit spectacular beaches, go walking in the hills, sightseeing in historic Noto.
- 7 nights in an apartment with sea views.

ACTIVE WRITING | A blog post

1 Plan your blog post.

Use these ideas to help you plan your writing.
- Say where you went and why.
- Mention how you got there and what the journey was like.
- Talk about how you spent your time.
- Sum up your overall experience; mention the people and their behaviour towards you.

2 Write your blog post.
- Use positive adjectives to make your blog post more interesting.
- Use phrases from the Writing box in the Student's Book and from this page.

3 Check your blog post. Check that:
- all the relevant information is included.
- there are clear paragraphs in your writing.
- there are no spelling or grammar mistakes.
- there is interesting and relevant topic vocabulary.

1 3A GRAMMAR AND VOCABULARY **Complete the holiday 'to-do list' with one word in each gap.**

> Things to do before I go
> **1**Pack my bags.
> Ask Mum to **2**d_____ me to the airport.
>
> When I'm there
> **3**R_____ a bike along the coast.
> **4**S_____ on the beach. (Take sun cream!)
> Get up early and **5**w_____ the sunrise.
> **6**S_____ the sights.
> **7**S_____ to an island on a ferry.
> **8**T_____ lots of photos.

2 3B VOCABULARY **Complete the texts with the words from the box.**

> board   break   cruise   fully   in   journey   landed
> missed   on   ~~package~~

Tell us about your holidays!

I like to relax on holiday, which is why I always choose a **1***package* holiday with everything organised for me, or a **2**_____ on a ship around the Mediterranean. I don't have to worry that the hotel will be **3**_____ booked or that there isn't a bus to the airport. *Akim, Leeds*

We nearly **4**_____ the plane because we were busy buying duty-free at the airport. We were the last people to **5**_____ the plane and everyone looked at us as we got on. Luckily, we took off **6**_____ time and we **7**_____ in Greece ten minutes early. *Gareth, Cardiff*

3 3C SPEAKING AND VOCABULARY **Complete the mini-conversations with one word in each gap.**

Tourist	Excuse me. Where's the subway station?
Londoner	I'm sorry? What's a subway station?
Tourist	Oh, of course. In Britain, you say **1***underground* station.
Londoner	Oh – you mean the **2**t_____ station! It's on Holland Park Avenue.

Tourist	I can't climb these stairs with my heavy suitcases. Is there an elevator?
Londoner	An elevator?
Tourist	You know. To take me up to the Left **3**L_____.
Londoner	Oh, you mean a **4**l_____. Sure – it's over there.

Tourist	Let's take a **5**c_____ to Buckingham Palace.
Londoner	A taxi? OK. There's a taxi **6**r_____ over there.

4 3E LISTENING AND VOCABULARY **Choose the correct words to complete the sentences.**

1 It's easy to __ a flight on the Internet.
   a book   **b** land   **c** miss

2 Print your boarding __ before you go to the airport.
   a pass   **b** review   **c** passport

3 Budget __ are usually very cheap.
   a aircraft   **b** airlines   **c** airports

4 Our flight was __ by a few hours.
   a cancelled   **b** delayed   **c** boarded

5 Put your suitcase on a __ and you won't have to carry it.
   a trolley   **b** package   **c** security

6 When you're meeting people off a plane, wait for them __.
   a at the gate   **b** in arrivals   **c** in the departure lounge

7 Tickets cost a lot more money in the __ season.
   a big   **b** high   **c** tall

8 I never take much __ luggage on a plane – just a book and my phone.
   a small   **b** left   **c** hand

5 3F READING AND VOCABULARY **Choose the correct words to complete the sentences.**

1 Trains are expensive, so why don't we try *boarding / hitchhiking*?

2 They didn't let me into the country because I didn't have a *trolley / visa*.

3 I like travelling *solo / up-to-date* because it gives me time to think.

4 My passport is only *valid / cancelled* for five months, so I need to get a new one.

5 The explorers *picked up / set out* on the first day of their mountain hike.

6 Wake up! We're crossing the *budget / border* from China into Vietnam.

7 Lots of young people travelled *overland / underground* to India through Afghanistan and Iran.

8 Many people want Scotland to be an independent *state / border* and not part of the UK.

6 3G WRITING AND VOCABULARY **Match adjectives 1–5 with places, people or things a–e.**

1 ☐ spectacular   **a** the journey by train
2 ☐ hospitable   **b** the day at the adventure park
3 ☐ scenic   **c** the view from the mountain top
4 ☐ fun   **d** our hotel room
5 ☐ attractive   **e** the people we stayed with

7 ON A HIGH NOTE **Write a short paragraph about what you did to get ready for a holiday. Did you look up the place you were going to on the Internet? Did you buy anything special for the journey? What did you pack?**

1 **For each learning objective, write 1–5 to assess your ability.**

1 = I don't feel confident. 5 = I feel confident.

	Learning objective	Course material	How confident I am (1–5)
3A	I can use Past Simple and Past Continuous to talk about past experiences.	Student's Book pp. 34–35	
3B	I can talk about holiday activities, transport and accommodation.	Student's Book p. 36	
3C	I can ask for information in situations related to travelling.	Student's Book p. 37	
3D	I can use relative pronouns to talk about people, things and places.	Student's Book p. 38	
3E	I can find specific details in a conversation and talk about problems while travelling.	Student's Book p. 39	
3F	I can get the main idea and find specific details in an article and talk about travelling and charities.	Student's Book pp. 40–41	
3G	I can write a blog post.	Student's Book p. 42	

2 **Which of the skills above would you like to improve in? How?**

Skill I want to improve in	How I can improve

3 **What can you remember from this unit?**

New words I learned and most want to remember	Expressions and phrases I liked	English I heard or read outside class

GRAMMAR AND VOCABULARY

1 **Complete the conversation with one word in each gap.**

Mandy Shall we go on a city **¹**b<u>reak</u> next month?

Steve OK. How about Venice? We could **²**s_____ in a nice hotel.

Mandy Wonderful. If we use a budget **³**a_____ , it will be cheap too.

Steve You have to pay a lot to take a suitcase, though.

Mandy We can just take **⁴**h_____ luggage. Then we won't need to queue up at the **⁵**c_____ -in desk.

Steve **⁶**B_____!

/ 5

2 **Complete the sentences with one word in each gap.**

1 What time do we arrive <u>*in*</u> New York?

2 I always feel nervous when the plane takes _____.

3 The bus leaves _____ the beach in ten minutes.

4 Because of fog, we arrived _____ Birmingham Airport instead of Heathrow Airport.

5 The explorers set _____ for the coast at the beginning of January.

6 We sailed around the island _____ a ferry.

/ 5

3 **Choose the correct words to complete the sentences.**

1 We were putting up the tent when we *were seeing / saw* a snake in the grass.

2 *As / While* we were waiting for the train, we bought some sandwiches.

3 A cruise is a holiday *which / where* you spend on a boat.

4 While I *was packing / packed* my suitcase, I found some shells from my last holiday.

5 I was waiting in the departure lounge *when / while* I lost my passport.

/ 5

4 **Complete the text with one word in each gap.**

One of these days ...

It was a day when everything seemed to go wrong. We **¹**<u>*were*</u> visiting my aunt **²**_____ lived in a small village in the mountains. After a while, we got to a place **³**_____there was a beautiful view of the town and sea. It was a great place for a photograph, so we stopped. We were getting out of the car **⁴**_____ Mum suddenly shouted. The car **⁵**_____ going backwards down the hill! Luckily, it didn't go very far and it was OK. We drove on but when we reached my aunt's house, she wasn't there. She was **⁶**_____ holiday!

/ 5

USE OF ENGLISH

5 **Choose the correct words a-c to complete the texts.**

1
> **Changes to the __**
> From 1st June the 10.24 train to London will leave at 10.22.

a timetable   **b** transport   **c** platform

2
> Because of bad weather, all today's flights are __.

a boarding   **b** cancelled   **c** booked

3
> You are approaching an international __. Please have your passport ready for inspection.

a destination   **b** expedition   **c** border

4
> **DISTANCE AND JOURNEY TIMES**
> __ car: 11 km, 6 minutes   On foot: 9 km, 2 hours

a With   **b** By   **c** On

5
> NO ROOM AVAILABLE.
> We are now fully __ until August 24th.

a boarded   **b** crowded   **c** booked

/ 5

6 **Complete the text with one word in each gap.**

It was 10th August and my family and I **¹**<u>*were*</u> waiting for the train to take us to the seaside. We **²**_____ the eleven o'clock train because Dad couldn't find the tent **³**_____ we needed for our camping holiday! We finally arrived at the campsite in the evening, **⁴**_____ up our tent and cooked our evening meal. Personally, I prefer **⁵**_____ holidays which include your travel, hotel and food, but it was OK. There was a nice beach near the campsite so I spent a lot of time **⁶**_____ on the beach. I met some nice people and we had fun.

/ 5

/ 30

A good buy

4A GRAMMAR AND VOCABULARY

Comparison of adjectives

1 ★ **Choose the correct forms to complete the sentences.**

1 Which of these three snacks is the ___?
  a tasty   **b** tastier   **c** tastiest

2 Children should eat something ___ than crisps.
  a healthy   **b** healthier   **c** healthiest

3 This meal isn't as ___ as I thought, but it's really good.
  a cheap   **b** cheaper   **c** cheapest

4 The film *The Chef* was ___ than I expected.
  a good   **b** better   **c** best

5 British breakfasts are much ___ for you than continental breakfasts.
  a bad   **b** worse   **c** worst

6 I was the ___ person in the restaurant and I'm only thirty-five!
  a old   **b** older   **c** oldest

2 ★ **Match the two parts of the sentences.**

1 ☐ Carrots are healthier
2 ☐ Coffee is more
3 ☐ This is the most
4 ☐ The restaurant is too
5 ☐ Dark chocolate is the least
6 ☐ The Jolly Frog is the furthest
7 ☐ This café isn't big
8 ☐ Restaurant pizzas aren't as

a expensive restaurant in our town.
b busy – let's eat at home.
c enough for all the customers.
d than crisps.
e tasty as yours.
f sweet kind of chocolate.
g restaurant from my house.
h popular than tea in my family.

3 ★★ **Put the words in order to make sentences.**

1 biggest / in the world / is / hot dog / this / the
  This is the biggest hot dog in the world.

2 I / can / less / something / fattening / have / ?
  _____

3 the / your meal / least / is / on the menu / nutritious
  _____

4 is / fruit juice / fruit / for / than / better / you
  _____

5 as / in other restaurants / expensive / aren't / the burgers here / as
  _____

6 tastiest / in this place / the / pizza topping / what's / ?
  _____

4 ★★ **Complete the sentences with the correct forms of the adjectives in brackets.**

1 Some special coffees are *more fattening* (fattening) than a burger and fries.

2 This is the _____ (cheap) supermarket in the area.

3 Are sweet potatoes _____ (good) for you than normal potatoes?

4 This low-fat yoghurt isn't as _____ (tasty) as normal yoghurt.

5 Experts say that broccoli is the _____ (nutritious) vegetable in the world.

6 Home-made soup is _____ (healthy) than soup from a tin.

5 ★★ **Complete the text with the correct forms of the adjectives in brackets. Add any other necessary words.**

Why try a gourmet burger?

They are **1** *more expensive than* (expensive) normal burgers; even **2** _____ (cheap) gourmet burger costs about £10 compared to 99p for a 'regular' burger. It's hard to believe, but **3** _____ (good) gourmet burgers can cost £100 or more! They use one of **4** _____ (fine) types of beef in the world – Wagyu beef from Japan. Wagyu beef is **5** _____ (health) normal beef and it's much **6** _____ (juicy), too.

One reason it costs more is that the Wagyu cows live **7** _____ (long) other beef cows and need a special diet. **8** _____ (famous) kind of Wagyu beef is Kobe beef, which comes from the Kobe area of Japan. But is it **9** _____ (good) as the experts say?

Some people are disappointed because you need an expert chef to cook it properly. It is **10** _____ (difficult) to cook well than normal beef and the correct temperature is essential. So, for the best gourmet burger, go to the best restaurant with the best chef and enjoy a special treat.

6 ★★ **Complete the text with the words from the box. There are two extra words.**

as (x2) best enough good more most ~~than~~
the (x2)

KEITH FLOYD – celebrity chef

My favourite TV chef was Keith Floyd. His programmes were more interesting **¹** _than_ other cookery shows. I don't think other TV chefs are **²**_____ passionate about food as he was. I think he was also **³**_____ friendliest chef and he loved chatting to people from all over the world on his show. I think today's cookery shows are **⁴**_____ serious than Floyd's shows.

The **⁵**_____ series he presented was when he went to the USA – he showed the culture and people as well as the food and cooked everything from barbecued meat to delicious sea food. The **⁶**_____ exciting place he visited was Memphis – he met people who knew Martin Luther King, went to Elvis Presley's home and watched a blues concert. **⁷**_____ funniest programme was somewhere in the wild west. He cooked something for two cowboys, but they didn't like it and gave it to their dog – but Keith still showed that part on his programme. Not many TV chefs would be as brave **⁸**_____ that nowadays!

7 ★★★ USE OF ENGLISH **Complete the second sentence using the word in bold so that it means the same as the first one. Use no more than three words including the word in bold.**

1 My bread is nicer than the bread from the bakery. **AS**
The bread from the bakery isn't _as nice as_ my bread.

2 Chips in the UK aren't as thin as French fries in the USA. **THINNER**
French fries in the USA _____ chips in the UK.

3 No restaurant in our town is better than this one. **THE**
This is _____ in our town.

4 Dark chocolate is healthier than milk chocolate. **AS**
Milk chocolate is _____ as dark chocolate.

5 I think that rice isn't as filling as bread. **MORE**
I think that bread is _____ rice.

8 ★★★ **Use the information and the prompts to write sentences.**

🍴 FOOD REVIEWS

CLICK HERE to write a fast food review

	Meal deal	Light bite	Sweet treat
Price:	£2.20	£2.80	£2.45
Taste:	*	**	*****
Nutrition:	***	***	*

1 The meal deal / cheap / the light bite
The meal deal is cheaper than the light bite.

2 The meal deal / cheap / snack
_____

3 The light bite / not / tasty / the sweet treat
_____

4 The light bite / tasty / the meal deal
_____

5 The sweet treat / tasty / of all
_____

6 The meal deal / nutritious / the light bite
_____

7 The light bite / nutritious / the sweet treat
_____

8 The sweet treat / nutritious / of all
_____

9 ON A HIGH NOTE **Write a short paragraph comparing different fruit. Use adjectives from the box or other adjectives of your choice.**

cheap expensive nutritious popular tasty

4B VOCABULARY | Food and drink

1 ⭐ **Choose the word which does NOT fit in each sentence.**

1 I always put __ on my bread.
  a jam   **b** melon   **c** honey

2 No, I don't want __ – I'm a vegetarian.
  a sausages **b** mushrooms **c** bacon

3 I'd like something filling like a __.
  a muffin   **b** doughnut   **c** cucumber

4 We need some fruit. Can you buy some __?
  a beans   **b** lemons   **c** grapes

5 You will need __ and eggs to make a cake.
  a lentils   **b** sugar   **c** butter

2 ⭐ **Complete the mini-conversations with the words from the box.**

bacon   cream   muffin   pancake   ~~roll~~

Adrian A ham sandwich, please.
Sally   White bread, brown bread or a **¹**_roll_?

Amy   Do you want a **²**_____?
Bill   No, thanks. I don't like cakes.

Brad   Do you want **³**_____ in your coffee?
Jill   No, thanks. I can't eat anything made from milk.

Ahmed   What do you want on your **⁴**_____?
Sarah   Lemon and sugar, please.

Paul   Do you want some **⁵**_____ with your eggs?
Pam   No, thanks. I don't eat meat.

3 ⭐ **Complete the words for these definitions with one letter in each gap.**

1 It's a fish with pink flesh. s_a_l_m_on
2 They grow on trees and are black or green.
   o__ __ __ __ s
3 It's a large fruit with a green skin and red inside.
   w__ __ __ __ __ __ __ __ n
4 It's a healthy breakfast food you mix with milk.
   p__ __ __ __ __ __ e
5 It's good on pancakes and comes from Canada.
   m__ __ __ e s__ __ __ p
6 This cold drink has different flavours like chocolate or banana.   m__ __ __ __ __ __ __ __ e

4 ⭐ **Match adjectives 1–8 with their opposites a–h.**

1 ☐ mild   **a** light
2 ☐ crunchy   **b** soft
3 ☐ fresh   **c** spicy
4 ☐ fizzy   **d** dry
5 ☐ delicious   **e** sweet
6 ☐ bitter   **f** disgusting
7 ☐ hard   **g** still
8 ☐ heavy   **h** smooth

5 ⭐⭐ **Complete the sentences with the adjectives from Exercise 4**

1 The food was delicious, but a bit _heavy_ – there was too much cream and cheese.
2 This dish is _____. Can you give me the recipe?
3 I didn't put any hot spices into the curry, so it's quite _____.
4 The bread is _____ – I made it this morning.
5 Don't put the butter in the fridge. It gets very _____ in there.
6 I only drink _____ water. I don't like the bubbles in fizzy drinks.
7 Do you prefer smooth or _____ peanut butter?

6 ⭐⭐ **Complete the text with the words from the box. There are three extra words.**

beans   bitter   ~~croissant~~   crunchy   grapes   lemons
mushrooms   porridge   salt   sugar

What's your favourite food?

For breakfast, I always have a **¹**_croissant_. It's a popular French breakfast food and it's delicious. I have that with a cup of coffee. I don't put any milk or **²**_____ in my coffee. I like the **³**_____ taste of black coffee.

For lunch, I often make an omelette. I sometimes put ham or cheese in it but, in September, I go into the forest to find **⁴**_____. They're delicious, but you have to be careful because some are very dangerous. I usually put a little sea **⁵**_____ on my omelette.

My favourite vegetables are **⁶**_____ – long green ones or small white ones. My favourite fruit are **⁷**_____ – I like both the green and the red ones.

7 ON A HIGH NOTE **Write a short paragraph about the last time you ate out. What did the food taste like?**

4C GRAMMAR

Quantifiers

1 ⭐ **Put the words from the box in the correct column.**

beans ~~cream~~ eggs fruit honey jam olives rolls
sausages sugar

There's some ...	There are some ...
cream	_____
_____	_____
_____	_____
_____	_____
_____	

2 ⭐ **Complete the sentences with *of*. Where *of* is not necessary, write –.**

1 Do you want a bit *of* ham?

2 Is there any bread? Oh, there's a little bit _____ but not much.

3 We've got a lot _____ eggs. Let's have an omelette.

4 I don't want any cake. I ate a lot _____ before you arrived.

5 Cerys eats lots _____ meat – her favourite is fried chicken.

6 I think I'll have a couple _____ eggs for breakfast today.

3 ⭐⭐ **Complete the sentences with the words from the box.**

enough few little lot lots of many much (x2)

1 How _much_ bread is there in the cupboard?

2 There isn't _____ sugar in my tea. Can I have some more?

3 There's a _____ salt in the soup but not much.

4 How _____ mushrooms did you find in the forest?

5 There's too _____ sugar in this tea – I don't like it so sweet.

6 Take as many rolls as you want – we've got _____ them.

7 You can have a _____ crisps, but not many – they're not good for you.

8 We need a _____ of eggs for this recipe.

4 ⭐⭐ USE OF ENGLISH **Complete the blog post with one word in each gap.**

5 ⭐⭐⭐ **Look at the picture and complete the questions and answers. Use *a lot (of)*, *a little*, *a few*, *any*, *couple* and any other necessary words.**

Ellis	Are **1**_there any_ rolls?
Joey	Yes, **2**_____ rolls.
Jack	How **3**_____ grapes **4**_____?
Leo	There **5**_____ grapes.
Max	How **6**_____ bacon **7**_____?
Luca	There **8**_____ bacon.
Blake	**9**_____ jam?
Louis	Yes, **10**_____ of jam.
Isla	How **11**_____ water **12**_____?
Lily	There **13**_____ water.
Toby	How **14**_____ sausages **15**_____?
Aisha	There **16**_____ of sausages.

6 ON A HIGH NOTE **Write a short paragraph about what food and drink there is in your fridge. Use quantifiers.**

WE ASKED ...

PEOPLE EAT TOO MUCH FAST FOOD. WHY? YOU TOLD US ...

There isn't **1**_enough_ time to cook a big meal in the evening because I don't leave work until eight p.m. There are **2**_____ of fast food restaurants so I can have something different each day. *Amanda*

There are too **3**_____ fast food restaurants in our cities. **4**_____ isn't enough choice. It's fast food or nothing. *Jake*

I think a lot **5**_____ people are just lazy. It only takes a **6**_____ time to cook rice and vegetables. *Jeff*

I really don't know. I don't like **7**_____ kind of fast food. I only eat healthy food – well, I have a little **8**_____ of cake with my mid-morning coffee but I eat salad and fish for lunch. *Tia*

4D READING AND VOCABULARY

1 Where would you find these products in a supermarket? Match products a–c with areas 1–3 on the supermarket floor plan. Then read paragraphs 2, 3 and 6 of the text to check your answers.

a ☐ bread **b** ☐ fruit **c** ☐ sweets

2 Read the text quickly and choose the best answer.

What is the text about?
- **a** How supermarkets make us spend more.
- **b** The advantages and disadvantages of supermarkets.
- **c** How to find the best offers in your supermarket.

3 Read the text again. Match headings A–G with paragraphs 1–6. There is one extra heading.

- **A** Offers that don't save us money
- **B** New products keep customers interested
- **C** Tempting treats while we wait
- **D** Some tips for customers
- **E** Some more tricks
- **F** Healthy options to start
- **G** Ways to keep us searching

4 Read the text again and answer the questions.

1 What are the first products you see in most supermarkets?
fruit and vegetables

2 Where do supermarkets place the most important items that most people need?
_____

3 What emotion do customers often feel when they see a special offer?
_____

4 According to the article, why are supermarket trolleys very big?
_____

5 Which product do customers sometimes buy while waiting at the checkout?
_____

6 Which two tips for spending less in the supermarket does the author give?
_____

Vocabulary extension

5 Find the words in the text that match these definitions.

1 The way a room or building is arranged. (intro.)
l*ayout*

2 A special price that is less than usual. (intro.)
o_____

3 Something you get because you are good. (para. 1)
r_____

4 The most important. (para. 2) k_____

5 Products set in a certain way to look attractive. (para. 4)
d_____

7 A thing on wheels where you put your shopping. (para. 4) t_____

ACTIVE VOCABULARY | Nouns with prepositions

Some nouns change their meaning or become a different part of speech in combination with prepositions.

6 Read the sentences including phrases with *date* and *point*. Match the underlined phrases with their meanings a–e.

1 ☐ When looking for the items you need in a supermarket, <u>at some point</u> you can put some unnecessary things in your trolley too.

2 ☐ This offer is <u>out of date</u>; it says 'Half price until 12th June' but today is 15th June!

3 ☐ The tricks used by supermarket managers are clever but if you're alert, they work only <u>up to a point</u>.

4 ☐ <u>To date</u> there are three supermarkets in our town, but I think they will build more soon.

5 ☐ Is all the information in your report <u>up to date</u>? It says here that Barack Obama is the president of the USA!

- **a** to some extent but not completely
- **b** at some moment in time
- **c** too old to sell
- **d** the most modern
- **e** up until now

7 ON A HIGH NOTE Describe a supermarket you go to. Write a short paragraph about what you can see when you first walk in and where the different products are. Do you think the layout of the shop is attractive or not? Why?

SUPERMARKET SHOPPING
TREAT OR TRICK?

When people talk about the things they dislike about food shopping, they often mention queues or bad service. Very few people mention the layout of their supermarket or the offers available … but maybe they should. Why? Because everything is carefully designed to encourage you to buy things you don't really need.

1 ☐ In many supermarkets, the main entrance leads directly into the fruit and vegetable section. There is a reason for this. Psychologists say that when we start by buying food which is good for us, we are more likely to feel better about ourselves. That's why, later on, when we pass the crisps or biscuits, we often take a packet as a reward for our earlier good behaviour.

2 ☐ Supermarket managers want customers to look at as many products as possible. While we are looking for everyday items which we need, we also notice other food items for sale. That's why key products such as dairy, bread and meat are right at the back of the store, so customers have to walk past lots of other different food items before they find the ones they actually need.

3 ☐ When we see a sign offering a discount, we often take the product without thinking. It isn't unusual to see a sign saying: '2 packets only £2!' and, in our excitement, we grab the product without noticing that the price for one packet is actually only £1! And be careful – these items are often very near their 'sell-by-date'. You might have to throw the product away the next day!

4 ☐ How else do supermarkets make us spend more? There are quite a few tricks. The smell of fresh bread can make us more hungry and make the shop seem more attractive. Displays at the end of each aisle are easy to see and, after seeing them three or four times, customers often take something. In addition, large supermarket trolleys make us think that we only have a few items and that we should buy more!

5 ☐ Finally, we reach the checkout. Perhaps we are having a bad day and don't feel so good. Perhaps we are just bored while waiting. And while we're waiting in that queue, what do we see? Chocolate bars. Without thinking, we pick one up and drop it into the trolley. More money spent!

6 ☐ How can we avoid these clever tricks? Make a shopping list – then you will only buy the things you need. And – good news for phone addicts! Looking at your phone while you are waiting at the checkout means you don't get bored and you might not even notice the chocolate bars all around you!

4E LISTENING AND VOCABULARY

1 🔊 **27** **Listen to Part 1 of a radio programme and choose the correct caption for the photo.**

jumble sale / jumble trail

2 🔊 **28** **Now listen to the whole programme and complete the notes with 1–3 words in each gap.**

Traditional jumble sales

1 The aim of traditional jumble sales was to raise money for organisations or *charity*.

2 Jumble sales often took place in community halls, churches or _____.

Jumble trails

3 These take place outside people's _____.

4 The first one, which was held in Clapton, London, happened in _____.

5 _____ came to the Clapton Jumble Trail two years later.

6 As well as unwanted items, some people make and sell _____.

7 It's a good way for people to meet _____.

3 🔊 **29** **Listen to two people talking at a jumble trail and tick the items that the girl is selling.**

☐ trousers ☑ kilt ☐ suit ☐ bracelets ☐ earrings
☐ rings ☐ belts ☐ blouse ☐ hat

Vocabulary extension

4 **Complete the sentences with the words and phrases from the box, which you heard in the radio programme in Exercise 2.**

donate fee free of charge ~~get rid of~~ household
stall

1 There are different ways to *get rid of* something you don't like – sell it, give or throw it away.

2 We're asking people to _____ old clothes and toys that they no longer need.

3 The organisers charge a _____ to the people selling things – not much, just a few pounds.

4 There are five people in this _____; two adults and three children.

5 Donna is selling cakes and sandwiches from the _____ in front of her house.

6 You don't have to pay to get into the concert. It's _____.

Pronunciation

5 🔊 **30** **Listen to some sentences from the radio programme in Exercise 2. Write *ch* if you hear the /tʃ/ sound and *sh* if you hear the /ʃ/ sound. Write both if you hear both sounds.**

1 *sh*

2 _____

3 _____

4 _____

5 _____

6 _____

6 🔊 **31** **Listen and wite down the three words from Exercise 5 which contain the /ʃ/ sound. What do you notice about the way this sound is spelled in each word?**

1 _____

2 _____

3 _____

7 🔊 **32** **Look at the pairs of words. Listen and choose the one you hear.**

1 share / chair   **4** shop / chop
2 ships / chips   **5** wash / watch
3 wish / which   **6** cash / catch

ACTIVE PRONUNCIATION | /tʃ/ and /ʃ/ sounds

The letters *ch* can be pronounced in three different ways:

- /tʃ/ (e.g. **ch**urch, **ch**eese, **ch**eap).
- /ʃ/, especially in words which originate from French (e.g. **ch**andelier, **ch**ef, bro**ch**ure).
- /k/, especially in words that originate from Greek and refer to science and education (e.g. s**ch**ool, te**ch**nology, **Ch**emistry).

---

8 🔊 **33** **Read, listen and complete the sentences. Use Active Pronunciation to help you.**

> A teacher, a chef and a mechanic went on holiday. The teacher went to China. The chef went to Chicago. The mechanic went to Munich. They all did different activities. Who visited a local school? Who decided to do a parachute jump? Who went to see how cheese is made?

1 The _____ visited a local school.

2 The _____ did a parachute jump.

3 The _____ went to see how cheese is made.

9 🔊 **33** **Listen again and repeat.**

10 🔊 **34** **In each sentence, find one example of each way of saying *ch*. Listen and repeat the sentences.**

1 Ask the chemist to check the machine.

2 Every person in the orchestra has a cheerful chauffer waiting in a car outside.

1 🔊 *35* Listen and repeat the phrases. How do you say them in your language?

SPEAKING | Opinions

ASKING FOR OPINIONS

What do you think?

Don't you think I look good in this dress?

What's your opinion/view?

GIVING OPINIONS

I think/believe this old jacket looks shabby.

In my opinion/view, designer labels are too expensive.

If you ask me, one sweater is enough.

Personally, I think it's good to buy from charity shops.

Frankly, I don't think that colour suits you at all.

To be honest, your jeans look scruffy.

It seems to me these shoes are very cheap.

AGREEING

Absolutely.

I agree (with you).

I totally agree.

Me too!

You're right.

I couldn't agree (with you) more!

PARTLY AGREEING

You've got a point but I couldn't wear second-hand clothes.

I suppose so.

Fair point, but these clothes are too informal for an interview.

DISAGREEING

I know what you mean but I don't think I could wear a hat like that.

I'm not sure about that.

I don't think so.

I don't agree.

I disagree.

No way!

2 Complete the conversation with the words and phrases from the box.

be honest   do you think   got a point
If you ask   my opinion   no   not sure   personally
seems to   suppose

Kylie Hi, Amelia. I'm looking for a present for Sarah. What **¹***do you think* of these bracelets?

Amelia To **²**_____, I think they're too big. She prefers thinner ones.

Kylie Yes, I **³**_____ so. Any other ideas? How about earrings?

Amelia I'm **⁴**_____ about that – I don't think she's got pierced ears. **⁵**_____ me, I don't think jewellery is a good idea. **⁶**_____, I think a book is a better choice. She loves reading.

Kylie Yes, you've **⁷**_____, but I don't know what books she's got already.

Amelia In **⁸**_____, a classic is best. Something by Dickens or Jane Austen.

Kylie **⁹**_____ way! She reads fantasy books and science fiction, not eighteenth and nineteenth century literature!

Amelia Well, it **¹⁰**_____ me that we should go to the bookshop and see what they've got.

Kylie You're right. Let's do that.

3 Rewrite the sentences using the phrases from the Speaking box.

1 This looks good. What do you think?
   This looks good. What's *your opinion/view*?
2 I totally agree with you!
   I couldn't _____!
3 I suppose so, but I think the white dress looks better.
   I know _____ but I think the white dress looks better.
4 If you ask me, I think the colour is too dark.
   To _____, I think the colour is too dark.
5 I suppose you're right, but it could be the wrong size.
   _____ point, but it could be the wrong size.

4 Choose the correct phrases to complete the mini-conversations.

Poppy Most of our classmates have no idea how to look cool.

Ava **¹***I don't agree. / Fair point.* A lot of my friends dress really fashionably.

Owen I don't usually follow fashion – I just wear what I want.

Seth **²***No way! / Me too!* The latest trends don't usually suit me.

Ivy What do you think about fashion shows?

Amber **³***I disagree, / Frankly,* I find them quite boring and I never watch them.

Ryan Do you ever buy designer labels?

Leon **⁴**No, I *think / suppose* they're a waste of money.

4G WRITING AND VOCABULARY | A formal letter of complaint

Begin your letter appropriately with a formal expression.	Dear Sir/Madam,
Give your reason for writing.	I am writing to **1**complain / respond about an item which I bought from you online.
Describe what went wrong and what happened.	On 2 December this year, I purchased an HD13 camera from your website and paid an extra £5 for 'next-day delivery'. **2**Suddenly / Unfortunately, the delivery van did not arrive the next day and they phoned to say that it would come on the 9th. In the end, it arrived on the 7th when I wasn't at home. The driver left a note telling me to collect the camera from the local office which is over ten kilometres away! This was most **3**annoyed / inconvenient as I don't have my own transport.
Describe what other problems you had.	When I arrived at the office, I waited over an hour before they found the camera. To make **4**matters / service worse, the camera wasn't the model I ordered – it was an H13X, which is a cheaper model. This is **5**typical / unacceptable, but the delivery company told me they couldn't return the product to you and that I should arrange to send the camera myself.
Give suggestions on ways the company can improve.	I **6**feel / mean that you should find a delivery company which can deliver products on the date they promise and which delivers the correct items.
Say what compensation you want.	I believe you should replace the camera you sent me with the correct one which I ordered and also apologise for the inconvenience you caused. I look **7**ahead / forward to your reply.
End your letter appropriately with a formal expression.	Yours **8**carefully / faithfully, Kelly Pelham

1 Read the letter of complaint quickly. Which two things is the writer complaining about?

a receiving something which is broken
b a delivery on the wrong date
c rude service from the company's staff
d getting the wrong product

2 Read the letter again and choose the correct words to complete the letter.

3 Complete the sentences with the words from the box.

believe   complain   forward   ~~improve~~   matters

1 I feel that you should _improve_ your customer service.
2 I look _____ to your reply.
3 I _____ that you should refund the cost of the shirt.
4 To make _____ worse, when I phoned you, I had to wait thirty-five minutes on the line.
5 I am writing to _____ about a T-shirt I bought from your website.

4 Complete the sentences with a, an or the.

1 I bought _a_ watch from _____ company on _____ Internet. When _____ watch arrived, it didn't work.
2 I bought _____ shirt from _____ shop in _____ town centre but, when I got home I found that there was _____ hole in _____ shirt.
3 _____ man in our street complained about us. _____ man doesn't like our dog. _____ dog ran into his garden last week and chased his cat. _____ cat was alright. It ran up _____ tree.

5 WRITING TASK Read the information and write a letter of complaint. Use the notes below to help you.

Last month you bought a book online for a friend as a present.
• The book wasn't new. There were words written inside.
• You phoned the company and they apologised and asked you to send it back.
• You got a new copy of the book too late for your friend's birthday and you had to buy something else.
• You want a refund for the book which you don't need now and an apology.

ACTIVE WRITING | A formal letter of complaint

1 Plan your letter.
Include the following information:
• Your reason for writing.
• The problems you had.
• Ways that the company can improve its service.
• What you want from the company.

2 Write the letter.
• Remember to start and finish appropriately.
• Use formal language and avoid using contractions.
• Be polite.

3 Check that ...
• You have included all the relevant information.
• There are no spelling or grammar mistakes.
• You have used formal language.

UNIT VOCABULARY PRACTICE

1 4A GRAMMAR AND VOCABULARY **Complete the sentences with the words from the box. There are two extra words.**

~~expensive~~ fattening good jar nutritious packet
popular salad sandwich weigh

1 This caviar can cost thousands of pounds for one kilo –
it's very _expensive_.
2 Fruit is _____, but it's got a lot of sugar in it.
3 Lots of my friends eat at the local pizza restaurant – it's
very _____.
4 Fish is _____ for you and you should eat it quite
often.
5 I'm on a diet so I don't want to eat anything that's
_____.
6 Let's get a _____ of crisps on the way home.
7 We've got some bread and tuna. Let's make a tuna
_____.
8 These chips _____ about 200 grams.

2 4B VOCABULARY **Match sentence beginnings 1–8 with endings a–h.**

1 ☐ When you like food, you say it is
2 ☐ When you put sugar in your tea,
it becomes
3 ☐ Cola and lemonade are
4 ☐ Neil can't eat fish, so don't cook
him
5 ☐ The best thing to put on toast is
6 ☐ I'd like a slice of
7 ☐ The only fruit we've got is a
8 ☐ I can't eat anything that comes
from milk, so I can't have

a salmon.
b jam.
c sweet.
d lemon.
e bread.
f fizzy drinks.
g delicious.
h cream.

3 4D READING AND VOCABULARY **Choose the correct words to complete the sentences.**

1 Marks and Spencer is a famous *chain / focus* store – you
can find one in every town.
2 You can only take two things to try on in the *waiting /
changing* room.
3 Shop *assistants / agents* should be nice to the
customers / visitors in their shop.
4 Why is the *queue / discount* for the supermarket *mall /
checkout* always so long?
5 Selfridges is a *supermarket / department store* – it sells
books, clothes, cosmetics and toys.
6 The clothes here are cheap but the *bargain / quality* is
terrible.

4 4E LISTENING AND VOCABULARY **Complete the conversations with one word in each gap.**

Erin Why are you wearing those old jeans?
Ali The invitation said 'informal clothes'.
Erin Yes, but that doesn't mean you can wear old,
[1]s_scruffy_ jeans. It means you don't need to wear
a jacket or a [2]t_____. Why don't you wear
your new [3]d_____ jeans, a nice, white shirt
and your black shoes? Then you'll look really
[4]f_____!
Ali OK.

Ben Nice dress.
Megan Thanks. It's [5]b_____new. I bought it this
morning. It was a [6]b_____ – only £19.99.
And it fits perfectly.
Ben Yes, it's just [7]p_____ for you.
Megan I'm glad you like it. I want to go back to the
shops after lunch to get some accessories to go
with it – a [8]h_____ to keep my things in and
some new earrings.

5 4G WRITING AND VOCABULARY **Complete the conversations with the words from the box. You may have to change the form of the words.**

exchange ~~policy~~ receipt refund

Customer Excuse me, what's your [1]_policy_ on giving
[2]_____ for unwanted items?
Assistant You can [3]_____ them for a different item
in the shop, or we can give you your money
back. You must have your [4]_____, though.

discount order receive return

Woman Excuse me. Last week, I [5]_____ a shirt from
your online store. The shirt I [6]_____
yesterday wasn't the same colour as the one
I wanted. Can I [7]_____ it here or do I have
to send it back?
Assistant Yes, of course. What colour did you want? We
might have it in the shop.
Woman The dark blue one.
Assistant Here it is. I can give you a 10 percent
[8]_____ too as it was our mistake.

6 ON A HIGH NOTE **Write a short paragraph about the shops, cafés and restaurants you think your town needs. Explain why.**

1 For each learning objective, write 1-5 to assess your ability.

1 = I don't feel confident. 5 = I feel confident.

	Learning objective	Course material	How confident I am (1–5)
4A	I can use comparatives and superlatives to compare things.	Student's Book pp. 48–49	
4B	I can talk about food and drink.	Student's Book p. 50	
4C	I can use quantifiers to talk about countable and uncountable nouns.	Student's Book p. 51	
4D	I can understand the main idea of a text and a paragraph and talk about shopping.	Student's Book pp. 52–53	
4E	I can understand the main idea and find specific details in a conversation about shopping.	Student's Book p. 54	
4F	I can express, agree or disagree with opinions politely.	Student's Book p. 55	
4G	I can write a simple letter of complaint.	Student's Book p. 56	

2 Which of the skills above would you like to improve in? How?

Skill I want to improve in	How I can improve

3 What can you remember from this unit?

New words I learned and most want to remember	Expressions and phrases I liked	English I heard or read outside class

GRAMMAR AND VOCABULARY

1 Choose the correct answers to complete the sentences.

1 Make sure you get real __ syrup from Canada.
   a pancake   **b** maple   **c** muffin

2 This bread isn't very __. I think it's from yesterday.
   a fresh   **b** spicy   **c** heavy

3 You should buy this dress – it's a __.
   a bargain   **b** reduction   **c** discount

4 I can't eat any more – it's delicious, but also very __.
   a nutritious   **b** healthy   **c** filling

5 I can't find the __ for my phone. I hope I can still get my money back.
   a refund   **b** receipt   **c** response

/ 5

2 Complete the sentences with one word in each gap.

1 Bennetts d_epartment_ store is pleased to announce the opening of our new restaurant.

2 Try this delicious h_____ from our own bees.

3 I love real French c_____ made with butter.

4 When you p_____ any products for £20 or more, you get a free bottle of shampoo.

5 Oh dear. This dress doesn't f_____ – it's too small.

6 I don't go to the supermarket on Saturday because the q_____ are very long.

/ 5

3 Choose the correct words to complete the sentences.

1 How _much / many_ sugar do you have in your coffee?

2 It's the _more / most_ expensive thing on the menu!

3 I haven't got _time enough / enough time_ to cook dinner after work.

4 This fried rice is as _tasty / tastier_ as the food they sell in the Chinese restaurant.

5 This cola is _less / least_ fizzy than when we opened it.

/ 5

4 Complete the sentences with the correct words from each pair in the box.

a couple of / a lot of
Are there enough / ~~Is there enough~~
is too little / are too few
less dry / least dry
more annoyed / the most annoyed

1 _Is there enough_ sugar in your coffee or do you want some more?

2 I was _____ than my friend when the shop assistant refused to give us a refund.

3 This is the _____ bread in the shop, but it still isn't very fresh.

4 There _____ ketchup on my plate. Can I have some?

5 My dad's got _____ ties but not many.

/ 4

USE OF ENGLISH

5 Complete the text with one word in each gap.

The clothes at our local **1**_shopping_ mall aren't **2**_____ cheap as the clothes in the market, but I often shop there. Firstly, there are changing **3**_____ where I can try on clothes and make sure they fit.

Also, there isn't **4**_____ choice at our market and some of the clothes look quite old-fashioned. The people who work there are friendly, though.

5_____ worst thing about the shops at the mall is the service. The shop **6**_____ always say, 'Oh, it's perfect **7**_____ you, even when you know that it really isn't!'

/ 6

6 Complete the second sentence so that it means the same as the first one. Use no more than three words.

1 There isn't much to eat.
   There _aren't many_ things to eat.

2 Nothing at the Indian restaurant is as spicy as their vindaloo.
   Their vindaloo _____ thing on the menu.

3 The portions of chips are smaller than they used to be.
   The portions of chips are _____ as they used to be.

4 There isn't much water so don't drink it too quickly.
   There is only _____ water so don't drink it too quickly.

5 This jar isn't big enough to keep pasta in.
   This jar _____ to keep pasta in.

6 The other dresses are more expensive than this red one.
   This red dress _____ expensive of all.

/ 5

/ 30

51

05 Fit and well

5A GRAMMAR AND VOCABULARY

Modal verbs

1 ⭐ Complete the sentences with the modal verbs from the box.

could   don't have to   has to   mustn't   should   ~~shouldn't~~

1 You _shouldn't_ keep all these clothes on the sofa – it's so untidy.

2 I _____ help you tidy up your flat if you want.

3 I think you _____ get a new wardrobe – this one isn't very nice.

4 You _____ take your dog into the furniture shop!

5 You _____ take the rug with you now – we can deliver it to your home.

6 Carla _____ tidy up her room before her mum gets home!

2 ⭐ Match the two parts of the sentences.

Housework

1 ☐ Kate must
2 ☐ Meg has
3 ☐ Nina mustn't
4 ☐ Anne doesn't have

a to tidy her room every Saturday.
b leave bits of food in her room.
c to wash her windows – someone cleans them for her.
d clean the floor – it's sticky.

Friends

1 ☐ You could
2 ☐ You should
3 ☐ You don't have
4 ☐ You shouldn't

a to be friends with everybody.
b say nasty things to your friend.
c explain that your friend's behaviour is hurting you.
d listen when a friend has a problem and try to help.

3 ⭐ Choose the correct modal verbs to complete the sentences.

1 Who _must / has to_ do the washing up this evening?

2 I _must / have to_ learn how to cook – it will be very useful when I go to college.

3 Kitty can't come. She _must / has to_ study.

4 In this country, you _must / have to_ buy a TV licence every year.

5 Dan _must / has to_ get his hair cut because he's joining the army.

6 I _must / have to_ remember to buy some more hangers for my clothes.

7 How often _must Lucy / does Lucy have to_ make dinner?

8 We _must / have to_ clean this carpet – it's so dirty!

4 ⭐⭐ Read the rules for rooms in student accommodation. Complete the sentences with _have to_, _mustn't_ or _don't have to_ and a suitable verb.

STUDENT ACCOMMODATION

RULES

1 No smoking anywhere in the building.
2 No loud music after 10 p.m.
3 No overnight guests.
4 Pay for the room on the first day of the month.
5 No need to pay a deposit!
6 Clean the kitchen after use.
7 Leave the building if you hear the alarm.
8 Stay out as long as you like! Return at any time.
9 Stay one extra week after the academic year for no extra charge.

1 You _mustn't smoke_ anywhere in the building.

2 You _____ loud music after 10 p.m.

3 Guests _____ in the room overnight.

4 You _____ for the room on the first day of the month.

5 You _____ a deposit.

6 All students _____ the kitchen after using it.

7 All students _____ the building when they hear the alarm.

8 You _____ to your room at any special time.

9 You _____ the building when the term ends. You can stay one extra week for free.

5 ⭐⭐ Complete the text with the modal verbs from the box.

~~could~~   don't have to   have to   must   mustn't   should

FENG SHUI – how to organise your home

Feng Shui is an ancient Chinese philosophy which translates as 'wind-water'. One of the main ideas is that good energy in your home will make you feel happier. Today, people use a form of Feng Shui to organise their houses. Follow our top tips!

- Before you start, check your 'birth element'. This **¹could** be fire, wood, metal, water or earth. If your birth element is fire, then you **²_____** decorate your home in red and yellow. Those are probably the best colours. If your birth element is water, you certainly **³_____** use red or yellow decorations.

- Ask a Feng Shui expert to make you an energy map. You **⁴_____** do this, but it can sometimes be helpful.

- You **⁵_____** throw out objects which you don't love. This is a very important rule.

- Although it isn't always possible, you **⁶_____** have lots of natural light and fresh air in your home.

6 ⭐⭐ Choose the the correct modal verbs to complete the text.

I feel unfit and unhealthy. What advice can you give me? What do you think I **¹__** do? Thanks for your help. *RayBoy*

You **²__** join a sports club if you like. I go to a running club and I really enjoy it. *Cookie12*

Well, first of all, you **³__** go to bed late, especially if you **⁴__** to get up early for work or school. *Gym45*

You **⁵__** do anything extreme. Don't go on a 25 km run or stop eating for two days or anything like that! You **⁶__** have to become a super hero! Just eat well, sleep well and get plenty of exercise. *KittyCat*

I agree with KittyCat. You **⁷__** be careful and you really **⁸__** follow any foolish advice from the Internet! Lol! *lisaT*

1	**a** have	**b** should	**c** must
2	**a** could	**b** must	**c** have to
3	**a** shouldn't	**b** must	**c** don't have to
4	**a** must	**b** have	**c** should
5	**a** don't have	**b** couldn't	**c** mustn't
6	**a** mustn't	**b** don't	**c** can't
7	**a** mustn't	**b** should	**c** could
8	**a** shouldn't	**b** couldn't	**c** don't have to

7 ⭐⭐ Complete the conversation with one word or a negative contraction in each gap.

Nathan What do we **¹_have_** to wear for your brother's wedding?

Simon You **²_____** have to wear anything special, but you **³_____** look quite smart.

Nathan I've got a nice jacket and a white shirt. I **⁴_____** iron it tonight. Do you think I **⁵_____** wear a tie?

Simon It's up to you. My brother **⁶_____** to wear a tie, but you don't!

Nathan What time does the wedding start?

Simon Three o'clock. You **⁷_____** be late. We **⁸_____** take you in our car if you like.

Nathan That would be great. Thanks.

8 ⭐⭐⭐ USE OF ENGLISH Complete the second sentence using the word in bold so that it means the same as the first one. Use no more than three words including the word in bold.

1 One possibility would be for us to donate these old toys to charity. **COULD**

We _could donate_ these old toys to charity.

2 It is necessary for us to buy a new fridge. **TO**

We _____ a new fridge.

3 In my opinion, it would be a bad idea to paint your bedroom black. **SHOULDN'T**

You _____ your bedroom black.

4 Stacy isn't allowed to stay out after midnight. **HAS**

Stacy _____ home before midnight.

5 It's not necessary for my room to be very tidy. **HAVE**

My room _____ to be very tidy.

6 We can't wear our shoes in the house. **MUST**

We _____ our shoes in the house.

9 ON A HIGH NOTE Write a short paragraph about what you have to, don't have to and mustn't do at home. Then write another paragraph about your brother/sister/friend. Does he/she have to do the same things as you?

5B VOCABULARY | Household chores

1 ⭐ Put the words from the box in the correct column.

a cup of tea   a meal   a sandwich   breakfast
the cleaning   the dishes   the housework   the ironing
the windows   your bed

do	make
	a cup of tea

2 ⭐ Choose the correct words to complete the list of chores.

Today, I have to ...

1 walk *my bed / the rubbish / the dog.*

2 empty *my bed / the rubbish / the washing machine.*

3 polish *the furniture / the carpets / the rubbish.*

4 tidy up *the dog / my room / the carpets.*

5 make *my bed / the furniture / the table.*

6 take out *my shoes / the dishes / the rubbish.*

7 vacuum *the carpets / the furniture / the bed.*

8 dust *the carpets / the furniture / the dishes.*

3 ⭐⭐ Complete the conversation with one word in each gap.

Pauline Are you OK, Mum? You look tired.

Mum I'm exhausted, but I have to do a lot of chores.

Pauline Don't worry. You should lie down. I can ¹m*ake* dinner and the others can help me. Matt can ²s_____ the table before dinner. Leanne can ³c_____ the table after dinner and they can both ⁴w_____ u_____ the dishes while I ⁵c_____ the cooker and ⁶w_____ the surfaces. Do you want a cup of tea now?

Mum No, thank you. I just want to sleep. Thanks for helping.

4 ⭐⭐ Read the blog post about home appliances. Complete the words with one letter in each gap.

The house I lived in when I was a student wasn't great. There was no ¹w*ash i ng* m*ach ine*, so I used to take my dirty clothes home to my parents every second weekend. We didn't have a ²_ i _ _w_ _h_ _ of course, so there was always a lot of washing up to do, but nobody did it! There was a ³v_ _ _ _ _m c_ _a_ _r, but I don't remember using it. We didn't have a ⁴_ _ c_ _ _ _ _v_ ; we just had a normal ⁵_ _ e_, but nobody cooked – we had takeaway food every day.

There was an ⁶_r_ _ and we all used that for our clothes because we wanted to look good in the evenings. We used the ⁷_ _ _ _d_e in the kitchen, but it wasn't always a good idea to keep milk or food in there, because other people used to take it! We had a ⁸k_ _ _l_ and we made a lot of tea and coffee (without milk because it always disappeared). We didn't have a ⁹_r_ _z_r, so we couldn't buy ice cream. That was the worst thing about the house. No ice cream!

5 ⭐⭐ Complete the conversation with the words from the box.

did   d̶o̶   emptied   make   take out   tidy   vacuum
walk   wipe

Ali What time do you want to go out?

Cass About two o'clock.

Ali Two! Can't you come earlier?

Cass No, I have to ¹*do* some chores. I have to ²_____ up my room – I do that every Saturday. I have to ³_____ all the surfaces, ⁴_____ the floor and put my clothes away.

Ali Do you have to ⁵_____ your bed?

Cass Oh, yes. I forgot. Then I have to ⁶_____ the rubbish. Don't you have to do anything?

Ali I have to ⁷_____ the dog every morning, but I did that at 6.30 today. Then I ⁸_____ the washing up and ⁹_____ the washing machine.

Cass Wow! Well, I hope I can meet you earlier than two o'clock, but I can't promise.

6 ON A HIGH NOTE Think about chores which you don't like and write a short paragraph about ways in which they could be made easier using technology.

5C GRAMMAR

Past modal verbs

1 ⭐ Choose the correct modal verbs to complete the sentences.

1 I was allowed to stay for the night at my cousin's house when I was five. *Did you have to / Could you* stay overnight with friends when you were younger?

2 We *didn't have to / couldn't* wear a school uniform; we were allowed to wear what we wanted.

3 You didn't hand in your History project again. *Did you have to / Could you* stay behind after school to finish it?

4 Most of my friends *didn't have to / couldn't* go to the party because it was on a school night.

5 We *had to / could* walk into town yesterday evening because there was no bus.

6 *Did you have to / Could you* do homework when you were at primary school?

7 At summer camp, Josh *had to / could* get up at seven o'clock every morning – he hated it!

8 When Melissa was young she *had to / could* watch TV when she came home from school – now she has to do homework.

2 ⭐⭐ Complete the questions with the correct forms of *could* or *have to* and the words in brackets. Then write answers which are true for you.

1 What <u>could you do</u> (you/do) when you were younger that you can't do now?

_____

2 What _____ (your parents/wear) to school that you don't have to wear today?

_____

3 When _____ (you/go) to bed when you were younger?

_____

4 What _____ (your parents/do) for you when you were very young?

_____

3 ⭐⭐ Complete the text with *could, couldn't, had to* or *didn't have to*.

When I was younger, I **1**<u>had to</u> wash up every day because we didn't have a dishwasher. Some children had to walk the family dog. I **2**_____ walk our dog because … we didn't have one! I **3**_____ tidy my room every weekend, but I didn't have to vacuum the floor.

On Fridays and Saturdays, I **4**_____ go out with my friends until 10 p.m., but if I had school the next day, I **5**_____ go out at all. On school days, I **6**_____ finish my homework before I **7**_____ watch TV.

My friends **8**_____ stay for the night and we **9**_____ watch films in my bedroom, but we **10**_____ be quiet.

4 ⭐⭐⭐ Complete the conversation with the correct forms of *could* or *have to*. Add any other necessary words.

Adrian I went to stay with my cousins in the USA for two months. I **1**<u>didn't have to do</u> any chores or homework or anything! It was great – really relaxing. How about you? How was your summer?

Charles OK, but I **2**_____ French in the evenings twice a week. Mum said my grades weren't good enough.

Adrian Oh, poor you!

Charles Well, it wasn't so bad. I **3**_____ in August because the teacher went on holiday.

Adrian What about Julie? **4**_____ camping with her parents again? I know she doesn't really like camping.

Charles No, she didn't. She **5**_____ on a beach holiday with her friends.

Adrian Great. What else happened? How was Paul's party?

Charles It didn't happen. He **6**_____ a party at home because his dad said no. And some people **7**_____ to the party anyway because they had to do some revision.

Adrian They were studying? In the summer? Who **8**_____?

Charles Samantha and Matt **9**_____ for their exams because they both failed Physics.

5 ON A HIGH NOTE Write a short paragraph about your last school holidays using *could, couldn't, had to* and *didn't have to*.

5D **SPEAKING**

1 🔊 **36** Listen and repeat the phrases. How do you say them in your language?

SPEAKING | Permission

QUESTION

Can I have this banana?
Is it alright if I change the channel?

RESPONDING 'YES'

Yes, of course./Sure, go ahead.

RESPONDING 'NO'

Sorry, you can't. That's my breakfast.
I'm afraid not. This is my favourite show.

QUESTION

Do you mind if I open the door?
Do you mind if I smoke?

RESPONDING 'YES'

No, of course not./No, I don't mind.

RESPONDING 'NO'

Please don't. It's a bit cold./Yes, I do. I hate the smell.

2 Choose the response which is NOT appropriate in each situation.

1 Can I have something to eat?
  a Sure, go ahead.
  b Sorry, you can't.
  c No, I don't mind.

2 Is it alright if I leave my bag here?
  a Yes, I do.
  b Yes, of course.
  c Sorry, I'm afraid it isn't.

3 Is it a problem for you if I arrive late in the evening?
  a No, of course not.
  b Yes, of course.
  c I'm afraid it is.

4 Do you mind if I bring a friend?
  a Yes, I do.   **b** I'm afraid it is.   **c** No, I don't.

5 Can I use your laptop?
  a Yes, of course.   **b** Sure, go ahead.   **c** No, I don't.

3 Match questions 1–5 with responses a–e.

1 ☐ Is it alright if I send a couple of emails?
2 ☐ Do you mind if I use this towel?
3 ☐ Can I borrow this book?
4 ☐ Is it a problem if I don't stay for dinner?
5 ☐ Can I turn off the radiator?

a Sorry, you can't. I haven't finished it.
b Of course not. I know you have to leave early.
c No, I don't mind.
d Please don't. I'm cold.
e Yes, of course. You can use my computer.

4 Complete questions 1–5 with the words from the box. There are two extra words. Then match the questions with responses a–e.

~~alright~~ afraid can buy ~~drive~~ go if leave mind open problem say

1 ☐ Is it *alright* if I *drive* the car?
2 ☐ Do you _____ if I _____ something?
3 ☐ Is it a _____ for you if I _____ the party early?
4 ☐ Mum, _____ I _____ out tonight?
5 ☐ Do you mind _____ I _____ the window?

a No, of course not . Is everything alright?
b Yes, I do. It's freezing in here.
c I'm afraid not. It's my parents' car and I have to be very careful with it.
d Sorry, you can't. You've got too much homework to do.
e No, I don't mind. It's interesting to hear what other people think.

5 Complete the questions with the correct forms of the words in brackets. Add any other necessary words. Then complete the answers with one word in each gap.

Ella Do you **1** *mind if I borrow* (mind/borrow) your phone?

Ruby No, of **2**_____ not.

Amy **3**_____ (problem/you) if I make myself something to eat?

Leo No, it isn't. Go **4**_____.

Ezra **5**_____ (alright/if) we stop for a rest? I'm exhausted.

Luke I'm **6**_____ we can't. We have to catch the train.

Holly **7**_____ (I/change) the channel on the TV?

Mia **8**_____, go ahead. Nobody's watching it.

5E LISTENING AND VOCABULARY

1 🔊 *37* **Listen to Part 1 of Beth's podcast and put the pictures in the order that she tried the activities.**

☐  ☐  ☐

2 🔊 *37* **Listen to Part 1 again and choose the correct answers.**

1 Beth went to the swimming pool
  a early in the morning.
  b during the week.
  c at the weekend.

2 Beth went to the gym because
  a her friends recommended it.
  b it was a warm place to go in the winter.
  c it was local and easy to get to.

3 Which of these things did NOT happen at the gym?
  a Beth compared her fitness to other people's.
  b Beth found the exercises boring.
  c The trainer criticised Beth's fitness levels.

3 🔊 *38* **Listen to Part 2 of Beth's podcast and complete the notes with 1–3 words in each gap.**

1 Beth's home is on *three* floors.
2 She started by ＿＿＿＿＿＿ in every room.
3 There was some ＿＿＿＿＿＿ stuck to the cooker.
4 Vacuuming was difficult because she had to ＿＿＿＿＿＿ cleaner up and down the stairs.
5 She found one of her ＿＿＿＿＿＿ behind a wardrobe.
6 Now, when Beth is in her bedroom, she has to go down to ＿＿＿＿＿＿ to answer her phone.
7 She has to do a sit-up in order to switch off her ＿＿＿＿＿＿ in the morning.
8 Her next podcast will be about how to make a ＿＿＿＿＿＿ in your home.

Vocabulary extension

4 **Match the words from the box, which you heard in the podcast in Exercises 2 and 3, with the definitions.**

aching exhausting freezing ~~rushing~~ strengthening
sweating

1 Moving quickly because you're in a hurry. *rushing*
2 Very tiring. ＿＿＿＿
3 Hurting because of physical exercise. ＿＿＿＿
4 Making something stronger. ＿＿＿＿
5 Feeling very cold. ＿＿＿＿
6 Having liquid on your body because you are hot.
＿＿＿＿

Pronunciation

5 🔊 *39* **Listen to the extracts from Beth's podcast in Exercises 2 and 3 read in two different ways. Choose the version, a or b, which you think sounds correct.**

1 a / b
2 a / b
3 a / b
4 a / b
5 a / b
6 a / b

ACTIVE PRONUNCIATION | /ŋ/ sound

You can hear the sound /ŋ/ in words like *rang*, *sing*, *English* and *singing*. In writing it is usually followed by the letter *k* (e.g. ta**nk**) or *g* (e.g. lo**ng**).

6 🔊 *40* **The sentences in Exercise 5 which sound correct use the /ŋ/ sound at the end of -ing words. Listen and repeat the words.**

swimming
jogging
stretching
emptying
feeling
morning

7 🔊 *41* **Listen to some more extracts from Beth's podcast. Write down the words you hear in each sentence which contain the /ŋ/ sound.**

1 *along* ＿＿＿＿ ＿＿＿＿ ＿＿＿＿ ＿＿＿＿
2 ＿＿＿＿ ＿＿＿＿
3 ＿＿＿＿ ＿＿＿＿
4 ＿＿＿＿ ＿＿＿＿
5 ＿＿＿＿ ＿＿＿＿
6 ＿＿＿＿ ＿＿＿＿ ＿＿＿＿

8 🔊 *42* **Read the sentences and find the words with the /ŋ/ sound. Listen and check.**

1 I like jogging in the morning.
2 Mum will be angry if you bang the door like that!
3 During the winter holidays, I went skiing and snowboarding.
4 In the evening, I enjoy watching TV, listening to music and surfing the Internet.
5 Yesterday evening, we went to a karaoke night and sang along to all the songs.
6 Don't forget to bring your swimming things with you.

9 🔊 *42* **Listen again and repeat the sentences. Try to pronounce the /ŋ/ sound correctly.**

UNIT VOCABULARY PRACTICE > page 61

5F READING AND VOCABULARY

1 Read the text quickly and match the numbers from the box with what they refer to.

1/3   5 billion   150   ~~22~~   2

1 The percentage of boys who do the recommended amount of exercise. _22_

2 The amount of exercise an adult should do per week in minutes. _____

3 The number of hours of P.E. that most school pupils do every week. _____

4 The cost of obesity to the National Health Service each year in pounds. _____

5 The proportion of children aged two to fifteen who are obese. _____

2 Read the text again and choose the correct answers.

1 According to the writer,
  a more young people are overweight compared to the past.
  b more young people are overweight than adults.
  c obesity is a problem that mainly affects 2–15 year olds.

2 One problem the writer identifies is that
  a some medical staff are unable to work because of obesity.
  b medical staff are depressed because of the situation.
  c obesity can also cause psychological problems.

3 The writer's view of packaged food is that
  a it doesn't fill people up as much as 'real' food.
  b it contains too many unhealthy ingredients.
  c parents give it to their children because they don't know how to cook.

4 The government has introduced a law which
  a forces students to take part in active after-school activities.
  b increases the number of hours of P.E. students have a week.
  c raises the price of unhealthy drinks so that people drink less of them.

5 In the article, the author
  a explains the reasons for obesity and what can be done to improve the situation.
  b blames parents for not caring enough about their children's diet.
  c criticises the government for not doing more to deal with the problem of obesity.

Vocabulary extension

3 Match the highlighted words from the text with the definitions.

1 Describing food which makes your stomach feel full. _filling_

2 A person's emotional and psychological state. _____

3 Illnesses or other health problems. _____

4 Things in food which help us live and grow healthily. _____

5 To be heavier than you should be. _____

6 A feeling of being very sad that makes you feel there is no hope for the future. _____

7 Curing an illness or injury by using medicine or hospital care. _____

ACTIVE VOCABULARY | Prepositional phrases

A prepositional phrase is a group of words which includes a preposition (e.g. *in* love).

---

4 Replace the underlined parts in the sentences below with the phrases from the box.

in addition   in advance   in fact   ~~in other words~~
in the long run   in the wrong

1 <u>Another way of saying this is</u>, a person who is 'obese' is dangerously overweight. _In other words_

2 Some people believe fruit juice is healthy but <u>really</u> it is high in sugar. _____

3 An unhealthy lifestyle doesn't cause immediate problems but, <u>after some time</u>, it will make you ill. _____

4 We had to pay one month's gym membership <u>before we started</u>. _____

5 It is the producers of unhealthy products who are <u>to blame</u>. _____

6 People eat too much. <u>Also</u>, they don't do enough exercise. _____

5 ON A HIGH NOTE Write a short paragraph about the ways in which your diet and lifestyle are healthy and unhealthy. Give examples of your good and bad habits.

| **UNIT VOCABULARY PRACTICE > page 61**

OBESITY
IN THE UK

'Obesity' is the term used by health officials to describe a person whose body fat is at a level which can cause them serious health problems. In other words, a person who is 'obese' is dangerously overweight. Sadly, recent reports show that a third of all children and teenagers in the UK between the ages of two and fifteen are now 'officially obese' – the highest level ever. In addition, the age at which they are becoming obese is getting lower.

Obesity can lead to medical conditions such as heart disease and diabetes and doctors now know that there is also a direct link between obesity and depression – so the problem not only affects people's physical health, but their mental health too. The cost of treating weight-related conditions is more than £5 billion a year, which is one reason why the UK's National Health Service is having problems coping with the demand for hospital places and trained medical staff.

So why is the situation getting worse? One problem is that we aren't getting enough exercise. Experts recommend that adults get at least 150 minutes of exercise every week – that amounts to just half an hour every day for five days. However, surveys show that only 53 percent of the adult population do that amount of exercise, and as people don't always tell the truth in surveys like this, it's possible that the real numbers are even lower.

The figures for children are even more worrying. While medical experts recommend that children over the age of five should do at least one hour of exercise a day, only 15 percent of girls and 22 percent of boys get this amount. At the same time children and teenagers are consuming more calories, especially in the form of sugar. A single can of soft drink contains more sugar than the recommended amount for an entire day! Furthermore, working parents don't often have time to cook meals using fresh ingredients and are tempted by cheap packaged food which is filling but contains few nutrients and is often high in salt, fat and sugar.

So, what are the solutions? One idea suggested by government experts is a 'sugar tax'. This makes the price of fizzy drinks higher, and will lead to a fall in demand for these products. At the same time it has forced manufacturers to reduce the amount of sugar in their products. The government will spend the tax money on sports programmes in schools and school breakfast clubs with healthy food options.

At the same time, schools are trying to increase the amount of exercise that children do. Most schools offer about two hours of P.E. a week and it is often difficult to increase this because of the need to study other subjects. However, some schools are now trying to persuade students to have active breaks, rather than sitting in corridors looking at their phones, and they are also offering more after-school sports activities for those who are interested.

The problem of obesity is one that schools, parents, governments, health officials, and most of all, individuals must try and overcome by working together to find solutions.

5G **WRITING AND VOCABULARY** | A note/short message

You can leave out greetings and polite expressions.

You can leave out the verb *to be* and definite articles.

Use bullet points.

You can leave out pronouns and auxiliary verbs.

Use imperatives.

Use contractions, initials, emoticons and symbols.

Neil,
Working late tonight. Back about ¹8.
- Buy yourself pizza – money in kitchen drawer.
- Do homework.
- Keep kitchen tidy ²_____ look after Katie.
Back³_____. See you later.
Mum

Mum,
Had pizza. ⁴_____ for money! Tidied kitchen.
Now at Jack's doing homework. Katie here too.
Phone when ⁵_____ get home.
N. ☺

1 Read the note and the text message. Answer the questions.

1 Why did Neil's mum leave a note? *because she was working late*
2 What should he buy? _____
3 Where is the money? _____
4 What other things should he do? _____
5 Where are Neil and Katie? _____
6 What are they doing? _____

2 Complete the note and the text message with the contractions from the box.

asap   u   &   thx   &

3 Rewrite these phrases to get the number of words in brackets.

1 Dear Dad (1)
   Dad
2 I had to go out. (4)
   _____
3 I will be back at about seven o'clock. (3)
   _____
4 I'm eating with Sam. (3)
   _____
5 My phone is not working. (3)
   _____
6 Best wishes, Jack (1)
   _____

THX   YW☺

4 Replace the underlined parts in the note with the correct contractions.

Mel, sorry I didn't wait. Train ¹departure in 15 mins. Will phone ²as soon as possible. Hope ³you are OK. ⁴Thanks for everything. There are some ⁵chocolates for you on table. Great to see you again. Ian, ⁶kisses

1 *dep*   2 _____
3 _____   4 _____
5 _____   6 _____

5 WRITING TASK You want to cook dinner but you need to go out to buy some ingredients. Use the information below to write a note to your parents.

ACTIVE WRITING | A note/short message

1 Plan your note.
- Tell your parents what you're making for dinner.
- Explain why you have to go out.
- Tell them where you are going.
- Ask them to set the table.

2 Write the note.
- You can leave out greetings, pronouns and auxiliary verbs.
- Use contractions, initials and emoticons.
- Use imperatives and bullet points where appropriate.

3 Check that ...
- you have included all the relevant information.
- there are no spelling or grammar mistakes.
- you haven't used any unnecessary words.

UNIT VOCABULARY PRACTICE > page 61

1 5A GRAMMAR AND VOCABULARY **Complete the sentences with the words from the box. There are two extra words.**

curtains decorations drawer hanger radiator
rug sofa ~~surface~~ wardrobe windowsill

1 There are papers on every _surface_ in the house. Why don't you put them away?

2 We need to put up some _____ for the party.

3 Put your clothes in the _____.

4 It's sunny outside. Why don't you open the _____ and let some light in?

5 The knives are in the top _____.

6 We could put some plants on the _____ – they'll get a lot of sunlight there.

7 Your coat is on a _____ in the hall.

8 It's cold in here. Is the _____ on?

2 5B VOCABULARY **Choose the correct words to complete the sentences.**

1 I'm __ a cup of tea. Do you want one?

a making **b** doing **c** taking

2 You're still in your pyjamas! You should __ dressed before you have breakfast.

a keep **b** make **c** get

3 Can you __ out the rubbish, please?

a take **b** get **c** make

4 There's orange juice on the floor. __ it up please.

a Dust **b** Iron **c** Mop

5 Let's take a __ with us so we can make tea in the morning.

a dishwasher **b** kettle **c** freezer

6 __ your bed before you go to school.

a Do **b** Take **c** Make

7 You should __ the furniture in your bedroom.

a mop **b** vacuum **c** dust

8 Please __ this dusty floor.

a set **b** sweep **c** dry

3 5E LISTENING AND VOCABULARY **Complete the blog post with one word in each gap.**

4 5F READING AND VOCABULARY **Choose the correct words to complete the sentences.**

1 Jess wants to go *in / on* a diet so she can lose weight before her holiday.

2 *Soft / Dairy* drinks, which are high in sugar, cause a lot of people to be overweight.

3 One very important piece of advice is to stop eating before you feel full *through / up*.

4 It's important to get enough exercise – this helps us to get fit and then *stay / go* fit.

5 Unfortunately, a lot of teenagers spend their money on poor quality *fast / low* food.

6 Vegans don't eat *diet / dairy* products such as milk.

7 I should eat meals that are *full / low* in salt and fat.

5 5G WRITING AND VOCABULARY **Complete the text with the words from the box.**

ambulance appointment indigestion ~~pains~~ pills
prescription symptoms results temperature tests

A worrying morning

Dad felt ill this morning and had sudden **1**_pains_ in his chest. We thought he was having a heart attack, so we called a(n) **2**_____ and it took him to hospital. The doctors did lots of **3**_____ and we waited nervously for the **4**_____. Finally, Dad came out looking embarrassed. There was nothing wrong with him. He just had a bit of **5**_____.

However, while he was in the hospital, the doctor found some other **6**_____ – high blood pressure and a high **7**_____, so he gave my dad a **8**_____ for some **9**_____ and dad made an **10**_____ to see him again two weeks later. Now, for the next two weeks, dad can't eat any red meat, butter, cheese or other fatty food. He isn't happy but at least he won't get indigestion again!

6 ON A HIGH NOTE **Imagine that a friend is giving you advice about your lifestyle. Write a short paragraph about the advice they would give you about your diet, exercise, sleep and any other things?**

JENNY'S FITNESS BLOG

YOUR QUESTIONS ANSWERED. CLICK ON A QUESTION TO FIND MY TOP TIPS!

- What's the easiest way to **1**_get_ fit?
- Can you explain the difference between **2**p_____ -ups, **3**s_____ -ups and pull-ups? Which is the best for **4**b_____ off calories?
- Why do I need to **5**w_____ up before I start to **6**w_____ out? Is it to **7**s_____ my muscles?
- How can I choose a good **8**p_____ trainer? Is it best to have someone strict or relaxed?
- Will **9**w_____ training make me stronger?
- What's the best activity for a healthy heart? **10**A_____ in a gym to upbeat music or jogging?

1 **For each learning objective, write 1–5 to assess your ability.**

1 = I don't feel confident. 5 = I feel confident.

	Learning objective	Course material	How confident I am (1–5)
5A	I can use modal verbs to talk about suggestions and obligations.	Student's Book pp. 64–65	
5B	I can talk about household chores.	Student's Book p. 66	
5C	I can use modal verbs to talk about the past.	Student's Book p. 67	
5D	I can ask for, give and refuse permission.	Student's Book p. 68	
5E	I can work out the meaning of new words in a web podcast and talk about health and fitness.	Student's Book p. 69	
5F	I can find specific information in an article and talk about healthy living.	Student's Book pp. 70–71	
5G	I can write a short note or message.	Student's Book pp. 72–73	

2 **Which of the skills above would you like to improve in? How?**

Skill I want to improve in	How I can improve

3 **What can you remember from this unit?**

New words I learned and most want to remember	Expressions and phrases I liked	English I heard or read outside class

GRAMMAR AND VOCABULARY

1 Match questions 1–5 with the most sensible answers a–g. There are two extra answers.

1 ☐ Where's the patient?
2 ☐ Where's the ice cream?
3 ☐ Where's the student party?
4 ☐ Where's the shirt I ironed?
5 ☐ Where are the dirty cups?

a In the freezer.
b In the washing machine.
c On the hanger.
d In the dishwasher.
e In the ambulance.
f In the halls of residence.
g In the oven.

/ 5

2 Complete the text with one word in each gap.

I changed my life last year. I went **1**_on_ a diet and stopped eating unhealthy food. No more cakes for me! Now, I **2**_____ breakfast for my family every morning, then **3**_____ the table and **4**_____ the washing up. I even tidy my **5**_____ every Saturday. I **6**_____ well every night and wake up full of energy in the morning.

/ 5

3 Replace the underlined parts in the sentences below with the most appropriate modal verbs in the correct form.

1 <u>My advice</u> to you is to change your diet.
You **_should_** change your diet.

2 Throw the water bottle away! You<u>'re not allowed to</u> take it through security.
Throw the water bottle away! You _____ take it through security.

3 <u>One possibility is for us to</u> buy a microwave oven.
We _____ buy a microwave oven.

4 On holiday, <u>no-one told me to</u> get up early.
On holiday, I _____ get up early.

5 <u>It isn't a good idea to</u> eat fast food every night.
You _____ eat fast food every night.

/ 4

4 Complete the sentences with the words from the box. There are two extra words.

could ~~couldn't~~ didn't had has have must mustn't

1 I was so tired yesterday morning that I _couldn't_ get out of bed.
2 Milo _____ to be home before 10 p.m. His parents don't allow him to stay out longer.
3 You _____ stay up too late – you have an exam tomorrow.
4 Who _____ to stay behind after the lesson last Friday? Was it George?
5 Helen _____ speak Italian when she was five because her grandparents are Italian.
6 When I was ill last time, I _____ have to make my bed for a week.

/ 5

USE OF ENGLISH

5 Choose the correct words a–d to complete the text.

MOST PEOPLE AGREE THAT DOING THE HOUSEWORK HELPS YOUR PARENTS AND ALSO PREPARES YOU FOR WHEN YOU LEAVE HOME. SO WHAT CHORES CAN YOU **1**__?

The most important is tidying your bedroom. This means putting clothes away, **2**__ the bed and vacuuming the floor. You should also help a lot in the kitchen. For a long time the most important job was doing the washing **3**__ but, now, because of dishwashers, a lot of children **4**__ do this. More important is learning how to cook. If you don't know how to do this, you may end up eating nothing but **5**__ food in the future!

At the same time, learn how to **6**__ a good cup of tea or coffee. Then, when you have your own flat or room in the **7**__ of residence, you can invite your friends round for a hot drink.

1	**a** work	**b** make	**c** do	**d** throw
2	**a** cleaning	**b** making	**c** doing	**d** dusting
3	**a** up	**b** off	**c** down	**d** out
4	**a** mustn't	**b** don't have to	**c** shouldn't	**d** couldn't
5	**a** fast	**b** quick	**c** soft	**d** dairy
6	**a** do	**b** get	**c** have	**d** make
7	**a** flat	**b** house	**c** home	**d** halls

/ 7

6 Complete the second sentence so that it means the same as the first one. Use no more than three words in each gap.

1 It isn't necessary for Melissa to go to a gym to get fit.
Melissa doesn't **_have to go_** to a gym to get fit.

2 My advice to you is to get some weights.
You _____ some weights.

3 I'd like to throw away some of my old clothes that I never wear.
I'd like to get _____ some of my old clothes that I never wear.

4 We couldn't wear trainers at my primary school.
We _____ proper shoes at my primary school.

5 You could help me wash up if you like.
You could help me do _____ if you like.

/ 4

/ 30

6A GRAMMAR AND VOCABULARY

Future arrangements and intentions

1 ⭐ **Put the words in order to make questions and answers with *going to*.**

1 a shave off / his moustache / is / to / going / Harry / ?
Is Harry going to shave off his moustache?

b his beard / to / going / too / he / yes / is / shave off
_____

2 a are / get / your hair / to / cut / when / going / you / ?
_____

b grow / am / long / to / going / it / I
_____

3 a look for / a new job / to / is / going / your mum / ?
_____

b is / she / yes
_____

4 a work / going / are / in the summer / to / they / ?
_____

b are / going / in a café / they / to / work / yes
_____

2 ⭐ **Match questions 1–5 with answers a–e.**

1 ☐ When are you babysitting for your neighbours?
2 ☐ Why are you going to London this weekend?
3 ☐ Is your sister having a party this weekend?
4 ☐ Where are you meeting Russ?
5 ☐ Is your dad collecting us from the station?

a No, she isn't. She's having it in two weeks.
b On Saturday evening.
c I'm meeting him outside the school gate.
d We're going to see a play at the Royal Theatre.
e Yes, he is. I hope he isn't late.

3 ⭐⭐ **Choose *A* for arrangement or *FI* for future intention. Then complete the sentences with the correct forms of the verbs in brackets.**

1 Next week, we *'re going to start* (start) looking at holiday ideas. A / FI
2 I can't come tomorrow; Mum _____ (have) a birthday party. A / FI
3 Where _____ (you/meet) your group? A / FI
4 They _____ (have) a test on Friday. A / FI
5 One day, I _____ (run) my own business. A / FI
6 Bo doesn't like his hair. He _____ (change) his look completely. A / FI

4 ⭐⭐ **Complete the conversation with responses a–f.**

Dora Are you looking forward to the party on Friday?
Noah Yes, I am. Everybody's doing something to help.
Dora What are you doing?
Noah ¹c
Dora Wow – Noah the DJ! Is Jane making a cake?
Noah ²___
Dora What kind of cake?
Noah ³___
Dora Who else is helping?
Noah ⁴___
Dora That sounds interesting! I'd like to see that.
Noah ⁵___
Dora Of course! I'm going to stay at Amelia's for the night after the party. We're going to tidy up.
Noah ⁶___
Dora No, Jackie and Helen are going to help too.

a I don't know. It's going to be a surprise.
b How about you? Are you doing anything to help?
c ~~I'm organising the music.~~
d Are you and Amelia going to do that by yourselves?
e Steve and Jan are going to make a film.
f Yes, she is. I asked her to.

5 ⭐⭐ **Use Sophie's notes and the correct future forms to complete the sentences.**

My future intentions
1 Keep in touch with old friends.
  I *'m going to keep in touch* with old friends.
2 Not get upset at stupid jokes.
  I _____ at stupid jokes.

My appointments next week
3 Meet Joyce – Sat. 2 p.m.
  I _____ on Saturday at two o'clock.
4 Not play basketball – Sunday – match cancelled.
  I _____ because the match has been cancelled.

My future plans and ambitions
5 Learn to drive when I'm eighteen.
  I _____ when I'm eighteen.
6 Not get married until I'm thirty!
  I _____ until I'm thirty!

6 ★★ Choose the correct forms to complete the sentences. Sometimes both forms are correct.

1 I *'m meeting / 'm going to meet* some old friends next weekend.

2 My parents *are losing / are going to lose* weight next year.

3 We *aren't having / aren't going to have* a test next week.

4 I *'m working / 'm going to work* in a laboratory next year.

5 What *are you doing / are you going to do* next weekend?

6 When *are you giving / are you going to give* me my book back?

7 ★★★ Use the prompts and the correct future forms to complete the conversation.

Gemma **1** What / you / do / on Saturday?
What are you going to do/doing on Saturday?

Erin **2** I / visit / a new stylist. I phoned her last night and got an appointment for 10.30.

_____

Gemma Really? **3** you / get / your hair / cut?

_____

Erin Yes, but more importantly **4** I / get / some advice about my skin and nails.

_____

Gemma That sounds interesting.

Erin What about you? **5** you / get / a tattoo / like you said?

_____

Gemma No! **6** I / never / get / a tattoo.

_____

I don't know why I said that! But **7** I / get / a piercing tomorrow. I went to the salon yesterday and made an appointment. I was lucky there was a free place. Sometimes you have to wait a week or more.

_____

Erin What are you having pierced?

Gemma Just my ears!

8 ★★★ Rewrite the mini-conversations using the correct forms of *going to* or the Present Continuous. Make any other necessary changes.

Sally What are your plans for the summer?
1 *What are you going to do in the summer?*

Ethan My plan is to get a summer job.
2 _____

Max Have you got any arrangements for this Saturday?
3 _____

Kai Yes, Adrian and I arranged to meet in the evening.
4 _____

Isla What are your ambitions for the future?
5 _____

Ava My ambition is to become a doctor.
6 _____

Noah What are your arrangements for tomorrow?
7 _____

Zoe I've got an appointment with the dentist at 3 p.m.
8 _____

9 ★★★ Complete the conversation with the correct future forms of the verbs from the box.

become   buy   do   change   get   not eat   start   ~~take up~~

Ricky I **1** *'m going to take up* jogging.

Myra Great. When **2** _____?

Ricky Next week. My parents **3** _____ me a new pair of trainers at the weekend.

Myra So, why did you make this decision?

Ricky I want to get fit.

Myra **4** _____ your diet?

Ricky Yes, I **5** _____ fast food – well, not much – and I **6** _____ a vegetarian.

Myra Great. Good luck. Hey, **7** _____ anything this afternoon? We could go to the cinema.

Ricky Sorry, **8** _____ my hair cut at four o'clock. Maybe tomorrow.

10 ON A HIGH NOTE Write a short paragraph about your plans and arrangements for the rest of this week and the weekend.

6B READING AND VOCABULARY

1 Read the first two paragraphs of the diary and choose the best answer.

What is 'social anxiety'?

a Being afraid that you can't make new friendships.

b Feeling nervous when you have to interact with other people.

c Not having a good relationship with family members.

2 Read the whole text and match events 1–5 with dates a–e.

1 ☐ She showed a presentation to her family.

2 ☐ She gave her second presentation.

3 ☐ She talked to the life coach about social anxiety.

4 ☐ She talked to the life coach about her faults.

5 ☐ She gave her first presentation.

a Monday, 4th June

b Sunday, 3rd June

c Tuesday, 6th May

d Tuesday, 29th April

e Monday, 21st April

3 Read the text again. Match sentences A–H with gaps 1–5 in the text. There are three extra sentences.

A The topic is 'An invention that changed the world'.

B I tried to ignore the negative comments.

C I even told a couple of jokes.

D I thought she would give me advice, but it doesn't work like that.

E What was I doing there?

F Looking back, it wasn't as bad as I thought.

G I was really nervous and kept forgetting what to say.

H Now I know that identifying my anxieties is the best way to deal with them.

Vocabulary extension

4 Find words and phrases 1–5 in the text and decide which meanings are correct: a or b.

1 my mind went (completely) blank

a I had strange thoughts.

b I couldn't think of anything.

2 panicked

a couldn't think clearly

b made a silly mistake

3 embarrassment

a a feeling of being nervous

b a feeling of being angry

4 in tears

a confused

b crying

5 blush

a when cheeks go red

b when hands shake

ACTIVE VOCABULARY | Prefix over-

The prefix *over-*, when added to an adjective, means 'too much' or 'more than is necessary', e.g. if you are *overconfident*, you are *too* confident. You might make a mistake because you are not careful.

5 Complete the sentences with the adjectives from the box.

overconfident overcooked overdressed overpaid ~~overweight~~ overworked

1 Keith wants to lose a few kilos because he's a bit *overweight*.

2 The meal wasn't very good – the fish was too salty and the vegetables were _____.

3 In my opinion, some actors are _____; $20 million for one film is ridiculous.

4 Tom was _____ and lost the match – he was so sure of winning that he became careless.

5 I'm _____ at the moment because I'm doing my own and my colleague's work.

6 Don't you think that you're a little _____? You don't need to wear a suit and tie for a children's birthday party!

6 ON A HIGH NOTE Write a short paragraph about a social situation in which you felt anxious.

UNIT VOCABULARY PRACTICE > page 73

HOW I BECAME A BETTER SPEAKER

Monday, 21st April

I gave a presentation to the class today. It was awful. **1**___ At one point, my mind went completely blank and I stared at my notes and couldn't say a word! Then I accidentally switched off the laptop halfway through the presentation – I just panicked and couldn't manage to switch it back on. I felt myself going bright red with embarrassment. My friends were very sympathetic and my teacher gave me a B, but I still felt dreadful. I was in tears when I got home. I told Mum and Dad all about it during dinner and Mum suggested I go to see her 'life coach' next week. What's a life coach?!

Tuesday, 29th April

I had my first session with the life coach today. She asked me what I wanted to talk about so I told her all about my presentation and what had gone wrong. **2**___ A good life coach knows exactly what questions to ask so that you can work out the answers to your problems yourself. She asked me how I had felt, and if I often feel like that. Then she explained that I have a condition called 'social anxiety'. She said that a lot of people feel the same way as I do – nervous and upset if they have to meet new people or speak in public. I felt a lot better about myself after that – now I know I'm not the only one!

Tuesday, 6th May

I had another great session with the life coach today and, with her help, found out more about myself; I give up too easily and I think too much about other people's opinions. I spend a lot of time worrying about how my family and friends see me. I found it really helpful to work out what exactly makes me feel so upset and nervous. **3**___

Sunday, 3rd June

I'm giving another presentation tomorrow for History. **4**___ This time I followed the advice of my life coach who told me that being well-prepared would help me to feel more confident. I got on with the project immediately and finished it three days ago. Now I feel ready and I'm about to present it to my first audience – my parents and grandparents!

Well, that went quite well and they gave me good advice about how to stand, where to look and what to say at different times. I still look at my notes too much and, even with my family, I blush when I make a mistake, but I'm much better prepared than last time. I think I'll try again in my bedroom now and watch myself in the mirror while I talk.

Monday, 4th June

The presentation is over. What a difference! I was confident, but not overconfident. I looked directly at the other students while I was speaking and didn't need my notes at all. **5**___ At the end, everyone started clapping. I couldn't believe it! The teacher gave me an A and suggested that I give a presentation at the next school open day when new students and their parents come to see what the school is like. Six months ago, that was my biggest nightmare, but now I'm quite excited about the idea!

6C GRAMMAR AND VOCABULARY

Future predictions: *going to* and *will*

1 ⭐ Look at the pictures. Complete the sentences with the correct future forms of the verbs in brackets.

1 Do you think he *will pass* (pass)?

2 I'm sure his parents ＿＿＿＿＿＿ (buy) him a car.

3 He ＿＿＿＿＿＿ (probably/phone) us when the test finishes.

4 Oh dear! He ＿＿＿＿＿＿ (crash).

5 He ＿＿＿＿＿＿ (not pass) his test!

6 The other driver ＿＿＿＿＿＿ (be) very upset.

2 ⭐⭐ Complete the dialogue with the correct future forms of the verbs in brackets.

Archie This is a great wedding.

Dana Yes. Do you think they **1** *will be* (be) happy?

Archie Who?

Dana Your brother and his wife, of course.

Archie I guess so.

Dana Do you think they **2** ＿＿＿＿＿＿ (start) a family soon?

Archie I don't think so.

Dana Where do you think **3** ＿＿＿＿＿＿ (they/live)?

Archie They **4** ＿＿＿＿＿＿ (probably/move) to London. They like big cities. Oh, my dad's calling us. That means we **5** ＿＿＿＿＿＿ (eat) soon.

Dana What kind of food **6** ＿＿＿＿＿＿ (we/have)?

Archie I'm not sure but there **7** ＿＿＿＿＿＿ (be) a lot. Dad told me not to eat any breakfast today!

3 ⭐⭐ Complete the mini-conversations with the correct future forms of the words from the box.

I/probably/wait   he/fly   it/probably/be   it/rain
it/stop   she/say   they/put on   sure/he/have
~~you/invite~~   you/start

Tom Who **1** *are you going to invite* to the end of year ball?

Jack Rania probably, but I think **2** ＿＿＿＿＿＿ 'No'.

Kit When **3** ＿＿＿＿＿＿ studying for your exams?

Will I don't know. **4** ＿＿＿＿＿＿ until the last minute as usual!

Amy Look at those people over there. **5** ＿＿＿＿＿＿ some kind of show. Do you want to watch it?

Rick No. **6** ＿＿＿＿＿＿ boring. Let's go.

Alan It's very dark this morning. I think **7** ＿＿＿＿＿＿. What about our camping holiday?

Sue Relax, it's only Monday today. I'm sure **8** ＿＿＿＿＿＿ before the weekend.

Kim My brother is very excited because **9** ＿＿＿＿＿＿ to New Zealand next week.

Mel Really? I'm **10** ＿＿＿＿＿＿ the time of his life there.

4 ON A HIGH NOTE Write a short paragraph about two things you hope will happen in the next week and two things you know are going to happen.

UNIT VOCABULARY PRACTICE > page 73

1 🔊 43 **Listen to Part 1 of a podcast and choose the best answer.**

What will the main point of the podcast be?
- **a** How we use weather words in different languages.
- **b** How the weather can affect our behaviour.

2 🔊 44 **Listen to Part 2 of the podcast and decide if statements 1–8 are true or false.**

1 ☐ People only suffer from SAD in the autumn and spring time.

2 ☐ The speaker doesn't believe that the condition really exists.

3 ☐ Scientists are not completely sure about the exact cause for SAD.

4 ☐ In the dark winter months, the balance of hormones in our bodies changes.

5 ☐ Most people who suffer from SAD live in the UK.

6 ☐ Changing your daily routine can help you to feel better.

7 ☐ You should exercise outdoors even when the weather is cold.

8 ☐ Vitamin D can only be found in certain foods.

Vocabulary extension

3 **Match the words from the box with the definitions.**

depression   disorder   ~~hormone~~   mood swings
suffer from

1 A chemical produced by the body that affects our mood. *hormone*

2 To feel physical or psychological pain. _____

3 A feeling of being unhappy. _____

4 An illness or medical condition. _____

5 Sudden changes in emotion, e.g. from happiness to sadness. _____

4 🔊 45 **Complete the extracts from the podcast in Exercise 2 with the words from Exercise 3. Listen and check.**

1 Some people have a feeling of tiredness, a lack of energy, and sudden *mood swings*.

2 You may be suffering from Seasonal Affective _____.

3 Studies have shown that when there's less sunlight, our bodies produce more of a _____ called 'melatonin'.

4 SAD often improves and disappears in the spring and summer, which is why it's also known as 'winter _____'.

5 Experts estimate that between three and twenty percent of people in the UK _____ SAD.

Pronunciation

ACTIVE PRONUNCIATION | /θ/ and /ð/ sounds

In English, we pronounce *th* as /θ/ in *th*ink or /ð/ in *th*is.

5 🔊 46 **Listen and repeat.**

/θ/ <u>th</u>ink   /ð/ <u>th</u>is

6 🔊 47 **Look at these sentences from the podcast in Exercises 2 and 3. How is *th* pronounced in the underlined words? Choose the correct phonetic symbol. Listen and check.**

1 We often use <u>weather</u> phrases to describe a certain character trait or behaviour.   /θ/ or /ð/

2 From the beginning of the autumn <u>through</u> to spring time.   /θ/ or /ð/

3 People who are affected by this condition say that during the winter <u>months</u> they feel anxious and miserable!   /θ/ or /ð/

4 When I first heard about this, I <u>thought</u>, 'Just a minute, this can't be an actual medical problem'.   /θ/ or /ð/

5 <u>Although</u> the exact cause of SAD isn't completely clear, scientists think that this lack of sunlight may be the problem.   /θ/ or /ð/

7 🔊 48 **Match the words from the box with the correct phonetic symbols. Listen, check and repeat.**

clo<u>th</u>es   ~~ma<u>th</u>ematics~~   mo<u>th</u>er   smoo<u>th</u>   sunba<u>th</u>e
too<u>th</u>paste   <u>th</u>rilled   <u>th</u>row

/θ/ *mathematics* _____ _____ _____

/ð/ _____ _____ _____ _____

8 🔊 49 **Listen. How is the pronunciation of the word *the* different before a consonant sound and before a vowel sound? Practise saying the sentence.**

From the beginning of the autumn through to spring time.

ACTIVE PRONUNCIATION | /ðə/ and /ðiː/ sounds

The word *the* is pronounced
- /ðə/ before a consonant sound (e.g. *the b*eginning).
- /ðiː/ before a vowel sound (e.g. *the a*utumn).
- /ðə/ and not /ðiː/ before a word beginning with *u* pronounced as /juː/ (e.g. *the u*niform).

9 🔊 50 **Practise saying these sentences. Listen and check.**

1 The exact cause of SAD isn't clear, but scientists think that this lack of sunlight may be the problem.

2 Experts estimate that between three and twenty percent of people in the UK suffer from SAD.

3 When the weather is bad, you probably won't feel like going outside, but it's important to make the effort.

UNIT VOCABULARY PRACTICE > page 73

1 ⭐ Choose the words with the same meaning as the underlined parts in the sentences below.

1 Were you <u>uninterested</u> during the film?
  a stressed   **b** excited   **c** bored

2 Mum was <u>very pleased</u> with her present.
  a delighted   **b** surprised   **c** worried

3 Steve is <u>very upset and miserable</u> about losing his job.
  a disappointed   **b** depressed   **c** amazed

4 I'd love to be <u>unstressed</u> like Megan during exams.
  a relaxed   **b** worried   **c** depressed

5 Cath <u>wanted to know more about</u> the paintings in the gallery
  a was amazed by **b** was interested in
  c was surprised by

6 The kids were <u>very happy and restless</u> when they got the invitation.
  a depressed   **b** excited   **c** relaxed

2 ⭐ Complete the words in the text with one letter in each gap.

I always get ¹a_n_x_i_o_u_s_ when I have an exam or a test – it's the only time I ever get really ²s___r_____s___ ___. During my driving test, I was so nervous that my hands were shaking! I felt ³m___ ___ ___ ___ a b___ ___ because I was sure that I would fail. When the driving instructor said 'Congratulations', I was ⁴a___ ___z___ ___!

Mum was really proud that I'd passed my driving test, but I could see that Dad wasn't so ⁵pl___ ___s___ ___. I couldn't understand it. Why wasn't he happy for me? Then I realised what the problem was. He was ⁶w___r r___ ___ ___ about me driving his new car!

3 ⭐ Complete the sentences with the words from the box.

amazing   boring   ~~disappointed~~   exciting   exhausted
pleased   relaxing   worried

1 When Mark didn't get into the basketball team he was *disappointed*.

2 My friend dyed her hair. She looked great – really _____.

3 I didn't really like the book – it was really _____.

4 We liked the computer game because it was very _____.

5 The boys stayed up all night and the next day were _____.

6 I couldn't find my wallet. I was really _____.

7 When Steve got good marks, his parents were very _____.

8 After a difficult year at school, the holidays were very _____.

4 ⭐⭐ Complete the texts with the correct adjectives formed from the verbs in bold.

I went to see the new *Star Wars* film last week. My friends said it was ¹*amazing* (**AMAZE**), but I have to say I was ²_____ (**DISAPPOINT**). I found it quite ³_____ (**BORE**) really. I prefer horror films. I like to feel ⁴_____ (**FRIGHTEN**) on the way home from the cinema!
May, aged 15

My parents booked a package holiday last summer. They think package holidays are ⁵_____ (**RELAX**) and ⁶_____ (**INTEREST**). I don't know why. I was ⁷_____ (**BORE**) for most of the two weeks. How long can you spend lying in the sun? My parents were ⁸_____ (**SURPRISE**) when I told them that I didn't enjoy the holiday.
Tom, aged 16

5 ON A HIGH NOTE Write a short paragraph about two of the things and situations from the box and how they make you feel. Use adjectives from this lesson.

a book you don't like   a film you really like
a subject at school   getting a new haircut
meeting somebody new   something you do on holiday
sports

1  🔊 *51* Listen and repeat the phrases. How do you say them in your language?

SPEAKING | Expressing probability

VERY LIKELY

You'll definitely win.
You'll (almost) certainly win.
I'm sure you'll win.

LIKELY

I think you'll win.
You'll probably win.

POSSIBLE

Perhaps/Maybe you'll win.
It's possible (that) you'll lose.
You may/might lose.
Perhaps/Maybe you won't win.

UNLIKELY

I don't think you'll win.
You probably won't win.

VERY UNLIKELY

You definitely won't win.
You (almost) certainly won't win.
I'm sure you won't win.

---

2 Put the words in order to make sentences.

1 they / give / good advice / will / definitely / you
They will definitely give you good advice.

2 sure / you / a great time / have / I'm / will
_____

3 be / will / arrives / tired / he / Roman / when / probably
_____

4 will / something interesting / there / almost / you / find / certainly
_____

5 probably / visit / this weekend / my cousins / us / won't
_____

6 is / late / the plane / be / that / will / possible / it
_____

3 Complete the conversations with the words from the box.

~~definitely~~ don't it's maybe might possible sure will won't

Cath	Rob's coming home tomorrow after six months in Thailand. I wonder what he'll look like.
Lucy	He **1** *definitely* won't be pale! I'm sure he'll have a great suntan.
Cath	Yes, and he **2**_____ definitely be thinner after six months of swimming and hiking.
Lucy	Hey! He **3**_____ have blond hair or a pierced nose or something.
Cath	**4**_____ he will. Wow. That would be funny!
Sam	Are you going to watch the football match this evening?
Tom	Yes, I'm **5**_____ it will be a good match.
Sam	I hope so, but it's **6**_____ that the match will be disappointing. Our team haven't been playing very well recently.
Adrian	Jason's got his driving test today. He definitely **7**_____ pass. He's only had three lessons.
Paula	I **8**_____ think he'll pass either, but I guess **9**_____ possible that he'll be lucky and have a kind examiner.

4 USE OF ENGLISH Complete the second sentence so that it means the same as the first one. Use no more than three words in each gap.

1 It's very likely that Grace will wait until the last minute.
I'm *sure Grace will* wait until the last minute.

2 It's possible that the gym will be closed.
The gym _____ closed.

3 It's unlikely that I'll find a job.
I _____ that I will find a job.

4 It's likely that you'll pass your driving test.
You'll _____ your driving test.

5 It's very unlikely that Anna will get a piercing.
Anna almost _____ get a piercing.

Give your email a title.

Explain what the event is.

Give the place, date, time and contact details.

Encourage your friend to accept.

Sandra Rivera
To: Lori Collins
Re: Meal on Saturday

Hi Lori,

My dad's cooking a big Spanish meal on Saturday. ¹*Would* you like to come? My dad's a really good cook and it'll ²_____ great fun. Sam is inviting one of his friends too and my dad's sister from Valencia is going to come with my Spanish cousins.

The ³_____ is 27, Orchard Way. It's going to start at three o'clock, but you can come round earlier if you want. Phone or text me on 0717345623 to let me know if you can come.

I really ⁴_____ you can make it.

All the best,
Sandra

Thank your friend for the invitation.

Accept or decline the invitation.

Check the arrangements.

Lori Collins
To: Sandra Rivera
Re: Meal on Saturday

Hi Sandra,

Thanks so ⁵_____ for inviting me to your dad's meal.
I'll definitely come! I love Spanish food.

Three o'clock is fine, but I can't come earlier because my guitar lesson doesn't finish until two o'clock. Do I ⁶_____ to bring anything?

Thanks again,
Lori

1 USE OF ENGLISH **Complete the emails with one word in each gap.**

2 **Imagine that Lori couldn't come to the meal. Complete her reply with the words from the box.**

afraid   anyway   ~~appreciate~~   kind   love

Lori Collins
To: Sandra Rivera
Re: Meal on Saturday

Hi Sandra,

I really ¹*appreciate* the invitation to your dad's Spanish meal. It's really ²_____ of you. I'd ³_____ to come but I'm ⁴_____ I can't make it. We're going to visit my aunt this weekend.

Thanks ⁵_____. Have a good time!

Lori

3 WRITING TASK **You and your parents are going to London for the weekend to visit some museums and art galleries. Your parents have said that you can invite a friend. Use the information below to write an informal invitation.**

ACTIVE WRITING | An informal invitation

1 Plan your invitation.
- Invite your friend, briefly describing the weekend trip.
- Give details of how you're travelling, where you're going to stay, what you're going to do, etc.
- Sign off appropriately and encourage your friend to come.

2 Write the invitation.
- Begin and end your invitation appropriately.
- Use paragraphs to organise your invitation.
- Use phrases from the Writing box in the Student's Book.
- Use future forms.

3 Check that ...
- you have included all the relevant information.
- there are no spelling or grammar mistakes.
- there is a good range of vocabulary and structures.

UNIT VOCABULARY PRACTICE

1 6A GRAMMAR AND VOCABULARY **Choose the correct words to complete the sentences.**

1 Why don't you *take care of* / *take up* a new sport or hobby?

2 Are you trying to *grow* / *make* a beard?

3 I want to *dye* / *paint* my hair red, but I don't know if it will suit me.

4 Kerry wants to get in *weight* / *shape* so she's going to join a gym.

5 If you *take care of* / *take up* your skin, you will look much younger.

6 You'll definitely *lose* / *put on* weight if you stop eating sugary snacks.

7 This exercise is good for *building up* / *taking up* your muscles.

8 Jemma wants to *change* / *grow* her look by getting her hair cut short.

2 6B READING AND VOCABULARY **Complete the Internet forum with one word in each gap.**

YOUR PROBLEMS

I'm **¹***about* to start my final year at school. How can I **²**_____ out more about university courses?

Sol, 18

....

I'm really having problems with Maths. I still have two more years before my final exams. Should I carry **³**_____ and hope that it gets easier or **⁴**_____ up and study something else?

Jack, 17

....

I'm looking **⁵**_____ a summer job. Last year I worked in a restaurant. It was hard work and not very interesting, but they want me to work for them again. Should I go **⁶**_____ there or try to find something else?

Beth, 18

....

Every time I try to **⁷**_____ on with my homework, I find some reason to **⁸**_____ it off until later. Usually I find something to **⁹**_____ out about on the Internet – TV programmes, film reviews, music videos – anything except do my homework. What can I do?

Mark, age 16

3 6C GRAMMAR AND VOCABULARY **Complete the diary entry with the words and phrases from the box.**

engaged have kids married middle-aged ~~move away~~ rent retire settle down twenties university

Next month I'm going to be eighteen and here's what I predict I will do in my life …

Next year, I'm going to **¹***move away* from home and go to **²**_____. I hope that I'll be able to **³**_____ a flat together with some other students. After I finish my studies, it's difficult to say what will happen, but I don't want to **⁴**_____ too quickly. I'd like to live abroad for a while. I'm not going to get **⁵**_____ before I reach my late **⁶**_____ or early thirties. Then I hope I'll get **⁷**_____ and **⁸**_____ before I reach the age of forty. I'd like to earn a lot of money and **⁹**_____ when I'm still **¹⁰**_____ – about fifty-five.

4 6D LISTENING AND VOCABULARY **Put the words from the box in the correct column.**

~~adore~~ affectionate can't stand cheerful hate look forward to loving miserable pessimistic tense

Positive meaning	Negative meaning
adore	

5 6E VOCABULARY **Complete the sentences with the correct words formed from the verbs in bold.**

1 I feel *worried* about the future because I have a lot of difficult decisions to make. **WORRY**

2 Sam is _____ in Biology and is planning to study Medicine at university. **INTEREST**

3 Lying in the garden reading a book is a _____ way to spend the afternoon. **RELAX**

4 If you're _____, you should find something to do – call a friend or go for a walk. **BORE**

5 My makeover was a bit _____ – I think I look exactly the same as I did before! **DISAPPOINT**

6 How can you be so _____ just before the exams? Everyone else is really stressed! **RELAX**

7 I'm _____ that so many people came to my party! **AMAZE**

8 Going away to university for the first time is an _____ experience. **EXCITE**

6 ON A HIGH NOTE **Write a short paragraph about an experience from your life that taught you something important and explain why.**

1 **For each learning objective, write 1–5 to assess your ability.**

1 = I don't feel confident. 5 = I feel confident.

	Learning objective	Course material	How confident I am (1–5)
6A	I can use the Present Continuous and *going to* to talk about future arrangements and intentions.	Student's Book pp. 78–79	
6B	I can work out the meaning of new words in a text and talk about procrastination.	Student's Book pp. 80–81	
6C	I can use *going to* and *will* to talk about future predictions.	Student's Book p. 82	
6D	I can understand the main points and identify specific information in a talk and talk about pessimism and optimism.	Student's Book p. 83	
6E	I can describe people's appearance and emotions using adjectives with *-ed* and *-ing* endings.	Student's Book p. 84	
6F	I can make predictions about the future.	Student's Book p. 85	
6G	I can write a reply in an email or letter accepting or declining an invitation.	Student's Book pp. 86–87	

2 **Which of the skills above would you like to improve in? How?**

Skill I want to improve in	How I can improve

3 **What can you remember from this unit?**

New words I learned and most want to remember	Expressions and phrases I liked	English I heard or read outside class

GRAMMAR AND VOCABULARY

1 Complete the sentences with the words from the box. There are three extra words.

anxious ~~cautious~~ celebrate find move pass put settle turn vote

1 In new situations it's a good idea to be _cautious_ and not to make any sudden decisions.

2 Who are you going to _____ for in the school council elections?

3 I don't think I'll be ready to _____ down until I'm in my thirties.

4 Can we _____ out what time the last bus leaves?

5 How are you going to _____ your dad's birthday this year?

6 Be polite and give a good reason when you _____ down your friend's invitation.

7 My brother wants to _____ away from home and start living on his own.

/ 6

2 Complete the email with one word in each gap.

> Hi Nick,
>
> I know you're **1**_keen_ on sports and fitness, so I'm writing to you for some advice. I started jogging a few weeks ago, but I've got a problem. I'll almost certainly have to **2**_____ up because it's really hurting my knees. I'd like to **3**_____ up a different sport because I really want to **4**_____ into shape before the summer. I'd like to **5**_____ up my muscles and **6**_____ a bit of weight at the same time.
>
> What sport would you recommend?
>
> Ray

/ 5

3 Complete each group of three sentences with the correct forms of the words in brackets and the Present Continuous, *going to* and *will*.

1

a This evening I _'m going to try_ (try) to finish my History project.

b Tomorrow, Helen _____ (get) her hair cut.

c I think my dad _____ (retire) in about five years.

2

a Where do you think _____ (we/be) in thirty years' time?

b _____ (you/work) harder this year?

c Who _____ (you/meet) this evening?

/ 5

4 Use the prompts to write sentences using future forms.

1 Oh no! Look at that boat! It / hit / the bridge!
It's going to hit the bridge!

2 I'm sorry, but I can't meet you today. I / work / until nine.

_____

3 I / grow / my hair long / this year.

_____

4 it / be / sunny / in Greece / in February?

_____

5 I / think / I / rent / a flat / with / my friends / when / I / go / to university

_____

6 Sam and Jane / get / married / next / month

_____

/ 5

USE OF ENGLISH

5 Complete the text with the correct words formed from the words in bold.

> The person I admire most is my older brother. He left home three years ago and went to university, but I still see him in the holidays. He's now in his early **1**_twenties_ (TWENTY). I like his **2**_____ (APPEAR) – he's tall with long, brown hair and brown eyes. Jason is very **3**_____ (RELAX). He doesn't worry about anything and he's always very **4**_____ (OPTIMIST) about the future. I don't know what he's going to do when he finishes university. I miss him, although I have to make a **5**_____ (CONFESS) – I'm secretly **6**_____ (DELIGHT) that I don't have to share a room with him anymore!

/ 5

6 Complete the text with one word in each gap.

> We all worry a little about what is **1**_going_ to happen to us in the future. Here are some of the things you shouldn't put **2**_____ for long:
>
> • Exams – there's a lot to learn so get on **3**_____ it now and do a little every day.
>
> • Getting in **4**_____ – you might regret not doing more exercise when you're older.
>
> • Saving for your retirement – the earlier you start, the more money you **5**_____ have at 65.
>
> Will you be prepared or not? It's up to you.

/ 4

/ 30

07 A job for life?

7A GRAMMAR AND VOCABULARY

Present Perfect (1)

1 ⭐ **Rewrite the sentences with the word in brackets in the correct place.**

1 I've had a part-time job. (never)
I've never had a part-time job.

2 Has your dad sacked one of his employees? (ever)
_____

3 I don't need a job. I've got one. (already)
_____

4 I can't meet you now. I haven't finished work. (yet)
_____

5 I've heard about your pay rise. (just) Congratulations!
_____

6 Has Jack started his new job? (yet)
_____

2 ⭐⭐ **Complete the sentences with the correct Present Perfect forms of the words in brackets.**

1 *Have you started* (you/start) looking for a job yet?
2 Antonia _____ (never/work) in a factory.
3 I _____ (not decide) which job I want to do yet.
4 _____ (the business/ever/make) a profit?
5 My friends and I _____ (never/have) summer jobs.
6 Cath is only seventeen and she _____ (already/have) five jobs!
7 My aunt _____ (just/open) a café.
8 _____ (the staff/have) a pay rise this year?

3 ⭐⭐ **Choose the correct time expressions to complete the mini-conversations.**

Olga	You've ¹*just / ever / never* tried to find a job before. Why are you looking now?
Bella	Alison has ²*already / just / ever* told me about her idea for a summer holiday together. I need some money.
Interviewer	Have you ³*already / just / ever* worked in a restaurant before?
Leon	Yes, I have, but in the kitchen doing the washing up. I've ⁴*already / just / never* worked as a waiter before.
Noah	Have you asked Mr James about a job ⁵*already / yet / ever*?
Jimmy	Yes, I have. He's ⁶*already / never / ever* told me I can start next week.

4 ⭐⭐ **Use the prompts to write questions in the Present Perfect. Then write short answers.**

1 you / ever / do / a job that you really loved?
Have you ever done a job that you really loved?
Yes, _____.

2 your mum / ever / tell / you to get a job?
_____
No, _____.

3 your neighbour / find / a new job yet?
_____
No, _____.

4 your boss / take on / any more staff yet?
_____
Yes, _____.

5 your teachers / ever / talk / to you about job interviews?
_____
Yes, _____.

6 you / change / your mind about becoming a police officer?
_____
No, _____.

5 ⭐⭐ **Choose the correct forms to complete the sentences.**

1 *Did you finish / Have you finished* your careers project yet?
2 Melissa *has never worked / never worked* in a café before, but she's really enjoying it.
3 What *have your friends done / did your friends do* last Saturday?
4 I *have worked / worked* in a sports shop last summer.
5 *Has your uncle ever sacked / Did your uncle ever sack* one of his employees?
6 This is my first morning at the café and I *have already served / already served* twenty customers!

6 ⭐⭐ Match the two parts of the sentences.

A

1 ☐ Did you   **a** been to London?
2 ☐ Have you ever   **b** you do in London?
3 ☐ What did   **c** go to London last year?
4 ☐ What have   **d** you done this year?

B

1 ☐ I've already seen   **a** this film yesterday.
2 ☐ I haven't seen   **b** this film in my life.
3 ☐ I've never seen   **c** this film so I don't want to see it again.
4 ☐ I saw   **d** this film yet.

7 ⭐⭐ Choose the correct forms to complete the sentences.

1 *Did you feed / Have you fed* the cat yet?
2 I *worked / have worked* as a babysitter last year.
3 William *hasn't never worked / has never worked* in a factory.
4 Why can't I go out? I've *tidied already / already tidied* my room.
5 *Did you ever have / Have you ever had* a holiday job?
6 What *did you do / have you done* at work yesterday?

8 ⭐⭐ Complete the email with the correct Present Perfect or Past Simple forms of the verbs in brackets.

Hi Olivia,
Great news. I ¹*'ve just found* (just/find) a job. I ² _____ (not start) working yet, but the manager ³ _____ (phone) me yesterday and ⁴ _____ (tell) me that I can start on Friday. It's lucky because I ⁵ _____ (already/spend) my first week's wages! I ⁶ _____ (go) shopping last weekend and bought a dress, some shoes and a shirt. I ⁷ _____ (not wear) the dress yet. I think I'll wear in to work on Friday.
Bye 4 now,
Katie

9 ⭐⭐⭐ Use the prompts to write the conversation. Use the Present Perfect and the Past Simple.

Louis you / ever / have / a job before?
¹*Have you ever had a job before?*

Maya Yes / I
² _____

I / sell / ice creams / last summer
³ _____

Louis Really? / you / enjoy / it?
⁴ _____

Maya Yes / I
⁵ _____

It / be / great fun
⁶ _____

Louis How long / you / do / it / for?
⁷ _____

Maya I / work / in the café / for four weeks
⁸ _____

Louis your boss / nice?
⁹ _____

Maya No / she
¹⁰ _____

She / not be / very friendly
¹¹ _____

10 ⭐⭐⭐ Complete the sentences with the correct forms of the words from the box.

already/start   go   ~~just/give~~   not come   you/buy   you/ever/see

1 My dad's boss *has just given* him a pay rise.
2 I'm cooking dinner because my parents _____ home from work yet.
3 You're late – all the other members of the team _____ work.
4 I _____ to bed early last night because I was so tired.
5 _____ the film *The Devil Wears Prada* with Meryl Street in it as a terrible boss?
6 _____ anything interesting at the shopping centre yesterday?

11 ON A HIGH NOTE Think about your plan for this week. Write a short paragraph about what you have and haven't done yet.

7B GRAMMAR

Present Perfect (2)

1 ⭐ Complete each pair of sentences with *for* and *since*.

1
a We've been in this room <u>for</u> an hour and a half.
b We've been in this room _____ 9.30 a.m.

2
a I've had my Saturday job _____ January.
b I've had my Saturday job _____ three months.

3
a I've had this idea _____ my birthday.
b I've had this idea _____ a long time.

4
a Tom has wanted to be a police officer _____ he was a young boy.
b Tom has wanted to be a police officer _____ ages.

2 ⭐ Complete the texts with *for* or *since*.

The bad job
I've been here **1**<u>*for*</u> six months. The company hasn't made a profit **2**_____ 2016 and the boss keeps sacking employees. I haven't had any money **3**_____ January. There should be four people working here today, but I've been on my own **4**_____ 9 a.m and I'm exhausted.

The good job
I've been at this restaurant **5**_____ June and my friend has been here **6**_____ the last two months. I've learned a lot **7**_____ I started and I've met lots of interesting people. Today has been a quiet day. I've been here **8**_____ two hours and there's only been one customer, so my boss has taught me how to cook Spanish paella.

3 ⭐⭐ Complete the sentences with the correct Present Perfect forms of the verbs in brackets.

1 How long <u>has he worked</u> (he/work) as a truck driver?
2 My dad _____ (own) this company since 2014.
3 Tom and Julie _____ (be engaged) for three months.
4 How long _____ (you/know) Casey?
5 I _____ (know) Simon since we worked at the garage together.
6 My parents _____ (be married) since they were twenty-five.

4 ⭐⭐ Use the prompts to write mini-conversations. Use the Present Perfect and the Past Simple.

Kelly How long / you know / each other?
1<u>*How long have you known each other?*</u>

Max We know / each other / two years
2_____

We / meet / at a party
3_____

Sarah How long / your mum / be a doctor?
4_____

Zoe She / be / a doctor / 2007
5_____

She / finish / her studies / in June of that year
6_____

Gillian How long / this factory / be here?
7_____

Noah It / be / here / 2006
8_____

They / open / it / in the year I was born
9_____

5 ⭐⭐⭐ USE OF ENGLISH Complete the second sentence using the word in bold so that it means the same as the first one. Use no more than three words including the word in bold.

1 I met Anita in 2013. **KNOWN**
I've <u>*known Anita since*</u> 2013.

2 My parents bought me this laptop two years ago. **HAD**
I _____ laptop for two years.

3 My grandparents moved to Spain in 1996. **LIVED**
My grandparents have _____ since 1996.

4 Paulina became a fan of Johnny Depp when she was thirteen. **LIKED**
Paulina _____ Depp since she was thirteen.

5 They took Alexis to hospital three hours ago. **IN**
Alexis has been _____ three hours.

6 ON A HIGH NOTE Write questions using *How long ...?* and the verbs from the box. Then write answers to your questions that are true for you using *for* and *since*.

be   have   know   like   live

7C LISTENING AND VOCABULARY

1 Tick the factors which you think are important for job satisfaction.

- ☐ boring work
- ☐ friendly co-workers
- ☐ good career prospects
- ☐ having full-time work
- ☐ long hours
- ☐ low salary
- ☐ working in a team
- ☐ working with customers

2 🔊 52 Listen to a talk about job satisfaction and answer the questions.

1 Who do you think the speaker is talking to?

_____

2 What is the main purpose of her talk?

_____

3 🔊 52 Listen to the talk again and choose the correct answers.

1 At the beginning, the speaker says how long
- **a** the listeners will work for.
- **b** she's been a career advisor.
- **c** it takes to choose the right job.

2 According to the speaker, surveys show that
- **a** job satisfaction rates are falling.
- **b** a good salary affects our job satisfaction the most.
- **c** more people are unhappy than happy at work.

3 What does the speaker say about her work?
- **a** She doesn't like giving speeches.
- **b** She has a job that everyone would enjoy.
- **c** She gets satisfaction from helping other people.

4 What do we learn about job satisfaction rates?
- **a** Doctors are happier at work than teachers.
- **b** The firefighting career gives the most satisfaction.
- **c** 80 percent of people would enjoy being firefighters.

5 At the end of the talk, what does the speaker say?
- **a** Some jobs aren't pleasant for anybody.
- **b** It's better not to work in an office.
- **c** It's important to find a job you enjoy.

Vocabulary extension

4 🔊 53 Complete the extracts from the talk in Exercise 2 with one word in each gap. Listen and check.

1 That means that more than 50 percent of people … get up every morning with a heavy _heart_.

2 For me, standing here giving this talk to a hall full of sixteen-year-olds is right up my _____ …

3 Of course, that doesn't mean that 80 percent of us are _____ about becoming firefighters, …

4 … let me just say that a job which suits one person might be another person's worst _____!

5 Don't _____ do with something that's not right for you.

6 It's your life – make the _____ of it.

5 ON A HIGH NOTE Choose a job which you think you'd like to do. Write a short paragraph about why you think it would give you satisfaction.

Pronunciation

6 🔊 54 Look at some words which contain the /ɜː/ sound. Try and guess what sound this symbol represents. Listen, check and repeat the words.

bird
third
heard
learn
burn
turn

ACTIVE PRONUNCIATION | /ɜː/ sound

The /ɜː/ sound can be heard in many different words in English, but the words in which it appears are not all spelled the same.

7 🔊 55 Look at these sentences from the talk in Exercise 2. Find the words which contain the /ɜː/ sound. Listen and check.

1 Your head teacher has invited me to talk to you today about career choices and your future in the <u>world</u> of work.

2 Work will take up a large part of your lives and really shapes who you are as a person.

3 Different surveys give us different information about which jobs give the most job satisfaction.

4 Not everybody likes giving talks though, or even working with people, so – as I say – your career is a very personal choice.

5 As you can imagine, a lot of research has been done into which careers give the most satisfaction and why.

6 Before I finish, let me just say that a job which suits one person might be another person's worst nightmare!

8 In Exercises 6 and 7, you heard the /ɜː/ sound in words with different spellings. Look at these groups of words and find one word in each group which does NOT contain the /ɜː/ sound.

1 girl	firm	shirt	(pirate)
2 earth	heart	heard	learn
3 return	burger	hurry	hurt
4 worm	worn	worse	world
5 very	hers	German	nervous

9 🔊 56 All these words have the /ɜː/ sound. Complete each word with one or two vowels. Listen and repeat the words.

1 s<u>u</u>rgery
2 j__rnalist
3 n__rse
4 s__rvice
5 e__rn
6 __rthquake
7 adv__rt
8 th__rties

7D **VOCABULARY** | Workplaces

1 ⭐ Put the words from the box in the correct column.

agriculture building site department store
education finance fisherman ~~health care~~
manufacturing miner nurse

Industry	Workplace	Job
¹*health care*	hospital	²
mining	mine	³
⁴	factory	factory worker
⁵	school	teacher
⁶	bank	bank worker
construction	⁷	building engineer
⁸	farm	farmer
fishing	fishing boat	⁹
sales	¹⁰	shop assistant

2 ⭐ What jobs do these people do? Match sentences 1–6 with jobs a–f.

1 ☐ I help people to choose books to read.
2 ☐ I do operations in a hospital.
3 ☐ I write articles for a newspaper.
4 ☐ I help guests when they arrive at the hotel.
5 ☐ I wash, cut and dye people's hair.
6 ☐ I drive an ambulance and try to save people's lives.

a journalist
b paramedic
c receptionist
d hairdresser
e librarian
f surgeon

3 ⭐ Match the two parts of the job words.

LOOKING FOR A JOB?

WE HAVE JOBS TO SUIT EVERYONE. COME AND FIND YOUR PERFECT JOB TODAY! WE NEED ...

1 ☐ bike
2 ☐ tour
3 ☐ shop
4 ☐ social
5 ☐ building
6 ☐ flight
7 ☐ estate
8 ☐ car

a workers
b assistants
c couriers
d mechanics
e guides
f attendants
g engineers
h agents

4 ⭐⭐ Replace the underlined parts in the sentences below with the phrases from the box.

at night from home in a team
is working to a deadline ~~long hours~~ part-time
under pressure works as works hard

1 We often work <u>for more than ten hours a day</u>.
   long hours
2 Sasha prefers working <u>together with other people</u>.
   _____
3 I don't go out to an office – I work <u>in my living room</u>!
   _____
4 Charles <u>is never lazy</u> at the garage.
   _____
5 Since her son was born, Clare only works <u>three hours a day</u>.
   _____
6 The interviewer asked David if he was good at working <u>in stressful situations</u>.
   _____
7 Tim <u>is</u> a journalist for a national newspaper.
   _____
8 I work <u>from the evening until the next morning</u>.
   _____
9 The sales team <u>has to be finished before a certain date</u> so they are all quite stressed.
   _____

5 ⭐⭐ Label the industries and workplaces with the words from the box.

forestry laboratory ~~nursery~~ oil platform

1 *nursery*

2 _____

3 _____
4 _____

6 ON A HIGH NOTE Write a short paragraph about the type of industry you would like to work in, e.g. health care, education, etc. Explain the reasons for your choice.

1 🔊 *57* **Listen and repeat the phrases. How do you say them in your language?**

SPEAKING | Describing photos

DESCRIBING WHAT THE PHOTOS SHOW IN GENERAL

The photo shows a group of skydivers.

GIVING MORE DETAIL

In the foreground/centre/background, there's some countryside.

At the bottom/top, there's an interesting poster.

On the right/left, there's a man with a tablet.

USING THE CORRECT TENSES

They've just jumped out of a plane.

They're falling down.

MAKING GUESSES

There might be fifteen of them.

It's hard to say how many **but** I think there are twenty.

It looks like Britain or Ireland.

Perhaps/Maybe it's Scotland.

I think they're having fun.

They look/seem happy.

GIVING YOUR OPINION

It looks quite cool.

It's really/very colourful.

It's/It looks quite/really/very unusual.

---

2 **Complete the description of Photo A with the words from the box.**

> background   centre   foreground   might   perhaps
> quite   right   shaking   ~~shows~~   think

The photo ¹*shows* a group of people having a meeting in an office. In the ²_____, we can see seven people sitting and standing around a table. They have laptops and tablets. In the ³_____, there is a chart with graphs and diagrams on it.

In the ⁴_____ of the photo, there's a man with glasses and a beard. On the ⁵_____, there's another man with glasses. They're ⁶_____ hands and the other people are clapping.

3 **Use the prompts to write sentences about Photo B. Add any other necessary words.**

1 picture / show / two people in a clothes shop
The picture shows two people in a clothes shop.

2 shop / look / very modern
_____

3 left / is / young sales assistant / and / right / is / customer
_____

4 shop assistant / smile
_____

5 customer / just / buy / something
_____

6 she / give / her credit card / to the shop assistant
_____

7 hard / say / what / she / buy / but the bags are small
_____

4 **Complete the sentences about Photos A and B with *a*, *an*, *some* or *the*.**

1 We can see *an* open laptop. I think _____ laptop is off because _____ screen is dark.

2 Two men are standing up. I think _____ man on _____ right is _____ other man's boss.

3 _____ office in _____ photo looks nice, but I wouldn't want to work in _____ office.

4 The woman is buying _____ clothes. _____ clothes are in bags.

5 She is using _____ credit card to buy _____ clothes. _____ credit card is in her hand.

6 I can see _____ shoes behind the sales assistant. _____ shoes look like my new shoes!

I ⁷_____ one man has just given a presentation. ⁸_____ he and his team have done well recently and the other man is congratulating him. The meeting looks ⁹_____ informal. No-one is wearing a jacket or tie. The office is very bright with white furniture and big windows. The people ¹⁰_____ work in sales or IT. It looks like a nice place to work.

7F READING AND VOCABULARY

1 Look at the photos, the title and the first paragraph of the article and answer the questions.

   1 What is WWOOF?

   _____

   2 How is volunteer work with WWOOF similar to/
different from the work for other volunteer
organisations?

   _____

   _____

2 Read the text quickly. Match headings A–F with paragraphs 1–5. There is one extra heading.

   A Why should I become a WWOOFer?

   B How do I find a job?

   C When is the best time to go?

   D Who can volunteer?

   E What does 'WWOOF' mean?

   F Who will I work for?

3 Read the text again and choose the correct answers.

   1 Why did the organisation change its name two times?

     a The original choices didn't accurately describe what the organisation does.

     b Paid employees of the organisation weren't happy with the name.

     c The aims of the organisation have changed three times.

   2 Which statement about WWOOF is true?

     a Volunteers work with other volunteers of their own age.

     b Retired volunteers aren't popular amongst employers.

     c Under eighteens can work for the organisation, but not everywhere.

   3 What is one benefit of reading the WWOOF website carefully?

     a You are able to get in touch with other volunteers.

     b You can avoid doing jobs which you aren't keen on.

     c You can find out information about the local climate.

   4 According to the text, what are the benefits of working on a large farm?

     a The work isn't as difficult.

     b You get more free time to enjoy.

     c You have a more lively social life.

   5 How does the writer claim that volunteer work can help you?

     a You can learn things that may be useful for you when you return home.

     b You can go travelling with your hosts when your volunteering time has finished.

     c You may be offered full-time, paid employment by your hosts if you are a good worker.

Vocabulary extension

4 Match the highlighted words and phrases from the text with the definitions.

   1 It doesn't cost anything.

     free

   2 To be in a better situation, or have more money.

     _____

   3 To ask for money for a product or service.

     _____

   4 Workers who earn money for what they do.

     _____

   5 An organisation whose aim is not money-making.

     _____

   6 Not to have enough money for something.

     _____

ACTIVE VOCABULARY | _maximum vs minimum_

Maximum means 'the largest amount, size, etc., that is allowed',
There's no maximum age limit.

Minimum means 'the smallest amount, size, etc., that is allowed',
A lot of countries have a minimum age of eighteen for volunteers.

5 Match sentences 1–6 with their meanings a–f. Are these statements true in your country?

   1 ☐ There is a maximum speed limit of 70 miles per hour on British roads.

   2 ☐ The minimum wage in 2018 was £7.83 per hour.

   3 ☐ The maximum working hours for doctors is 48 hours per week.

   4 ☐ There is a minimum speed you can drive on some roads.

   5 ☐ There is no maximum temperature for school classrooms.

   6 ☐ Some theme park rides don't have a minimum age. They have a minimum height.

   a Employers can't pay less than this.

   b You can't drive more slowly than this.

   c It doesn't matter how hot it is.

   d You can't drive faster than this.

   e You can't go on them if you are too short.

   f They can't work longer than this.

6 ON A HIGH NOTE Write a short paragraph explaining why you would or wouldn't like to become a WWOOFer.

I'M A WWOOFER AND IT'S GREAT!

WWOOF is a **non-profit organisation which brings volunteers together with organic farmers all over the world who need help, but can't find or can't afford to employ workers.** There are a lot of volunteer organisations and in some ways, WWOOF is no different to them. Volunteers don't get paid, they do it to see the world and meet new people. However, many organisations ask for money when you volunteer. WWOOF farmers don't charge anything. You work and they give you free food and accommodation.

1 ☐ Interestingly, the same letters have been used for three different names. Originally, the organisation's title was Working Weekends On Organic Farms. This showed that the experiences were temporary, but wasn't very accurate as most volunteers stay for longer than a weekend – a few weeks or months is a more usual length of time. So, the new title became Willing Workers On Organic Farms. However, it was felt that the use of the word 'workers' could make people think this was an organisation for paid employees. So, now, WWOOF stands for World Wide Opportunities on Organic Farms.

2 ☐ Anyone! A lot of countries have a minimum age of eighteen for volunteers, but in some countries such as Germany, Italy, Portugal and the UK, under-eighteens can also volunteer. There's no maximum age limit. I've worked with a lot of people in their twenties, middle-aged people who have decided to change their lives and even retired people who have decided to have an adventure in their old age! In fact, many hosts liked having older people because they often had more skills.

3 ☐ This is easy. On the WWOOF website, there is a map of the world showing all the countries you can work in. Just click on one and you'll see all the opportunities available with descriptions of the work and reviews from people who have worked there. You can often see what work needs doing at different times of the year which makes planning even easier, especially if there are some tasks you would prefer not to do. It's also good to check the climate of the country you choose on other websites because some places can get incredibly hot in the summer.

4 ☐ You can choose. Even though all the work is farm work, it doesn't mean that every experience is the same. Some places are very small. They may be run by an older couple or a family with young children who haven't got the time or strength to do everything necessary. They may be looking for just one or two volunteers to help them. It's a great way to get to know someone well and learn the language, but some volunteers would be better off on a bigger farm with lots of volunteers where the evenings and weekends are much more lively and sociable!

5 ☐ Working abroad gives you tremendous opportunities. You may not want to become a full-time farmer when you return home, but the training you get and key skills you learn could still be useful. It's also a great opportunity to learn a new language and visit new places. If you like travelling, find hosts who offer to take you to places of local interest on your days off. My host in Greece had a yacht and taught me how to sail in my free time.

So, that's a short introduction to WWOOF. Read about my experiences as a WWOOFer here.

7G **WRITING AND VOCABULARY** | A formal email of application

Give a clear reason for writing in the subject box.

Begin your email with a formal greeting.

Explain why you are writing.

Mention your age, education and previous experience.

Mention your personal qualities.

Say that you hope to receive a reply.

End your email with a formal greeting.

From: amy_bishop@hol.com
To: c.ennis@ewrite.com
Subject: Job application

Dear Mr Ennis,

I am writing to you to **1**a*pply* for the job as part-time office receptionist.

I am a seventeen-year-old student from Hereford. Although I haven't had any previous **2**e_____ as a receptionist, I have had several part-time jobs in the last two years. I have worked as a waitress, I have worked in a shop and I have done babysitting for neighbours. I have also **3**c_____ a course in effective online communication and can write eighty words per minute accurately on a computer keyboard. I finish school in June and I am hoping to study for a teaching degree from September.

I **4**c_____ myself to be organised and reliable. I can work alone or as part of a team and I am friendly with good communication skills.

I look forward to **5**h_____ from you.

Kind regards,

Amy Bishop

---

1 Complete the email with one word in each gap.

2 Read the email and complete the interviewer's notes.

Name:	Amy Bishop
Job/Position:	**1***office receptionist*
Work experience:	**2**_____, **3**_____, **4**_____
Qualifications and skills:	**5**_____, **6**_____
Future plans:	**7**_____
Personal qualities:	**8**_____, **9**_____, can work alone or as part of a team, friendly with **10**_____

3 Put the words and phrases from the box in the correct column.

~~accepting criticism~~ animals children computers creative enthusiastic hard-working solving problems working in a team

I'm good at ...	I'm good with ...	I'm ...
accepting criticism		

4 WRITING TASK Use the information below to write an email of application.

PART-TIME RADIO PRESENTERS REQUIRED

We're looking for young, chatty, friendly people to host our summer radio shows. No previous experience needed but you should be interested in music. Apply in writing to Katie Stephens, Radio Tayfield. Katie.S@radiotayfield.com

ACTIVE WRITING | A formal email of application

1 Plan your email.
   Use these ideas to help you plan your writing.
   - Explain clearly why you are writing.
   - Give details about yourself and your experience.
   - Mention three or four of your personal qualities.
   - Say that you hope to receive a reply.

2 Write the email.
   - Start and finish the email appropriately.
   - Don't use emoticons, exclamation marks or informal language.
   - Use paragraphs to organise your email.
   - Use the Present Perfect to describe your experiences and achievements.

3 Check that ...
   - all the relevant information is included.
   - there are clear paragraphs in your writing.
   - there are no spelling or grammar mistakes.
   - you have made yourself sound like a good candidate for the job.

1 7A GRAMMAR AND VOCABULARY Match the the two parts of the sentences.

1. ☐ Do you think we should take
2. ☐ Can this business ever make
3. ☐ When are they going to open
4. ☐ When are you going to give
5. ☐ Why did you lose
6. ☐ Have you ever been
7. ☐ Where can I find
8. ☐ Has your manager ever sacked

a us a pay rise?
b an employee?
c out of work?
d on more staff?
e a good job?
f the new factory?
g your job?
h a profit?

2 7C LISTENING AND VOCABULARY Choose the correct words to complete the sentences.

1. Colin doesn't *pay / earn* much money as a truck driver and wants to get a different job.
2. I work five days a week, but I would prefer a *part-time / full-time* job with more free time.
3. Some dangerous jobs have a very high accident *rate / death*.
4. Working *hours / conditions* here are great – a company restaurant, large offices and long breaks.
5. *Farmers / Miners* have to work underground doing a very dangerous job.
6. Inge works for a multinational *company / workplace* with over 3000 employees.
7. My *boss / employee* is great – she makes us work hard but she also cares about us.
8. I really like my *clients / co-workers* – they're great and I've made a lot of friends in my new job.

3 7D VOCABULARY Complete the mini-conversations with one word in each gap.

Nick Are you going to get a job in your parents' department ¹s*tore* when you leave school?
Becky No. I'd like to be a ²l_____ because I love books. What about you?
Nick I'd like to be a ³p_____.
Becky Good idea. I'll vote for you!

Aled You love writing. Why don't you get a job as a newspaper ⁴j_____?
Sue I don't think so. They have to work to a ⁵d_____ and finish their stories for the next day's paper. I couldn't work under ⁶p_____ like that.

Monia So, you're going to work in ⁷h_____ c_____ ? Do you want to be a doctor?
Artur No, I want to train as a ⁸p_____ .
Monia Oh – will you have to work ⁹l_____ hours?
Artur Yes, it's a difficult job.

4 7F READING AND VOCABULARY Complete the advert with the words from the box.

CV employers get key make making prospects ~~work~~

Volunteers needed

Do you ¹*work* well in a team? Are you good at ²_____ friends? Do you want a job that you like, but that will help others too? Why not try volunteering?

You won't ³_____ a lot of money. In fact, you won't ⁴_____ paid at all, but you will make a difference to the world around you. Volunteer work is also a great thing to put on your ⁵_____ and can help your future career ⁶_____ . You will learn ⁷_____ skills which will make future ⁸_____ choose you rather than someone else.

5 7G WRITING AND VOCABULARY Complete the definitions with the words and phrases from the box.

~~cheerful~~ good at accepting criticism
good at solving problems good with numbers
patient previous experience punctual sociable

1. She's always happy. She's *cheerful*.
2. I can do Maths well. I'm _____.
3. José has done this sort of work before. He has _____.
4. Katerina is always on time. She's _____.
5. My boss doesn't mind waiting. She's _____.
6. Ahmed likes meeting people. He's _____.
7. Felipe can always find the answer. He's _____.
8. I don't mind if you tell me what I'm doing wrong. I'm _____.

1 **For each learning objective, write 1–5 to assess your ability.**

1 = I don't feel confident. 5 = I feel confident.

	Learning objective	Course material	How confident I am (1–5)
7A	I can use the Present Perfect with *already*, *ever*, *just*, *never* and *yet*.	Student's Book pp. 94–95	
7B	I can use the Present Perfect with *for* and *since* to talk about a duration of time.	Student's Book p. 96	
7C	I can understand the main idea of a radio programme and talk about work.	Student's Book p. 97	
7D	I can talk about different jobs and workplaces.	Student's Book p. 98	
7E	I can describe people or things in a photo using correct tenses and phrase to make guesses.	Student's Book pp. 98–99	
7F	I can understand a factual text and talk about volunteering.	Student's Book pp. 100–101	
7G	I can write a formal email to apply for job or a course.	Student's Book pp. 102–103	

2 **Which of the skills above would you like to improve in? How?**

Skill I want to improve in	How I can improve

3 **What can you remember from this unit?**

New words I learned and most want to remember	Expressions and phrases I liked	English I heard or read outside class

GRAMMAR AND VOCABULARY

1 Complete each pair of sentences with the same word.

1

a I hope our company starts to *make* a profit next year.

b It's difficult to *make* friends when you go to a new school in the middle of the year.

2

a My mum's _____ hours are 9 a.m. to 5 p.m., Monday to Friday.

b We offer great _____ conditions including five weeks paid holiday a year.

3

a Do you think the factory will _____ on more staff this year?

b I'd like a job where I can _____ care of children.

4

a Doing volunteer _____ is a great idea.

b I'm looking for part-time _____ for the summer.

5

a There's a door _____ the left.

b I enjoy working _____ my own.

/ 4

2 Complete the second sentence with one word so that it means the same as the first one.

1 How much money do you get for doing your work?

How much money do you e*arn*?

2 What are the people you work with like?

What are your c_____-w_____ like?

3 How long have you been without a job?

How long have you been o_____ of work?

4 I think our boss is going to give us more money.

I think our boss is going to give us a pay r_____.

5 Can you help us to give people their meals?

Can you help to s_____ these meals?

6 I work for this organisation but I don't get paid.

I do v_____ work for this organisation.

/ 5

3 Complete the dialogue with one word in each gap.

Alisha Have you **1***ever* worked in a shop, Callum?

Callum Yes, I **2**_____. I worked in a clothes shop last year and now I'm working in a supermarket.

Alisha How **3**_____ have you worked in the supermarket?

Callum I've been there **4**_____ six months – **5**_____ October. How about you?

Alisha I've **6**_____ had a job, but I'm thinking of working in a department **7**_____ this summer.

Callum It's a good idea. You should do it.

/ 6

4 Use the prompts to write sentences.

1 We / just / finish / our dinner

We've just finished our dinner.

2 Rachel / already / write / three books

_____

3 you / ever / do / any volunteer work?

_____

4 They / never / have / a summer job

_____

5 How long / Sandra / be / a nurse?

_____

6 She / read / five / job adverts / but / she / apply for / any / of them / yet

_____

/ 5

USE OF ENGLISH

5 Complete the second sentence using the word in bold so that it means the same as the first one. Use no more than three words including the word in bold.

1 We arrived in Spain three hours ago. **FOR**

We've been *in Spain for* three hours.

2 This is the first time I've ever been late for school. **NEVER**

I _____ late for school before.

3 We had an exam a very short time ago. **JUST**

We _____ an exam.

4 I think I'm hard-working and confident. **MYSELF**

I _____ be hard-working and confident.

5 Ariadne is going to start her project soon. **STARTED**

Ariadne _____ her project yet.

6 When he gets down to work, he forgets about everything else. **HIMSELF**

When he gets down to work, he _____ it.

/ 5

6 Complete the text with the correct words formed from the words in bold.

I have applied for a job as a hotel **1***receptionist* (RECEPTION), and yesterday I attended the interview. The interviewer asked me the usual questions about my **2**_____ (EDUCATE) and experience. Then he wanted to know about my personality. I told him I was **3**_____ (CREATE), hard-working and **4**_____ (ENTHUSIASM), which is all true.

When the interviewer asked me if I was good at accepting **5**_____ (CRITIC) – without thinking – I replied, 'Why? Don't you like my hair style?' I hope my silly joke won't make any **6**_____ (DIFFER) to the interviewer and I can still get the job.

/ 5

/ 30

08 Switch on

8A GRAMMAR AND VOCABULARY

Verb patterns: the infinitive and the -ing form

1 ⭐ **Choose the correct forms to complete the sentences.**

1 Do you mind *to wait / waiting* for a few minutes?
2 I've decided *to study / studying* Physics in Edinburgh.
3 Have you finished *to read / reading* the report I gave you?
4 To learn a language, you have to practise *to speak / speaking*.
5 I promise *to be / being* more careful in the future.
6 Did you manage *to see / seeing* anything through the microscope?
7 I don't usually enjoy *to do / doing* experiments but today's was fun.
8 Would you like *to eat / eating* before the film or afterwards?

2 ⭐ **Match the two parts of the sentences.**

A
1 ☐ I can't stand
2 ☐ I hope
3 ☐ I might

a to study Physics at university.
b study Maths at university.
c studying Chemistry.

B
1 ☐ You must
2 ☐ You've finished
3 ☐ You promised

a to do the ironing.
b do the dishes.
c doing your homework.

C
1 ☐ Did you manage
2 ☐ Should I
3 ☐ Do you mind

a finishing the project?
b to finish the project?
c finish the project?

3 ⭐ **Complete the sentences with *about, at, in, on* or *up*.**

1 You have to keep _on_ trying.
2 Laura is going to give _____ studying Physics.
3 I'm not keen _____ working in a laboratory.
4 Are you good _____ proving hypotheses?
5 Is Harry thinking _____ going back to college?
6 Stella is interested _____ studying both Physics and Astronomy.

4 ⭐ **Choose the correct forms to complete the sentences.**

1 I continued ___ after we were told to stop because I was in the middle of a sentence.
  a writing   b write   c to write
2 The students have learned ___ different planets and stars in the sky.
  a identifying   b to identify   c identify
3 Mr Collins avoided ___ experiments after he caused a small explosion.
  a do   b to do   c doing
4 Why did you give up ___? You were really good.
  a swimming   b swim   c to swim
5 Never stop ___ to protect wildlife.
  a try   b to try   c trying
6 I don't mind ___ tests but we shouldn't have so many.
  a do   b to do   c doing

5 ⭐⭐ **Complete the texts with the correct forms of the verbs in brackets.**

You can't avoid ¹*meeting* (meet) Janice forever. You should ²_____ (talk) to her and try ³_____ (sort) out your relationship.

I tried ⁴_____ (do) the Chemistry test but it took me two hours just to finish ⁵_____ (answer) the first question. Could you ⁶_____ (help) me before the end of year exams?

This can't ⁷_____ (be) the right answer. Let's stop ⁸_____ (write) for a moment. We need ⁹_____ (go) online and find out more about the topic.

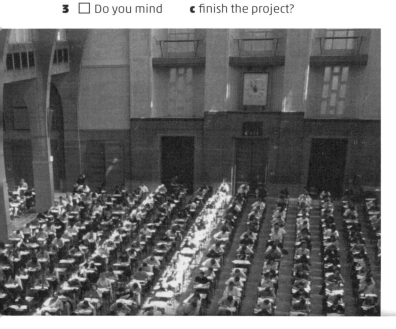

6 ★★ Complete the conversation with the correct forms of the verbs from the box.

do ~~explain~~ know (x2) move work

Amber You promised ¹*to explain* this theory to me.

Kyle Sorry, I forgot. What do you need ² _____?

Amber Newton's first law. Objects continue to move at a constant speed unless acted upon by a force. So why do things stop ³_____?

Kyle Because of friction. That's the force which acts between the road and your bike wheel and slows you down.

Amber So why don't I slow down when I go downhill?

Kyle Because of gravity. Amber, you agreed ⁴_____ hard this year. This is basic primary school science. You should ⁵_____ it.

Amber I haven't got time.

Kyle You've got time to play the guitar.

Amber Well, I enjoy ⁶_____ that!

7 ★★ Complete the text with the correct forms of the verbs from the box.

~~be~~ avoid collapse fall learn protect work

I'd like ¹*to be* an astronomer. I love ²_____ about space, even though the more you learn, the more there is to worry about! I don't know how the Earth has managed ³_____ being hit by another large meteor similar to the one which wiped out the dinosaurs. Another one could ⁴_____ from the skies at any time.

Another problem is solar storms. There was one in 1859 which damaged cables and wires. If there is a storm like that now, the Internet will stop ⁵_____. If we fail ⁶_____ our electronic systems, the world's economy could ⁷_____. It's frightening, but exciting at the same time!

8 ★★★ USE OF ENGLISH Complete the second sentence using the word in bold so that it means the same as the first one. Use no more than three words including the word in bold.

1 My ambition is to be an astronomer. **LIKE**
I *would like to* be an astronomer.

2 I succeeded in recognising Mars and Jupiter. **MANAGED**
I _____ Mars and Jupiter.

3 Try not to make him angry. **AVOID**
Try _____ him angry.

4 I said I would go with them. **AGREED**
I _____ with them.

5 What's the best thing for us to do now? **SHOULD**
What do you think _____ now?

6 I'm sorry. I didn't remember to buy shampoo. **FORGOT**
I'm sorry. I _____ shampoo.

7 I will work harder at school next year, Mum. **PROMISE**
I _____ harder next year at school, Mum.

9 ON A HIGH NOTE Write a short paragraph about the subjects you study at school and the activities you do after school. Use at least five of the verbs from the box.

can't stand don't mind enjoy give up learn might prefer try would like

8B VOCABULARY | Computers

1 ★ Match the two parts of the sentences.

1 ☐ Use your mouse to drag the image
2 ☐ When I play this game, my computer
3 ☐ It's difficult to expand
4 ☐ Be careful when you download
5 ☐ I never store images in
6 ☐ Use your mouse to click
7 ☐ You don't need these files now – you can
8 ☐ Don't type it again – just cut

a and paste.
b the cloud.
c delete them.
d images a lot without losing quality.
e to the place where you want it.
f free programmes.
g twice very quickly.
h always crashes.

2 ★ Complete the words in the conversation with one letter in each gap.

Aaron Your computer is very old-fashioned, Grandad. The problem with **1**de _skt_ _o_ _p_ computers is that they're heavy. Most people prefer a **2**l__ __ t__ __ or **3**t__ __ l__ __ nowadays.

Grandad I don't want to change now. I know what I'm doing on this.

Aaron Well, you could at least tidy up all the **4**c__ __ l__ __s. What's this one? Oh, OK. It connects the computer to the **5**p__ __ n__ __ __ __.

Grandad Yes, when people send me photos, I like to put them onto paper.

Aaron And this is for ...

Grandad That's for my **6**h__ __ __ds__ t. Here it is. It's got a pair of **7**h__ __ d__ __ o__ __s and a **8**m__ __ r__ __ h__ __ __ __.

Aaron Is that for talking to Debbie and her children in Australia?

Grandad No, that's for the online games I play. Sometimes I use the **9**s__ __ __ k__ __s, but not when your grandmother's at home. Some of the people I play against use very bad language and she gets annoyed!

3 ★★ Complete the conversation with the words from the box.

drive   flash   mouse   profile   screen   ~~wireless~~

Aaron So, I think you need to get rid of a few cables. First of all, you can use this **1**_wireless_ keyboard.

Grandad Oh, that's good.

Aaron It uses batteries, so you need to have some spare ones just in case it stops working. You can also have a **2**_____ without a cable. That will help with your gaming as sometimes the cable gets in the way. It works the same, when you move it, the arrow on your **3**_____ moves and you click right or left.

Grandad OK. And what's this?

Aaron This is a USB **4**_____ **5**_____ . When you visit people, you can put photos on this and take it with you. Then you connect it to their computer and they can look at them.

Grandad Great! Now, can you help me update my Facebook **6**_____?

Aaron You are on Facebook? I didn't know.

4 ★★ Which word doesn't collocate with the verb? Find the odd one out in each group.

1 open   a file   a document   (an icon)   a folder
2 post   a message   a folder   an image   a photo
3 save   a table   a photo   trash   a message
4 share   images   messages   hotspots   texts
5 create   a table   a screen   file   a folder
6 update   a text   a profile   a document   a disk

5 ON A HIGH NOTE Write a short paragraph about how you use your computer or smartphone on a typical day. Use verbs from Exercises 1 and 4.

1 (🔊) *58* **Listen and repeat the phrases. How do you say them in your language?**

SPEAKING | Explanations

ASKING FOR EXPLANATIONS

I'm sorry, I'm not sure I understand.

I don't know what you mean/what that means.

What is that (exactly)?

What does HD stand for?

Can you explain what that is?

Could you tell me what that is/does/means?

What do you mean?

What do you mean by turbocharger?

GIVING EXPLANATIONS

It's a kind/type/sort of operating system.

It's the kind/type/sort of camera you can use to take 3D photos.

It means 'fifth generation'.

It stands for High Definition.

It helps you to/lets you charge your phone battery fast.

---

2 **Complete the sentences with the words from the box.**

does exactly explain mean ~~means~~ stand type understand

1 I don't know what that *means*.
2 I'm not sure I _____.
3 What does UHD _____ for?
4 Can you _____ how it works?
5 What do you _____ by 'standalone'?
6 It's a _____ of programme.
7 What is that, _____?
8 Can you tell me what this programme _____?

3 **Complete the conversation with the words from Exercise 2.**

Customer Hello, I'm interested in buying a television. A 32 inch television.

Assistant Yes, of course. What **1** *type* of television? Do you want an HD screen?

Customer What does HD **2**_____ for?

Assistant High Definition.

Customer What do you **3**_____ by High Definition?

Assistant It has a very good picture quality.

Customer Oh, yes, OK. Perfect.

Assistant Great. 720 or 1080?

Customer I'm sorry. I'm not sure I **4**_____. Can you **5**_____?

Assistant Of course. It refers to the number of pixels.

Customer I don't know what that **6**_____. I'm sorry. I bought my last television in 1995.

Assistant Pixels are the little dots that the picture is made up of.

Customer Oh, yes, I see. What do you recommend?

Assistant I'd choose the 1080. It's much better quality. We've got a special offer on a 32 inch smart TV.

Customer What is that **7**_____? I mean, can you tell me what a smart TV **8**_____?

Assistant It can connect to the Internet and act like a computer.

Customer Oh, no. I'm sure it would be very complicated. I'm still having problems understanding my video recorder!

8D READING AND VOCABULARY

1 Read the text quickly. Find the names of three celebrities and match them with the information.

1 He/She has never used social media.

_____

2 He/She was angry at comments made by fans.

_____

3 He/She gave someone some good advice.

_____

2 Read the underlined sentences in the text and decide whether they are facts or opinions.

1 *fact*

2 _____

3 _____

4 _____

5 _____

3 Read the text again and complete the notes with 1–3 words in each gap.

1 Famous people use social media to keep themselves in *the public eye*.

2 As well as actors and singers, another group of people who try to control their public image are _____.

3 There are people whose job involves giving celebrities a more _____.

4 Justin Bieber was upset about comments made by his _____.

5 The writer believes that Selena Gomez's suggestion was _____.

6 Some celebrities don't like appearing in public because it is impossible for them to _____.

7 Celebrities can earn money just by writing a _____.

8 Daniel Radcliffe has always kept away from _____.

Vocabulary extension

4 Complete these phrases from the text with one word in each gap.

1 stay in the public *eye* (appear in magazines, social media, etc. so that people notice you)

2 _____ columnist (a person who writes about celebrities' private lives)

3 _____ a positive image (make sure a person's good points are shown)

4 be a _____ name (be well-known to most people)

5 _____ money (earn money from work or in other ways)

5 Complete the sentences with the phrases from Exercise 4.

1 Although it's possible to *make money* from writing a blog, it isn't as easy as it seems.

2 To _____ of our clients, we start by asking them to do some charity work. That always helps.

3 Celebrities do everything they can to _____ because people will forget them otherwise.

4 The radio DJ is a _____, but not many people know what he looks like.

5 The _____ lost her job when she wrote lies about two famous actors.

ACTIVE VOCABULARY | Prefixes *im-*, *un-*

We can add prefixes *im-* and *un-* to some adjectives to create their opposites. We use

- *im-* before adjectives beginning with *m* or *p* (e.g. **im**perfect).
- *un-* before a variety of adjectives (e.g. **un**reliable).

---

6 Complete the sentences with the opposite forms of the adjectives from the box. Use *im-* or *un-*.

fair ~~fortunate~~ mature necessary patient possible

1 The speaker made two *unfortunate* mistakes during his lecture.

2 He spoke so fast that it was _____ to understand what he was saying.

3 You seem very _____ - are you in a hurry to go somewhere?

4 He's eighteen but he seems quite _____ for his age.

5 Why do I always have to do the washing-up? It's so _____!

6 Paper and pencils were available, so it was _____ to bring our own drawing materials to the art class.

7 ON A HIGH NOTE Write a short paragraph about what you believe are the positive and negative aspects of being a celebrity.

No news is bad news ... usually

For celebrities there is a saying: 'No news is bad news'. This can have two meanings. If there is no news about a celebrity, it is bad for their career as they need publicity to stay in the public eye. It can also mean that every item of news, however bad it may seem at first, will be good because at least it makes people remember them. This is not always true, unfortunately, and some celebrities have seen their careers destroyed because of a particularly negative scandal.

[1]Singers, actors and even politicians have always tried to control what the public knew about them. In the past, this involved providing positive stories and photos to gossip columnists for magazines and newspapers. The rise of social media, though, has led to a number of changes in how celebrities use publicity for their own benefit. Now, celebrities employ whole teams of people to post messages about what's going on in their lives and careers, to update their profiles and maintain professional websites which promote a positive image.

The rise of social media also means that fans have become part of the publicity process – they can join in. This can have positive benefits as news and photos spread quickly around the world. However, Twitter feeds and online comments can sometimes turn into a battleground. When singer Justin Bieber posted photos of his new girlfriend on Instagram, he was upset to discover negative comments about her from his own fans. When he asked them to stop, his ex-girlfriend, Selena Gomez suggested that he should just stop posting the photos. [2]It seemed like sensible advice. However, although the two celebrities remained friends, almost immediately war broke out between Selena's fans and Justin's fans – it was a war which neither of them could control. Now that people everywhere own a smartphone, it's almost impossible for celebrities to control the photos and information which are published. If you are a household name, you can never fully relax in public because someone, somewhere will be there to capture the yawn or angry look and post it to their own online followers. [3]No wonder so many stars try to hide away from the public!

Another change is that social media gives celebrities the opportunity to make money by advertising their own or other companies' products. Several studies have shown that people remember products better if they are advertised by famous people. [4]This is true even if they aren't actually fans of that person. Advertising is not a new idea, of course, but now, as well as appearing in official adverts, a celebrity can write a simple comment about enjoying a particular chocolate bar or driving a certain car and get paid for it. [5]A company can also finance a video if it contains their product. To prevent this hidden advertising, governments have introduced laws saying that videos or tweets which a company has paid for must clearly state that they are adverts, but this doesn't reduce the stars' ability to make more and more money.

Despite the benefits to their career and the possibility of earning even more money from advertising, some celebrities have never been interested in using social media. British actor Daniel Radcliffe doesn't use Facebook, Twitter or Instagram and that's why his private life remains just that ... private.

8E GRAMMAR

The first conditional

1 ⭐ **Match the two parts of the sentences.**

1 ☐ If I'm not here when you arrive,
2 ☐ If you don't take care of your things,
3 ☐ If this doesn't fix the problem with my phone,
4 ☐ If I haven't got enough money to start a business,
5 ☐ If you have any problems with your website,
6 ☐ If my train is late,

a I'll take it back to the shop tomorrow.
b I'll call you from the station.
c let me know and I'll try to help you.
d my parents will let you in.
e I think I'll try crowdfunding.
f you'll lose them.

2 ⭐⭐ **Choose the correct forms to complete the sentences.**

1 If I *hear / will hear* more details about the gaming competition, I *let / will let* you know.
2 There *is / will be* a school trip if at least forty students *want / will want* to go.
3 If Dave *doesn't arrive / won't arrive* soon, we *go / will go* without him.
4 What *do you do / will you do* if you *won't know / don't know* the answers to the test questions?
5 If I *miss / will miss* the radio show, I *listen / will listen* to it online later.
6 *Will you still post / Do you post* the photos if Cathy *asks / will ask* you not to?

3 ⭐⭐ **Rewrite the sentences with the two clauses in reverse order. Be careful with commas.**

1 If your parents are late, will you order a pizza?
   Will you order a pizza if your parents are late?
2 I won't reply if I get nasty comments about my photo.
   _____
3 If I feel tired this evening, I'll go to bed at 10 p.m.
   _____
4 I won't open the link if I get another strange email.
   _____
5 If my sister argues with my parents, I'll shut my bedroom door and play loud music.
   _____

4 ⭐⭐ **Complete the sentences with the correct forms of the verbs in brackets.**

1 If you join Instagram, what *will your first photo be* (your first photo/be)?
2 You won't understand if you _____ (not listen).
3 What _____ (we/do) if the shops are shut?
4 We _____ (not have) time for lunch if we don't leave soon.
5 If Sara _____ (not reply) to my message soon, I'll send her another one.
6 If your post _____ (go) viral, what will you do?

5 ⭐⭐⭐ **Complete the conversation with the correct forms of the verbs from the box.**

be   have   not get   not see   ~~post~~   see   send

Grandad If I **1**_post_ a message, who will be able to read it?

Theresa That depends on your security settings. If you set it so that only friends can read it, then other people **2**_____ it at all.

Grandad I don't know what my settings are.

Theresa Well, if you click that button, you **3**_____ them.

Grandad It says 'only me'.

Theresa That means no-one can see anything you post except you.

Grandad That's why nobody ever comments when I post photos.

Theresa OK, I've changed it.

Grandad If I **4**_____ any comments now, I'll be very disappointed.

Theresa Oh, you've got a 'like' already. Eric Stephens. Who's that?

Grandad An old school friend. Great. If I have time later, I **5**_____ him a message.

Theresa OK, but not now. We have to meet Mum for lunch, remember? She'll be angry if we **6**_____ late. Bring your phone. If the restaurant **7**_____ wi-fi, you'll be able to check your account there.

Grandad Great!

6 ON A HIGH NOTE **Choose three situations from the box and write first conditional sentences about them.**

I have a lot of homework
I have some free time
my parents are angry with me
something goes wrong with my phone
there's something good on television

1 Match the questions from the box with the correct sets of three pictures below.

How did the boy spend the evening?
How many prizes has the girl won?
How old was the speaker when he started doing IT at school?
~~What has the girl already posted on social media?~~
What is the girl using to check her social media?

1 *What has the girl already posted on social media?*

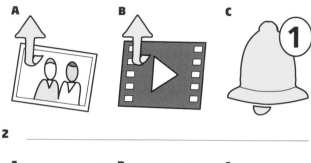

2 _____

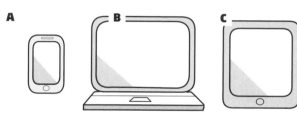

3 _____

4 _____

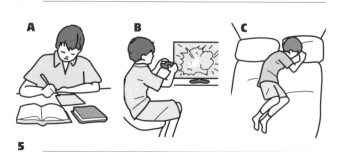

5 _____

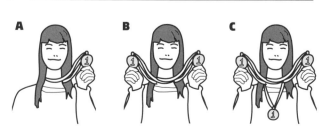

2 🔊 *59* Look at Exercise 1. Listen to five short recordings and choose the correct answer for each one.

Vocabulary extension

3 🔊 *60* Complete these sentences from the recordings in Exercise 2 with the words from the box. Listen and check.

aware ~~idea~~ jump message slipped

1 I've got no *idea* why.
2 … it completely _____ my mind.
3 Now I'm sixteen and I'm more _____ of the problems …
4 You shouldn't _____ to conclusions.
5 … the boys will finally get the _____ that we're just as good as they are.

Pronunciation

4 🔊 *61* Look at these sentences from the recordings in Exercise 2. How is the final vowel sound in the underlined syllables pronounced? Listen and check. Are these syllables stressed or unstressed?

1 He's going to Ma<u>la</u>ga soon with his parents.
2 I've got no ide<u>a</u> why.
3 Luckily, my bro<u>ther</u>'s old tablet was in the kitchen.
4 I think students should start having IT lessons youn<u>ger</u>.
5 I could even write some basic comp<u>u</u>ter code.
6 Oh, I remem<u>ber</u>.
7 I've won twice and ano<u>ther</u> girl has won once.

ACTIVE PRONUNCIATION | /ə/ sound

We often pronounce the vowel sound in unstressed syllables as /ə/ (e.g. *brother*, *about*).

5 🔊 *62* Now listen to the individual words from the sentences in Exercise 4 and repeat.

6 Find the stressed syllables in the words below. Then read the words. Which word has two /ə/ sounds?

1 <u>table</u>
2 people
3 forget
4 tablet
5 banana
6 students
7 today
8 problems
9 taken
10 again

7 🔊 *63* Now read the extracts which contain some of the words from Exercise 6. Then listen and repeat.

1 Yes, but it isn't easy finding a <u>table</u>.
2 <u>People</u> come in here with their laptops.
3 You didn't <u>forget</u> again, did you?
4 Luckily, my brother's old <u>tablet</u> was in the kitchen.
5 I think <u>students</u> should start having IT lessons younger.
6 Now I'm sixteen and I'm more aware of the <u>problems</u>.
7 Girls have won three out of the last four competitions which I've <u>taken</u> part in.

In your introduction, restate the question and give your own opinion.

Use an interesting question or comment to make your reader want to continue reading.

Give your own opinion with some arguments and examples.

Mention other arguments.

In your conclusion, summarise the arguments and state your opinion again.

WILL TECHNOLOGY DESTROY US OR SAVE US?

The human race is destroying the planet. Will technology help or make things worse? **1**___, it will make things better.

There are several advantages to technology. Firstly, electronic data has massively reduced our need for paper. **2**___, communication can reduce our need to travel. **3**___, why fly to the USA for a business meeting when you can talk over the Internet? **4**___, technology has made our lives much easier – gamepads in the car on long journeys, remote controls for lights, TVs, garage doors and sockets in trains, cars and planes if your phone needs charging.

5___, technology can cause problems too. Weapons have become more dangerous and millions of people may lose their jobs to robots. **6**___, governments can use technology to find out about our everyday lives and perhaps control us. It seems to me that people are too ready to give up their freedom and privacy.

7___, technology has both advantages and disadvantages. In the wrong hands, it can be very dangerous, but I am an optimist and **8**___ that people will understand how to control it and will use it for the good of society.

1 **Read the essay and tick the ideas the writer mentions.**

Advantages of technology

- ☑ Need less paper
- ☐ Need less travel
- ☐ Better health
- ☐ More renewable energy

Disadvantages of technology

- ☐ Addiction to smartphones
- ☐ More dangerous weapons
- ☐ Fewer jobs
- ☐ Governments using it against the people

2 **Match the words and phrases from the box with gaps 1–8 in the text and write them below. There may be more than one correct answer.**

after all   finally   however   ~~I believe~~   I think
in addition   in conclusion   in my opinion
on the other hand   to sum up   what's more

1 _I believe_ , _____, _____
2 _____, _____
3 _____
4 _____
5 _____, _____
6 _____, _____
7 _____, _____
8 _____, _____

3 WRITING TASK **Use the information below to write an opinion essay.**

People nowadays rely too much on technology for everyday tasks such as doing simple mathematics or map reading. Soon we will be unable to survive without technology. Do you agree?

ACTIVE WRITING | An opinion essay

1 **Plan your essay.**

- Read the essay question carefully and think about your opinion. Do you agree or not?
- Make a note of some arguments for and against the statement.
- Think about what you are going to write in your introduction and conclusion.

2 **Write the essay.**

- Write an interesting introduction restating the question and giving your opinion.
- Divide your essay into clear paragraphs.
- Use linking words to add, justify or contrast ideas.
- Summarise the arguments in your conclusion and restate your opinion.

3 **Check that ...**

- you have written an interesting introduction.
- your essay is organised into paragraphs.
- there are no spelling or grammar mistakes.
- you have used a good range of vocabulary and structures.
- you have made your opinion and reasons for it clear.

1 8A GRAMMAR AND VOCABULARY **Complete the sentences with the correct words formed from the words in bold.**

1 Do you need to be a _physicist_ in order to become a good engineer? **PHYSICS**

2 Pythagoras was one of the most famous _____ in the ancient world. **MATHS**

3 I heard a _____ talking about the danger of earthquakes in the Canary Islands. **GEOLOGY**

4 You don't have to be an _____ to know that the Earth is in danger. **ECOLOGY**

5 I'd like to be an _____ and create something that would make learning easier. **INVENT**

6 Adrian is interested in ocean life forms and wants to become a marine _____. **BIOLOGY**

7 Have you heard of the _____ Jane Goodall who studied chimpanzees in Africa? **NATURAL**

8 Frederick Sanger was a _____ who won the Nobel Prize two times! **CHEMISTRY**

2 8B VOCABULARY **Choose the correct words to complete the sentences.**

1 To go to the next photo, just _swipe / paste / copy_ left or right.

2 My laptop keeps _clicking / cutting / crashing_ and I don't know why.

3 Never click on a _site / link / text_ that you get in an email from an unknown person.

4 Check the _trash / cloud / file_ can before you _delete / empty / share_ it.

5 I usually receive one or two important emails and about ten _bad / trash / junk_ mails.

6 Abigail always _shares / saves / taps_ photos and film clips with her friends.

7 It's difficult to see where we are on this map. How can I _create / expand / store_ it to make it bigger?

8 Put all your documents in one _folder / page / profile_ and you'll be able to find them again easily.

3 8D READING AND VOCABULARY **Complete the sentences with one word in each gap.**

1 What do the initials 'UNICEF' _stand_ for?

2 We c_____ out two experiments yesterday, but we didn't get the results we wanted.

3 If something is t_____ on social media, it means that it is very popular at this time.

4 Our school project t_____ into a campaign involving the whole town!

5 Social n_____ is a great way to share ideas with people all over the world.

6 When a video suddenly becomes very popular on social media, we say that it has gone v_____.

7 If you want to put a photo or video, or anything else, on social media we say that you p_____ it.

8 Rachel Carson was a famous environmental c_____ who wrote about the damage which chemicals cause.

4 8F LISTENING AND VOCABULARY **Complete the sentences with the words from the box.**

3D ~~console~~ educational gamer genres handheld multiplayer virtual

1 I need to buy a new games _console_ – this one is out of date.

2 My favourite _____ of films are comedy, action and westerns.

3 Mum wants us to play an _____ game which teaches spelling, but it's really boring!

4 You should play a _____ game with your friends – it isn't right for you to play while they watch.

5 I enjoy watching _____ films, but I get a headache because of the glasses you have to wear.

6 In a _____ world you can see, hear and feel things that aren't really there.

7 My younger brother is a serious _____ and posts videos of himself playing on YouTube.

8 I'm going to spend my birthday money on a _____ device.

5 8G WRITING AND VOCABULARY **Complete the sentences with one word in each gap.**

1 I bought this laptop in the UK so it's got a British p_lug_ on it. Now I need an a_____ to charge it in France because the s_____ here are a different size.

2 There is no light s_____ in this room because they work using r_____ c_____ .

3 You don't need a c_____ to connect these g_____ to the console. They connect using wi-fi. Do you want to try them out? How about playing this new football game? I'll be Barcelona.

4 I often c_____ online with my friends but I prefer talking to them f_____ -to-f_____.

6 ON A HIGH NOTE **Write a short paragraph about what you think has been the most important invention or discovery in history. Explain why you think it is so important.**

1 For each learning objective, write 1–5 to assess your ability.

1 = I don't feel confident. 5 = I feel confident.

	Learning objective	Course material	How confident I am (1–5)
8A	I can use verb patterns with the infinitive and the *-ing* form to talk about different actions and states..	Student's Book pp. 108–109	
8B	I can talk about computer equipment.	Student's Book p. 110	
8C	I can ask for and give explanations about how to use a modern gadget.	Student's Book p. 111	
8D	I can tell facts and opinions in a short article and talk about social media.	Student's Book pp. 112–113	
8E	I can use the first conditional to talk about possible future situations.	Student's Book p. 114	
8F	I can identify specific information in conversations and talk about gaming.	Student's Book p. 115	
8G	I can write an opinion essay.	Student's Book pp. 116–117	

2 Which of the skills above would you like to improve in? How?

Skill I want to improve in	How I can improve

3 What can you remember from this unit?

New words I learned and most want to remember	Expressions and phrases I liked	English I heard or read outside class

GRAMMAR AND VOCABULARY

1 **Complete the sentences with the words from the box. There are two extra words.**

analyse danger data experiment fact laboratory result ~~scientist~~

1 I'd like to be a *scientist* and work in a _____.

2 Our Chemistry teacher wanted to do an _____. He lit some natural gas and made a ball of flame. Luckily, nobody was in _____.

3 Now that we've got all the _____, we have to _____ it carefully and see what it means.

/ 5

2 **Choose the correct words to complete the mini-conversations.**

Holly Do you need some help with your computer?

Brad Yes. If I want to move this photo into a different folder, I guess I have to [1]*cut / copy* and [2]*post / paste* it. Is that right?

Holly You can, but it's quicker to [3]*swipe / drag* it from one folder to the other – like this.

Raul Hey, Sara. How's your new smartphone?

Sara It's OK, but I don't know how to close the apps I've used.

Raul [4]*Tap / Click* on the little square at the bottom of the screen. Then you'll see everything that's open. Just [5]*swipe / share* each one – left to right or right to left, it doesn't matter – and they close.

/ 5

3 **Complete the text with the correct forms of the verbs in brackets.**

I'm now leaving this site. My friends can [1]*contact* (contact) me by email or phone. I've decided [2]_____ (leave) because some of the comments aren't nice. I don't mind [3]_____ (joke) with people, but some of the messages which people leave are horrible.

I managed [4]_____ (block) some of the users, but more kept [5]_____ (join) and I've given up [6]_____ (try) to stop them.

Best wishes and fight the hate!

/ 5

4 **Complete the sentences with the correct forms from the box. There are two extra forms.**

don't try to try ~~tries~~ try trying will try won't try

1 If Max *tries* harder, he will get the grades he needs to study Maths.

2 If we don't encourage her, Christina _____ at all.

3 Will you promise _____ harder next time?

4 I _____ to phone you from the hotel if there's a signal, but I don't know if it will be possible.

5 You won't know if it's possible if you _____.

/ 4

USE OF ENGLISH

5 **Complete the advert with one word in each gap.**

FED UP WITH YOUR SLOW COMPUTER? THEN READ ON!

[1]*If* you don't look after your computer, it will get slower and slower. Why? Well, most people keep [2]_____ adding and deleting programmes, downloading software, saving films and, basically, filling the computer up with rubbish. Many [3]_____ these programmes start working when you switch on your computer. If there are five new programmes all trying [4]_____ start at the same time, your computer [5]_____ take longer to come on.

People who know about computers can change settings, clean their computer and keep it in perfect condition. However, if you [6]_____ not an expert, you won't know what is safe to delete.

That's why MEGA CLEAN BOOST is the programme for you.
[7]_____ this link and download it today!

/ 6

6 **Choose the correct words a-c to complete the texts.**

1 All our laptops come with a free pair of ___ for a great listening experience.

a headphones **b** tablets **c** keyboards

2 ___ games to help students aged five and older with their studies.

a Educated **b** Education **c** Educational

3 A new theory of ___ – where did humans really come from?

a relativity **b** evolution **c** creativity

4 Don't _____ on a fantastic learning experience. Join our after-school computer club!

a stand for **b** miss out **c** go on

5 Two-player game. Try to beat your ___ in this race around the world.

a opponent **b** obstacle **c** subscriber

/ 5

/ 30

09 *Art lovers*

9A GRAMMAR AND VOCABULARY

Past Perfect

1 ⭐ Complete the sentences with the correct forms from the box.

> had already left   had looked   had come
> had forgotten   ~~had never been~~   had never learned
> had run out of   had seen   had spent   had started

1 Before our trip to London, Majid *had never been* to an art gallery before.
2 By the time we woke up, the bus to the seaside _____.
3 As soon as I got to the airport, I realised that I _____ to bring my passport.
4 Asmir couldn't buy a ticket because he _____ all his money.
5 By the time we arrived, the café _____ sandwiches.
6 After we _____ the Picasso exhibition, we left the gallery and went for lunch.
7 We finally got into the exhibition at 2 p.m. – four hours after we _____ queuing!
8 We met some people from Australia who _____ to Britain to see their grandparents.
9 Sarah _____ Spanish before she moved to Madrid.
10 Last year I found an old manuscript in the attic. I discovered that researchers _____ for it for centuries.

2 ⭐ Match sentences 1–6 with responses a–f.

1 ☐ John was tired when we saw him.
2 ☐ Why did Milo look so scared?
3 ☐ What was Russ worried about?
4 ☐ Nick ate lots of food at the barbecue! He was really hungry.
5 ☐ Do you know why Stephanie was angry yesterday?
6 ☐ Poor Laura was really wet when she arrived.

a That's right. He hadn't eaten breakfast that morning.
b Yes, he had stayed up studying until 2 a.m. the night before!
c Yes, her friend had borrowed her phone and lost it!
d I know. It was sunny when she left home, so she hadn't taken a coat.
e He had watched a horror film alone in the dark.
f He hadn't studied enough for his exam.

3 ⭐ Read the text and match questions 1–6 with answers a–f.

> In 2009, a Hungarian researcher discovered a long-lost painting known as 'Sleeping Lady with a Black Vase'. How did he do it?

1 ☐ Had he tried to find it before?
2 ☐ That was lucky! How long had it been lost for?
3 ☐ Where had it been all that time?
4 ☐ Where had she found it?
5 ☐ Had she known it was famous when she bought it?
6 ☐ Had the researcher contacted her about it?

a Nobody knows exactly, but it turned up in California; a woman who worked for Sony Pictures had it.
b No, she hadn't. She just thought it would look good in the film. A few years later she sold it and the painting returned to Hungary.
c No, he hadn't, but he'd known about it. Then, one day, he was watching a film with his daughter and he suddenly noticed the painting in the background.
d Yes, he had. He had sent her an email and she had replied that the painting was on her wall at home. She realised it was valuable and she sold it.
e About eighty years. It had disappeared in the late 1920s.
f She'd found it in an antiques shop.

4 ⭐⭐ Complete the sentences with the correct Past Perfect forms of the verbs in brackets.

When I got home, I realised that …
1 I *had left* (leave) my phone on the bus.
2 I _____ (forgot) my English books.
3 I _____ (not say) goodbye to my friends.
4 my parents _____ (ask) me to buy some milk on the way home.
5 I _____ (not take) my keys in the morning and there was no-one at home.
6 we _____ (arrange) to go to my grandparents' house for dinner – on the other side of town!

5 ★★ Complete the text with the correct Past Simple or Past Perfect forms of the verbs in brackets.

MY TOP FIVE ICONIC PHOTOS

Photography is my favourite art form. There are so many wonderful photos – the workers having lunch on the skyscraper, the train coming through the station wall – but here are my top five.

5 In 1968, two athletes **1** *had just received* (just/receive) Olympic medals when the national anthem started. They both **2** _____ (raise) their arms in the black power salute and became famous all over the world.

4 The photo of Albert Einstein that everyone knows was taken while he was sitting in a car. He **3** _____ (be) to a party to celebrate his seventy-second birthday and was about to go home when he **4** _____ (notice) the photographer trying to take his photo. Einstein stuck out his tongue and history was made.

3 By the time Nelson Mandela **5** _____ (be) set free in 1990, he **6** _____ (spend) twenty-seven years in prison, so it's amazing that he looks so relaxed, fit and healthy in this photo as he waves to the crowds who are there to welcome him.

2 There is a great photo of Neil Armstrong in the Apollo 11 spacecraft. His fellow astronaut, Buzz Aldrin **7** _____ (take) it. Armstrong is smiling but is a little shocked and confused. It isn't surprising. Earlier he **8** _____ (become) the first man to walk on the moon.

1 And now, my 'Number One'. It was August 14th, 1945 and the Second World War **9** _____ (just/finish). People were celebrating in New York and photographer Alfred Eisenstaedt was looking for the perfect photo. Suddenly, he **10** _____ (see) a man in a sailor's uniform kissing a young woman, both celebrating this wonderful day.

6 ★★ Rewrite the sentences in the Past Perfect.

1 I had breakfast, I listened to the radio and then I left home.
By the time I left home, *I had had breakfast and I had listened to the radio*.

2 I ran six kilometres and swam two kilometres. I was exhausted!
By six o'clock, I was exhausted. Earlier that day
_____.

3 On the first day of the camp, we got up, we tidied our rooms and then a bus came to take us on a trip.
On the first day of the camp, the bus arrived after
_____.

4 A few minutes after the exam started, the teacher took a phone from a student. Later he threw two students out for talking.
Before the end of the exam, the teacher
_____.

7 ★★ Complete the text with the correct Past Perfect forms of the verbs from the box.

~~arrive~~ hear offer phone see spend start take upload watch

It was 10 p.m. and the young artist finally put down his brushes and looked at his painting with a smile on his face. He **1** *had arrived* at the studio at five o'clock that morning. He **2** _____ the sky change colour from his balcony and **3** _____ several photos of the sky and the people below. Then he **4** _____ the photos to his computer and **5** _____ some time choosing the best. Finally, he **6** _____ painting at about 11 a.m.

He didn't like rushing, but this painting was for a customer who **7** _____ his paintings at a local exhibition and **8** _____ him $2000 for an original work of art. The customer **9** _____ the artist at five o'clock in the afternoon to say that he was leaving to Barcelona and needed the painting that night.

And now it was ready. There was a knock on the door, but the artist wasn't surprised. He **10** _____ the footsteps coming up the stairs. He opened the door with a smile.

8 ★★★ USE OF ENGLISH Complete the second sentence using the word in bold so that it means the same as the first one. Use no more than three words, including the word in bold.

1 When I sat down, I immediately realised I was on the wrong train. **GOT**
When I sat down, I realised *I had got* on the wrong train.

2 The first time I went to the gallery, I didn't enjoy it. **ENJOYED**
I had been to the gallery before, but I _____ it.

3 I saw a film about Van Gogh and that's why I bought a book about his life. **HAD**
I bought a book about Van Gogh's life because I _____ film about him.

4 Picasso was born in Spain, but moved to France when he was in his twenties. **LEFT**
By the time he was in his twenties, Picasso _____ and moved to France.

5 The first time I went to an exhibition of modern art was when I was at university. **NEVER**
Before I went to university, I _____ to an exhibition of modern art.

9 ON A HIGH NOTE Write a short paragraph about the things you had done before you left the house this morning. Include these linkers in your answer: *by the time*, *before*, *as soon as* and *after*.

9B VOCABULARY | Creative jobs

1 ★ **Choose the correct words to complete the sentences.**

1 A person who writes plays is called a __.
  a playwrite   **b** playwright   **c** playright

2 You're the lighting __; you fix the problem!
  a manager   **b** technician   **c** conductor

3 My favourite __ is Ed Sheeran; his songs are great.
  a conductor   **b** screenwriter   **c** songwriter

4 The stage __ has asked everyone to leave the stage for a few moments.
  a manager   **b** engineer   **c** director

5 The pop artist Andy Warhol painted famous __ of the actress Marilyn Monroe.
  a portraits   **b** landscapes   **c** oils

6 Beginner painters should experiment with different types and sizes of __ before they choose their favourite ones.
  a oils   **b** paints   **c** brushes

2 ★ **Match the jobs from the box with the sentences.**

camera operator composer conductor ~~director~~
extra screenwriter sound engineer stunt performer

1 I'm responsible for everything – actors, filming, lights, cameras, scripts. It's my film! _director_

2 I write classical music and film soundtracks. _____

3 I have to drive into that burning building really fast and jump out of the car at the last moment! _____

4 There I am – you can see the top of my head at the back of the crowd. I'm in a film! _____

5 If I wasn't there, you wouldn't hear the actors' voices and the background noise might be too loud. _____

6 I'm there to film people, make sure they're in focus and in the centre of the scene. _____

7 It's a very special feeling to stand in front of an orchestra and control that fantastic sound. _____

8 My job is to write the dialogues for films and TV series. _____

3 ★ **Complete the words with one letter in each gap.**

1 You really need a tr_i_ _p_ _o_d if you want to be a serious photographer. Anyone who t__ __ __s photos in poor l__ __ h__ needs one to keep the camera steady.

2 The singer felt sick and had to run off the s__ __ __e in the middle of the first song, so the rest of the band played their i__ __ t__ __ __ __ n__ __ for five minutes until he returned.

3 *Ocean's 8* isn't a r__ __ a _ e of *Ocean's 11*. It's a new story. *Ocean's 11* was s__ __ in Las Vegas but in *Ocean's 8* the action takes p__ __ __e in New York.

4 Most actors say that their worst moment is when they forget their l__ __ __s but the worst thing for me is when someone in the a__ __ __e__ __e starts coughing!

4 ★★ **Complete the texts with the correct forms of the words from the box.**

~~act~~ Art draw explain paint play remember
sing take tell

Matt is good at [1]_acting_. He played Romeo in the school play last year. He's really good at [2]_____ lines. He never forgets them. He'd like to be in a band, but he isn't very good at [3]_____ the guitar and he's terrible at [4]_____!

Elaine is very good at [5]_____. She is good at [6]_____ with watercolours and oils and she's also good at [7]_____ with a pencil. She wanted to teach other students to paint, but she isn't very good at [8]_____ things.

Sam is our school's official photographer. She's very good at [9]_____ photos of people. She's in charge of the photo pages on the school's website. She isn't very good with computers, but she's very good at [10]_____ people what to do!

5 ★★ **Complete the sentences with one word in each gap.**

1 What would you rather see? A p_lay_ at the theatre or a m_____ at the cinema?

2 I enjoy going to rock c_____; a good l_____ performance can be very exciting.

3 The best Robin Hood film was made in 1938! The p_____ of Robin Hood was played by Errol Flynn who was a huge s_____ at the time. Most films in the 1930s were made in b_____ and w_____ but this was a colour film. It cost Warner Bros an incredible $2 million to make!

4 *Mr Turner* was a British film which was b_____ on the life of the painter J.M.W. Turner. Turner often used w_____ although he used oils as well. He is famous for his l_____ of fields, towns and the sea. My favourite is 'The Grand Canal'.

6 ON A HIGH NOTE **Write a short paragraph about what is rewarding/challenging in the life of a professional dancer, musican or actor.**

Reported speech

1 ⭐ **Choose the correct forms to complete the sentences.**

1 'We'll be late!'
Tom told us that they *will / would* be late.

2 'I've finished my book.'
She told me that she *had / has* finished her book.

3 'We're having a lot of fun!'
They said that they *are / were* having a lot of fun.

4 'Ssh. The play is starting!'
He said that the play *is / was* starting.

5 'You can't leave in the middle of the play.'
My mum told me I *couldn't / can't* leave in the middle of the play.

6 'We always watch the news together in the evening.'
Jed said that they always *watched / watch* the news together in the evening.

2 ⭐⭐ **Read a speaker's words and complete the text with one word or contraction in each gap.**

'Sorry. I don't want to go to the concert. I've got lots of exams soon and the tickets are very expensive. I don't even like the band. I haven't listened to any of their music since their first CD. Anyway, I'm trying to save up for the summer holidays.'

Matt said that he **¹**<u>didn't</u> want to go to the concert. He told us that he **²**_____ lots of exams soon and that the tickets **³**_____ very expensive. He then said that he **⁴**_____ even like the band and that he **⁵**_____ listened to any of their music since their first CD. Finally, he told us that he **⁶**_____ trying to save up for the summer holidays.

3 ⭐⭐ **Complete the reported sentences with the words from the box. There are three extra words.**

after   before   couldn't   had (x2)   hadn't   have   he
his   my   she   their   ~~they~~   was   wouldn't

1 'We ate fish yesterday.'
The girls said that <u>they</u> _____ eaten fish the day _____.

2 'I'm watching the news.'
Beth told me that _____ _____ watching the news.

3 'I've had some problems with my back.'
Paul told us that _____ _____ had some problems with _____ back.

4 'I can't afford to eat out tomorrow.'
Kyle said that he _____ afford to eat out the day _____.

5 'Wow! We haven't heard a better concert in our town.'
The students said that they _____ heard a better concert in _____ town.

4 ⭐⭐⭐ **Rewrite the sentences in reported speech.**

1 'I'm not keen on modern art.'
Cath said that <u>she wasn't keen on modern art</u>.

2 'I didn't go out at all yesterday.'
Eric told us that _____.

3 'I haven't seen the film yet.'
Samantha said that _____.

4 'We'll be back tomorrow.'
Carly said that _____.

5 'We're having a meeting.'
Jackson told us that _____.

5 ⭐⭐⭐ **Read the conversation and rewrite it in reported speech.**

Adrian Hi, Emily. Real Madrid are playing Barcelona. I'll help you with your homework when it finishes.

Emily That's OK. I love Spanish football. I saw Girona play last year.

Adrian Really? Wow. I often go to watch our local team play, but I've never seen a big match.

Emily My dad's a Chelsea fan. I can get you tickets if you want.

Adrian Wow! Yes, please.

Emily went to Adrian's house because she needed help with her homework. When she arrived, Adrian said 'Hi' and told her that **¹**<u>Real Madrid were playing Barcelona</u> and that **²**_____ when the match finished. Emily didn't mind. She told him that **³**_____ and that **⁴**_____ before.
Adrian was surprised. He said that **⁵**_____, but that **⁶**_____. Emily told him that **⁷**_____ and that **⁸**_____ if he wanted. Adrian was very happy.

6 ON A HIGH NOTE **Think of five things people have told you and write them in reported speech.**

9D READING AND VOCABULARY

1 Look at the photo, the title and the first paragraph of the article and answer the questions.

  1 What kind of artist is Sixto Rodriguez?
    a singer-songwriter

  2 Where is he from? _____

  3 What are his songs about? _____

  4 In which country did he become famous?

    _____

  5 Did he make money from his music in the 1970s?

    _____

2 Read the whole article quickly and choose the best answer.

What is the writer's main purpose?

  a ☐ To encourage people to buy Sixto's music.

  b ☐ To show Sixto's character in a positive light.

  c ☐ To explain why Sixto's music wasn't popular in the USA.

  d ☐ To compare Sixto favourably with other musicians.

3 Read the article again and choose the correct answers.

  1 Why did Sixto become so successful in South Africa?

    a He wrote lyrics about South African politics.

    b The people there knew him and liked his personality.

    c His albums were easily available and on sale everywhere.

    d The people there had similar problems to the ones he wrote about.

  2 How did Sixto find out about his success in South Africa?

    a His daughter made a website about his music.

    b His daughter searched for information about him on the Internet.

    c His daughter discovered a website about him by accident.

    d A man called Stephen Segerman got in touch with his daughter.

  3 When he quit the music business, Sixto

    a had problems finding a job.

    b tried, and failed, to have a political career.

    c moved away from his home town.

    d also lost interest in politics.

  4 Despite his success, Sixto

    a has no interest in buying luxury items.

    b hasn't made much money.

    c can't afford a TV.

    d never goes to awards ceremonies.

  5 The most important thing for Rodriguez is that

    a he now makes a lot of money.

    b people enjoy his music.

    c he is now famous in his own country.

    d he has been able to record more albums.

Vocabulary extension

4 Match the highlighted words from the text with the definitions.

  1 An agreement between a record company and a musician to make and sell music. *recording contract*

  2 Take people's attention away from someone else who is more important. _____

  3 Money you earn every time someone buys your song, album, book, etc. _____

  4 An event where prizes are given for success in the music or film industry. _____

  5 Records produced/distributed illegally. _____

  6 Making something available to the public. _____

ACTIVE VOCABULARY | Prefix *re-*

We can add the prefix *re-* to nouns and verbs to mean 'again', (e.g. *discover – rediscover*).

---

5 Which verbs and nouns from the box can take the prefix *re-*? Put them in the correct column. There are four extra words.

advice ~~appearance~~ arrangement belief construction discovery marry perform start thank think use

Nouns	Verbs
reappearance	

6 Complete the sentences with the correct forms of the words from the table in Exercise 5.

  1 He made a *reappearance* on a TV series in 2015, ten years after he had left show business to become a teacher.

  2 If your computer screen has 'frozen', try _____ it. When it comes back on, the problem may be fixed.

  3 Why don't you _____ this old box as a bed for the cat?

  4 I don't like this new _____ of the furniture - it makes the room seem smaller.

  5 Digital _____ of old ruins help us learn about the civilisations that built them.

  6 Emma's parents got divorced in 2010 but they _____ two years later.

7 ON A HIGH NOTE Write a short paragraph about an interesting artist. Explain why you admire him or her and report some important things they have said.

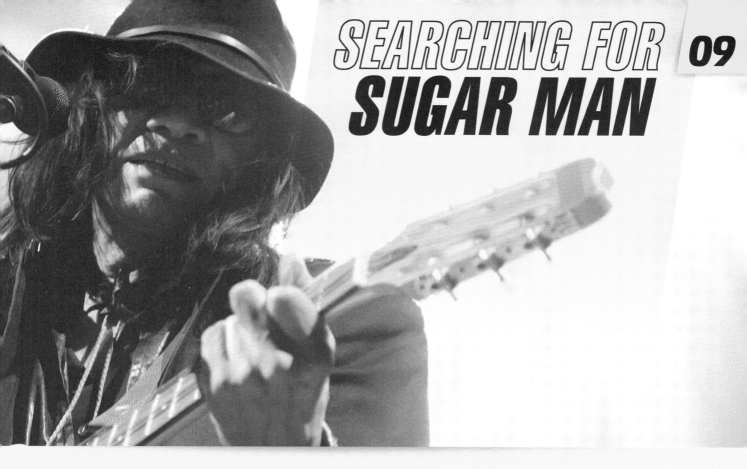

Sixto Rodriguez is an American singer-songwriter who grew up in the industrial town of Detroit. When he writes songs, he writes about the things he cares about – his home town, the anti-war protests against the Vietnam war, the civil rights movement in the USA and the fight for equality. In South Africa during the 1970s, many anti-apartheid supporters discovered his music and found that they could relate to Sixto's lyrics. He became extremely popular in that country, even though it wasn't easy to find his records. His fans had to make do with illegal copies of his albums, called bootlegs, so Sixto himself didn't receive any royalties and wasn't even aware of his own success.

Despite his popularity, not much was known about Sixto in South Africa. There were even rumours that he had died after releasing his first album. In 1997, Stephen 'Sugar' Segerman, more often known as Sugar Man, who was a songwriter, music shop owner and fan of Sixto, set up a website and named it 'The Great Rodriguez Hunt'. He wanted to find out more about his hero and hoped that the website would help. A year later, in Detroit, Sixto's daughter was surfing the Internet when she came across the site and was shocked to find that her father, who had given up his musical career many years earlier, was a star on the other side of the globe!

Sixto's musical career had started in 1968, when two record producers went to see him in concert and offered him a recording contract. He made two albums but they didn't sell many copies and, by the end of the decade, Sixto had retired. 'I didn't do any music,' he explains. 'I stayed pretty much out of it because there was nothing happening to me.'

He remained interested in politics and ran for mayor of Detroit twice but, when nothing came of his political ambitions, he found work in the construction industry and in factories. He bought a small house in a working class area of the city and settled down to family life, until his daughter clicked onto a website and changed his life completely.

Although Sixto's life has been transformed, he himself hasn't changed at all. He still lives in the same house, plays the same old guitar and prefers to give his money away than spend it on himself. He is also very modest. A film about his life called *Searching for Sugar Man* became a huge success and won an Oscar for best documentary in 2013. However, Sixto stayed away from the awards ceremony saying that the film was the director's achievement, not his, and that he didn't want to upstage him. He didn't even watch the ceremony on TV – he still hasn't got one!

Rodriguez is a star now. His two albums have both sold over 100,000 copies and his concerts attract audiences of 10,000 or more. 'This is what I always wanted, to make something of myself through music,' he says. He enjoys the success, not for himself or the financial rewards it can bring but because he can share his songs and his message and he now knows that people are listening.

The story of Sixto Rodriguez is a remarkable one. But perhaps the most remarkable thing is not the rediscovery of a talented musician after a quarter of a century, but the fact that Rodriguez has remained faithful to his beliefs during both good times and bad.

9E SPEAKING

1 🔊 **64 Listen and repeat the phrases. How do you say them in your language?**

SPEAKING | Informal invitations

MAKING INVITATIONS

Do you want to go to the cinema this evening?

Would you like to go to the theatre with me?

Do you fancy com**ing** to the concert tonight?

How about the exhibition at the Art Gallery?

ACCEPTING INVITATIONS

Sure, that sounds good/like a good idea.

Yes, I'd love to. Where shall we meet?

What a great idea! What time?

That's very kind of you, thanks.

TURNING DOWN INVITATIONS

No, thanks.

Thanks but I've already seen this film.

No, I'm sorry, I can't.

I'd love to but I'm busy tonight.

That sounds great/like a lot of fun but I'm already going out with Jake.

Maybe some other time.

GIVING REASONS

I don't really fancy it, to be honest.

I'm not really into classical music.

It's not my cup of tea.

I don't feel like go**ing** out tonight.

I've got other plans.

I've got to help my mum this evening.

---

2 **Match the two parts of the sentences.**

1 ☐ That's very kind	**a**	like to meet later?
2 ☐ I'm sorry,	**b**	cup of tea.
3 ☐ Would you	**c**	into sports.
4 ☐ Maybe some	**d**	I can't.
5 ☐ It's not my	**e**	going out tonight?
6 ☐ Do you fancy	**f**	like going out.
7 ☐ I don't feel	**g**	other time.
8 ☐ I'm not really	**h**	of you, thanks.

3 🔊 **65 Choose the correct words to complete the conversation. Listen and check.**

Lucas Do you fancy ¹*go / going / to go* out later?

Christie Sure, that ²*looks / is / sounds* great. Where ³*do / shall / will* we meet?

Lucas How about ⁴*meeting / meet / to meet* at the ice rink? We can go skating.

Christie I'm not really ⁵*into / up to / on for* skating. It's not my ⁶*mug / pot / cup* of tea. Do you ⁷*fancy / like / want* to go to the sports centre instead? We could play badminton.

Lucas ⁸*I'd / I'll / I'm* love to, but the sports centre closes at 6 p.m. I can't go out until seven o'clock. Why don't you just come round to my house and watch a film?

Christie ⁹*Which / How / What* a great idea! See you later.

4 **Choose the correct responses to complete the mini-conversations.**

1

John Do you want to go out later?

Amy ___

John About 8.30?

a Yes, I'd love to. Where shall we meet?

b Sure. What time?

c Maybe some other time.

2

Kate Do you fancy going to a classical music concert tomorrow evening?

Marie ___

Kate OK. Maybe some other time.

a That's very kind of you.

b I'm not really into concerts.

c No, I'm sorry. I've got other plans.

3

Tina Would you like to go shopping on Saturday?

Demi ___

Tina Well, let's just meet up for a coffee, then.

a How about next Saturday?

b I don't really fancy it, to be honest.

c Thanks, but I've got to go shopping.

5 **Complete the mini-conversations with one word in each gap.**

Alex ¹W**ould** you like to go out tonight?

Izzy I'd love to ²b_____ I haven't got time.

Otto ³D_____ you fancy going to the new exhibition at the art gallery?

Karl Sorry, I can't. I've got other ⁴p_____.

Marta Would you ⁵l_____ to come to dinner?

Ingrid That's very ⁶k_____ of you, thanks. What ⁷t_____?

Marta About seven o'clock.

9F LISTENING AND VOCABULARY

1 🔊 **66** Listen to Part 1 of an interview with a writer. What is the title of her novel?

2 🔊 **67** Listen to the whole interview and choose the correct answers.

1 Frances says that the events in the book
   a are all true but not about her life.
   b are not all about her own life.
   c are completely made up.

2 Frances decided she wanted to be an author
   a at the age of fifteen.
   b when she started her university course.
   c between leaving school and starting university.

3 We know that Frances' book includes a character
   a who meets someone famous.
   b who works in a library.
   c who is a writer.

4 It was the creative writing tutor who
   a encouraged Frances to finish her novel.
   b rewrote parts of the story to make it better.
   c contacted her with a publishing company.

5 The book would suit someone who likes
   a autobiographies.
   b novels about real life.
   c fantasy novels.

Vocabulary extension

3 Choose the correct words and phrases to complete the definitions of the words from the interview in Exercise 2.

1 Her debut novel is her *latest* / *first* novel.

2 If something is autobiographical, it's about *somebody else's* / *the author's* life.

3 Literature is the study of *great novels and poetry* / *important scientific texts*.

4 Your inspiration is the *idea* / *characters* for a novel or piece of writing.

5 Creative writing means writing *news stories* / *poetry and fiction*.

6 A manuscript is a piece of writing *after* / *before* it is printed.

7 A publicity tour is a series of interviews in different places to *advertise a book* / *meet fans*.

4 ON A HIGH NOTE Write a short paragraph about a book you have read which you really liked. Say why you liked it and how, if at all, it influenced your life.

Pronunciation

5 🔊 **68** Listen to some questions from the interview in Exercise 2. How is the intonation different in the questions beginning with a question word and in the *yes*/*no* questions?

ACTIVE PRONUNCIATION
Intonation for *wh-* and *yes*/*no* questions

- In *wh-* questions, which begin with *What*, *Who*, etc., the intonation goes down on the last word of the question.

- In questions which result in a *yes*/*no* answer the intonation goes up on the last word of the question.

6 🔊 **68** Listen again and choose ↓ for falling intonation or ↑ for rising intonation.

1 What is the book called and what's it about?   ↑/↓
2 Is it autobiographical?   ↑/↓
3 When did you decide you wanted to become an author?   ↑/↓
4 Was it difficult to find time for writing?   ↑/↓
5 So, when did you start writing your book?   ↑/↓
6 So, what now?   ↑/↓

7 🔊 **69** Listen to the intonation of some question endings and write the type of question, *wh-* or *yes*/*no*.

1 … you going out? *wh-*
2 … you meeting your friends? _____
3 … you got a phone? _____
4 … your homework? _____
5 … in your test? _____
6 … social media? _____

8 🔊 **70** Now listen to the whole questions and check your answers from Exercise 7. Listen and repeat.

9 🔊 **71** Listen to another question from the interview in Exercise 2 read with two different intonations. Choose the version, 1 or 2, in which the speaker knows the answer.

And this meeting is in your novel, isn't it? 1 / 2

ACTIVE PRONUNCIATION
Intonation for tag questions

In questions to which we already know the answer and just want to check information, the intonation usually goes down on the last word of the question.

In questions to which we really don't know the answer, the intonation usually goes up on the last word of the question.

10 🔊 **72** Listen to these sentences, each read with two different intonations. Choose the version, a or b, in which the speaker already knows the answer. Listen and repeat.

1 You're starting a new novel soon, aren't you?   a / b
2 You left school a year ago, didn't you?   a / b

Start with a heading that indicates your opinion.

Make some personal comments.

Give some factual details.

Give your opinion – positive, fifty-fifty or negative.

Use phrases to make comparisons.

Justify your opinion.

Give recommendations.

STEP BACK IN TIME AND ENJOY HOLLYWOOD'S GOLDEN AGE

If you're a movie fan like I am, you'll love the 'Hollywood History' season. There are three films a day and tickets cost £8 per film.

I must admit that the silent era films weren't really my cup of ¹*tea*. The comedies were absolutely hilarious, but the romances seemed slow and the acting over-dramatic.

The films of the 1940s and 1950s were wonderful. *La La Land* was great but, sorry Ryan and Emma, your singing and dancing were not ²_____ impressive as the great stars of the past!

There are some brilliant films still to come although, ³_____ my opinion, *The Sound of Music* is not ⁴_____ seeing. Don't ⁵_____ your time on it. It's slow and the songs are awful. It won five Oscars, but I think it seems ⁶_____ old-fashioned than films made ten or fifteen years earlier.

Go and see these Hollywood classics - you won't be disappointed!

1 USE OF ENGLISH **Complete the review with one word in each gap.**

2 USE OF ENGLISH **Complete the second sentence using the word in bold so that it means the same as the first one. Use no more than three words, including the word in bold.**

1 I don't really like musicals. **BIG**
I'm not *a big fan* of musicals.

2 The writer wrote two novels before this one. **THIRD**
It's the _____ novel.

3 I can't wait to read Frances' debut novel. **FORWARD**
I'm _____ reading Frances' debut novel.

4 The show was OK, but it was nothing special. **BAD**
The show _____, but it was nothing special.

5 It was a waste of time reading it. **WORTH**
It _____ reading.

3 **Find strong adjectives in the review.**

4 **Choose the word which <u>cannot</u> be used to complete the sentence.**

1 That's a ___ good idea.
a really   **b** totally   **c** very

2 Thanks, this is ___ perfect.
a totally   **b** absolutely   **c** very

3 What an absolutely ___ present.
a wonderful   **b** good   **c** brilliant

4 Some of the dancers were ___ awesome.
a very   **b** totally   **c** really

5 My meal was ___ tasty. How was yours?
a quite   **b** totally   **c** really

5 WRITING TASK **Think of an event you have been to recently. Use the information below to write a review.**

ACTIVE WRITING | A short review

1 Plan your review.

- Think of a good heading which indicates your opinion.
- Think about what was good and/or bad about the event.
- Think about how it compared to other similar events.
- Would you recommend a similar event to others? Why?/Why not?

2 Write the review.

- Give some personal information about why you saw the event, what you expected etc.
- Give some factual details about times, performers, venue.
- Give your opinion about the event and compare it to similar events.
- Justify your opinions.
- Use imperatives or phrases for giving advice to make recommendations.

3 Check that ...

- you have included all the relevant information.
- there are no spelling or grammar mistakes.
- there is a good range of vocabulary and structures.
- you have made your opinions and reasons clear.

1 9A GRAMMAR AND VOCABULARY **Complete the conversations with the correct words formed from the words in bold.**

Alan Well, this painting is certainly ¹*original* (**ORIGIN**). I've never seen anything like it. It's really thought- ² _____ (**PROVOKE**).

Cindy I disagree. I find it very ³ _____ (**IRRITATE**) when galleries put paintings like this on display. I think it's terrible.

Mary I love these pictures that little Emma has painted. They're so ⁴ _____ (**COLOUR**) and ⁵ _____ (**CHEER**).

Joss Frankly, I think they're a bit ⁶ _____ (**SOPHISTICATED**).

Mary Well, Emma is only five years old, you know!

Jack Tell me the truth – what do you think of our new painting?

Kim To be honest, I find it quite ⁷ _____ (**DEPRESS**). It makes the room look ⁸ _____ (**GLOOM**) and dark. It's almost ⁹ _____ (**SCARE**)!

Jack Exactly! That's why we bought it!

2 9B VOCABULARY **Match the two parts of the sentences.**

1 ☐ Their CDs are good, but their live
2 ☐ You can't take
3 ☐ The film is based
4 ☐ Tell the lighting
5 ☐ The film is set
6 ☐ You're good
7 ☐ Tell the sound
8 ☐ I don't understand why fashion

a photos during the show.
b models earn so much.
c engineer that we can't hear the actors.
d at acting and should have a better role.
e on a famous short story.
f technician that the stage is too dark.
g in the eighteenth century.
h performances are awesome.

3 9C GRAMMAR AND VOCABULARY **Match the TV programmes from the box with the sentences.**

chat show   documentary   quiz show   reality show
sitcom   ~~sketch show~~   the news

1 A group of comedians perform short, funny scenes in this popular half-hour show. *sketch show*

2 Today we look at schools around the world and what we can learn from them. _____

3 Can you answer the million dollar question this week? _____

4 The most important stories from around the world today. _____

5 Ten young men and women stay on a desert island for a week and see if they can survive. _____

6 Today, Emily talks to Johnny Depp, Adele and Cristiano Ronaldo. _____

7 This show is set in an office in Chester and is hilarious. All the characters are great, but the useless boss is definitely the funniest. _____

4 9D READING AND VOCABULARY **Complete the text with the words from the box.**

case   composer   concert hall   ~~orchestra~~   performance
rehearse   soloist   stared   talented

It was my first day with the ¹*orchestra* and we were in the vast ² _____ , sitting on the stage. It wasn't a ³ _____ in front of an audience; we were there to ⁴ _____ for a concert. I was the youngest and also the most nervous. We started with a ⁵ _____ singing on her own with just a piano. She was very ⁶ _____ and I sat and ⁷ _____ at her, wondering how she could be so calm. After a while, I started looking at the music in front of me. It was a piece by Bach – my favourite ⁸ _____ . I opened my violin ⁹ _____ to take out my instrument, but when I looked inside ... it wasn't there! I couldn't believe it! Then suddenly I heard laughter. The other musicians had played a trick on me by hiding my violin. I laughed too, and for the first time, I began to relax!

5 9F LISTENING AND VOCABULARY **Complete the text with one word in each gap.**

I'm not keen on old ¹n*ovels* by authors like Dickens. In *A Tale of Two Cities*, the opening ²l _____ starts quite nicely, 'It was the best of times, it was the worst of times', but the whole sentence is 119 words long! That isn't a sentence, it's a ³p _____ !

One of my favourite stories is called *Rikki-Tikki-Tavi*, by the ⁴a _____ , Rudyard Kipling. The main ⁵c _____ is a mongoose – a small animal which kills snakes. He's a real ⁶h _____ because he saves the family in the house where he lives from two cobras. The story has a very simple ⁷p _____ : the mongoose fights one snake, but the other one gets angry and at the end there's a big battle. Although Kipling wrote the stories over a hundred years ago, his writing ⁸s _____ is quite simple – much easier to read than Dickens! I guess that's because his stories were mainly written for children.

6 ON A HIGH NOTE **Write a short paragraph about something you would like to do in the arts or entertainment businesses and why.**

1 **For each learning objective, write 1–5 to assess your ability.**

1 = I don't feel confident. 5 = I feel confident.

	Learning objective	Course material	How confident I am (1–5)
9A	I can use the Past Perfect to tell stories from my life.	Student's Book pp. 124–125	
9B	I can talk about artistic professions and different types of art.	Student's Book p. 126	
9C	I can use *say*, *tell* and *ask* to report conversations.	Student's Book p. 127	
9D	I can understand a factual text and talk about music.	Student's Book pp. 128–129	
9E	I can make, accept and turn down invitations.	Student's Book p. 130	
9F	I can understand a conversation about an interesting book and talk about books.	Student's Book p. 131	
9G	I can write a review of a film, TV series, book or exhibition.	Student's Book pp. 132–133	

2 **Which of the skills above would you like to improve in? How?**

Skill I want to improve in	How I can improve

3 **What can you remember from this unit?**

New words I learned and most want to remember	Expressions and phrases I liked	English I heard or read outside class

GRAMMAR AND VOCABULARY

1 **Choose the correct words to complete the mini-conversations.**

Ali There was a guy near the beach doing **¹**portraits / landscapes of people. They were great.

Vic Painting or drawing?

Ali Painting. With a **²**brush / paint. He was making a lot of money.

Sam What are you watching?

Nell It's a crime film. It's based **³**in / on a song. The film is set **⁴**in / on Brazil and a lot of the action takes **⁵**part / place in Brasilia, the capital. That's where I used to live so I really enjoyed it.

Sam **⁶**Sounds / Speaks good. Maybe I can watch it.

Nell It's in Portuguese and it doesn't have subtitles.

/ 6

2 **Complete the sentences with the words from the box. There are three extra words.**

audience   conductor   ~~curtain~~   perform   rehearse
remake   saved   stunt   tripod

1 When the _curtain_ opens, the _____ will see you all standing in the middle of the stage having a loud argument.

2 You'll need a _____ for your camera if you want to get a good photo of the Northern Lights.

3 We need to _____ more often, otherwise we'll never be ready for the opening night.

4 The _____ performer almost fell out of the plane, but the director grabbed him and _____ his life.

/ 5

3 **Complete the sentences with the correct Past Perfect forms of the verbs in brackets.**

1 I didn't recognise the cinema yesterday. It _had changed_ (change) completely since my last visit.

2 By the time we arrived at the theatre, the play _____ (start) and they refused to let us in.

3 The drummer rejoined the band yesterday – he _____ (walked) out last year after an argument.

4 The director of the gallery found an old painting in the basement, but how long _____ (it/be) there?

5 I was surprised to see the spy in the second film as the agents _____ (kill) him at the end of the first film!

/ 4

4 **Read the conversation and complete the text with a word or phrase in each gap.**

Tommy I'm sorry. I woke up late. I'll just have some breakfast and then I'll be with you.

Director You haven't got time for breakfast. We have to film the wedding scene today.

Tommy I'm not starting without some food.

Director Well, in that case, I'll find another actor.

HOLLYWOOD GOSSIP

Tommy Jackson, star of the romantic comedy *Breakfast for Two* yesterday decided his own breakfast was more important than his director, co-stars and thirty-five technicians when he turned up an hour and a half late. He apologised and told the director that **¹**_he had woken_ up late. He said that **²**_____ some breakfast and then**³**_____ them. The director told Tommy that **⁴**_____ for breakfast because **⁵**_____ the wedding scene that day.

Tommy shouted that**⁶**_____ without some food and the director was so angry that he replied that he **⁷**_____ another actor.

/ 6

USE OF ENGLISH

5 **Complete the second sentence using the word in bold so that it means the same as the first one. Use no more than three words including the word in bold.**

1 The film was over before we arrived. **ALREADY**
By the time we arrived, the _film had already_ finished.

2 'I'm waiting for you at the art gallery,' Elaine said. **ME**
Elaine said that she was _____ at the art gallery.

3 I'm a terrible singer! **AT**
I'm _____ singing.

4 I didn't practise my lines, so I forgot them during the play. **PRACTISED**
I forgot my lines during the play because I _____ them earlier.

5 'The ending wasn't very good,' said Michelle. **BEEN**
Michelle said that the ending _____ very good.

/ 4

6 **Choose the correct words a-d to complete the text.**

By the time I sat down with director Steven Jennings, the audience **¹**___ the theatre and the actors were collecting their flowers and getting ready for the after-show party. So, in a deserted theatre, facing an empty **²**___, we sat and talked. For this production, Steven was working with teenagers who also had to attend school. 'I'm incredibly **³**___ of them,' he said and finished by saying that it **⁴**___ a wonderful experience for him and one he **⁵**___ love to repeat in the future.

1 **a** had left   **b** have left   **c** left   **d** would leave
2 **a** curtain   **b** movie   **c** stage   **d** landscape
3 **a** impressive   **b** shocked   **c** cheerful   **d** proud
4 **a** has been   **b** had been   **c** would be   **d** is
5 **a** had   **b** will   **c** did   **d** would

/ 5

/ 30

10 Crimewatch

10A GRAMMAR AND VOCABULARY

The passive

1 ⭐ **Put the words in order to make questions.**

1 filmed / the TV series / was / where / ?
Where was the TV series filmed?

2 was / first / when / on TV / shown / it / ?
_____

3 by / were / who / the main characters / played / ?
_____

4 based / a book / was / on / it ?
_____

5 shown / were / how many / episodes / ?
_____

6 the series / a film / has / made / into / been / ?
_____

7 the programme / a lot of people / was / watched / by ?
_____

2 ⭐ **Match the questions in Exercise 1 with answers a–g.**

a ☐ There were ninety-two altogether in four series.
b ☐ Starsky was played by Paul Michael Glaser and Hutch was played by David Soul.
c ☐ Yes, it was. It was a very popular programme.
d ☐ It was filmed in Los Angeles, California.
e ☐ No, it wasn't. It was a new idea for TV.
f ☐ Yes, it has. The film starred Ben Stiller.
g ☐ The first episode was shown in 1975.

3 ⭐ **Choose the correct forms to complete the text.**

Between 1888 and 1891, eleven women ¹*killed / were killed* in the Whitechapel area of London. The murderer ²*never caught / was never caught*.

In the autumn of 1888, several letters ³*sent / were sent* to newspapers from someone who ⁴*claimed / was claimed* to be the murderer. He ⁵*called / was called* himself 'Jack the Ripper'. The newspapers ⁶*printed / were printed* many stories about the murders. In fact, some people think that the letters ⁷*wrote / were written* by journalists who wanted to make the story more exciting for their readers.

Since that time many theories ⁸*have put forward / have been put forward* about who the murderer was and several films ⁹*have made / have been made* but who was Jack? No-one knows.

4 ⭐⭐ **Complete the sentences with the correct passive forms of the verbs in brackets.**

1 This is the weapon that *was used* (use) in the attack yesterday.
2 How many times _____ (Simon/arrest) since he lost his job?
3 I think a window _____ (leave) open when we went out.
4 How many crimes _____ (commit) each year in London?
5 The gang behaved badly but no laws _____ (break).
6 The Philip Marlowe detective novels _____ (write) by Raymond Chandler in the 1930s.

5 ⭐⭐ **Complete the text with the correct passive forms of the verbs in brackets.**

Who is your favourite fictional detective? We had hundreds of votes and they have now all been ¹*counted* (count). In first place is the TV detective, Columbo. The part ² _____ (play) by actor Peter Falk from 1971 to 2003 and episodes from the series ³ _____ (still/show) on different channels today.

In second place comes another TV detective, Veronica Mars. Veronica is a student who works as a private investigator in the evenings. The character ⁴ _____ (create) by writer Rob Thomas, who originally planned to make the investigator a boy. Luckily for us, he changed his mind. Veronica Mars started out as a TV series, but a film ⁵ _____ (also/make).

In third place is an Agatha Christie character, the elderly detective, Miss Marple. She lives in a world of English villages where people ⁶ _____ (murder) almost daily and crimes ⁷ _____ (solve) while eating cakes and drinking cups of tea!

6 ⭐⭐⭐ USE OF ENGLISH **Complete the second sentence so that it means the same as the first one. Use no more than three words.**

1 The police have found a clue under the sofa.
A clue _has been found_ under the sofa.

2 When they arrest someone, the police have to complete a lot of paperwork.
When someone _____, the police have to complete a lot of paperwork.

3 We keep all the evidence in this cupboard.
All the evidence _____ in this cupboard.

4 How many people at the festival did the police arrest?
How many people at the festival _____ arrested?

5 Basil Rathbone made fourteen Sherlock Holmes films.
Fourteen Sherlock Holmes films _____ with Basil Rathbone.

6 Criminals in the UK commit millions of crimes a year.
Millions of crimes _____ each year in the UK.

7 ⭐⭐⭐ **Complete the sentences with the correct passive forms of the verbs from the box.**

award   base   beat   ~~create~~   direct   play   sell

1 Tintin is a fictional detective who _was created_ by a Belgian cartoonist called Hergé.

2 The film _The Adventures of Tintin_ _____ by Steven Spielberg.

3 Spielberg _____ the 'Best Director' Oscar twice.

4 One of the directors who _____ by Spielberg in 1999 was Roberto Benigni.

5 The role of Lucius Detritus in _Asterix and Obelix Take on Caesar_ _____ by Benigni.

6 The film _____ on the books about Asterix the Gaul by René Goscinny.

7 More copies of the Asterix books _____ than any other comic book series ... apart from Tintin!

8 ⭐⭐⭐ USE OF ENGLISH **Complete the second sentence using the word in bold so that it means the same as the first one. Use no more than three words, including the word in bold.**

1 A left-handed man committed this crime. **COMMITTED**
This _crime was committed_ by a left-handed man.

2 The police questioned a man for several hours. **BY**
A man _____ the police for several hours.

3 The police haven't arrested anybody yet. **HAS**
Nobody _____ yet.

4 The story of the film came from a true story. **BASED**
The film _____ a true story.

5 Someone moved the body after the murder. **BODY**
The _____ after the murder.

6 Lots of tourists visit the Sherlock Holmes Museum every year. **VISITED**
The Sherlock Holmes Museum _____ lots of tourists every year.

9 ⭐⭐⭐ **Complete the text with the correct forms of the verbs from the box.**

ask   connect   enjoy   find   make   murder   play   ~~receive~~   write

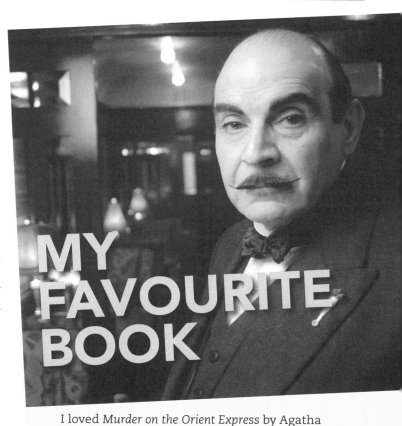

MY FAVOURITE BOOK

I loved _Murder on the Orient Express_ by Agatha Christie. Detective Hercule Poirot is in Istanbul when he **1**_receives_ a message asking him to return to London. He buys a ticket for the Orient Express train. On the train, he meets an unpleasant American man who **2**_____ for Poirot's protection. Poirot refuses and, that night, the man **3**_____. A note **4**_____ near the body on which the words, 'Remember Daisy Armstrong' **5**_____. It is an important clue.

Soon Poirot finds out that everyone in the train carriage **6**_____ to the murdered man in some way, and all of them had a reason to kill him. So, who did it? I'm not going to tell you! You'll have to read the book or you can watch the film _Murder on the Orient Express_ which **7**_____ in 2017. The part of the detective **8**_____ by Kenneth Branagh and the American by Johnny Depp. Although the film got mixed reviews, it **9**_____ by millions of people all over the world.

It is definitely worth watching.

10 ON A HIGH NOTE **Write about a fictional detective you have read about in a book or seen on television or in a film. Describe the detective, how he/she works and what you like about the character and the stories.**

10B VOCABULARY | Types of crime

1 ★ **Which word is not a crime? Find the odd one out in each group.**

1 assault   burglary   (murderer)
2 hacking   pickpocketing   thief
3 robbery   shoplifter   attack
4 murder   victim   theft
5 bank robbery   shoplifting   hacker

2 ★★ **Complete the sentences with the correct words formed from the words in bold.**

1 The _burglar_ must have got in through the back door. **BURGLE**
2 Have you heard? There's been a _____ at the bank! **ROB**
3 He's a criminal, but he isn't a _____ . **MURDER**
4 The _____ stole wallets on crowded buses. **POCKET**
5 I think a _____ has taken over my computer. **HACK**

3 ★★ **Complete the text with the words from the box.**

beaten   broken   cash   gang   purse   ~~victim~~   wallet

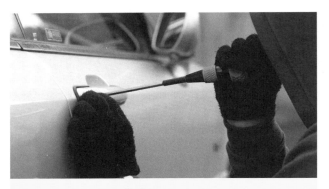

HAVE YOU BEEN THE ¹_VICTIM_ OF A CRIME?

Has someone ² _____ into your home
and taken ³ _____ or jewellery?
Have you been ⁴ _____ up by
a ⁵ _____ of hooligans?
Maybe a pickpocket stole your ⁶ _____
or ⁷ _____ with your money, credit
cards and documents inside while you were
in a crowded area.

Whatever the problem, you may need
counselling to help you overcome your
anxieties and fears.

Call us now for FREE help on 0322444

4 ★★ **Complete the text with the correct form of rob or steal.**

NEWS

Thieves ¹_stole_ a gold Ferrari from outside a house in central London last night …

Three people were ² _____ when they accepted a lift from a fake taxi driver …

A professional thief has become a security advisor and has shown bank officials how easy it is to ³ _____ their banks …

A major London art gallery admitted that three of its paintings have been ⁴ _____ this month …

A couple have been jailed after saying that they were ⁵ _____ while on holiday. They told their insurance company that thieves had ⁶ _____ a camera, laptop, jewellery and cash, but security cameras showed them hiding the valuables in a bag when the police came to investigate.

5 ★★ **Complete the words with one letter in each gap.**

Dear Sir/Madam,

I read your article about ordinary people trying to catch criminals and I was surprised by your negativity. You say that amateur crime fighters don't know for sure who the criminals are and only ¹su s pect the people they stop of committing crimes. You say this is unfair and should be left to the police.

I agree that people must be sure that someone has ²c__m____t_____ a crime before they do something. For example, if they see a ³s____p___f_____ taking things in a store without paying for them. But if people don't act, the criminals will ⁴g____ a__a__ with their crimes because the police aren't able to catch them.

I think you should save your sympathy for the ⁵v____t____s of a crime, not the people who cause it.

Yours

Arnold Green.

6 ON A HIGH NOTE **Write a short paragraph about crime in your area. What are the most common crimes and do you think the police do enough to protect people?**

1 🔊 73 Listen to Part 1 of a radio programme. Who are the Guardian Angels?

_____

2 🔊 74 Now listen to Part 2 of the radio programme and choose the correct answers.

1 Lucy says that
- **a** it is unusual for women to join the Guardian Angels.
- **b** people of any age can join the Guardian Angels.
- **c** to join the Guardian Angels, you must break the law.

2 From what Lucy says, we can assume that
- **a** many members broke the law at a young age.
- **b** she has just committed a crime.
- **c** the group attracts only poor people.

3 The Guardian Angels' most important work is
- **a** stopping knife and gun attacks.
- **b** helping communities to deal with crime.
- **c** making public transport safe for ordinary people.

4 The New York subway is safer now than it used to be
- **a** because the Angels can use modern technology.
- **b** because there are more police officers.
- **c** for a number of different reasons.

5 Lucy says that
- **a** people had the wrong idea about the Angels at first.
- **b** she worked at a school before she joined the Angels.
- **c** Mayor Koch never liked the Guardian Angels.

Vocabulary extension

3 Complete the sentences with the correct verbs from the box , which you heard in the radio programme in Exercises 1 and 2.

defend   deter   ~~patrol~~   prevent   vandalised

1 At our school, prefects *patrol* the corridors at break time to make sure there's no trouble.

2 If I were attacked, I would _____ myself using the skills I've learned in my karate lessons.

3 A sign saying 'Dangerous dog' will _____ burglars – even if you haven't got a dog!

4 I wanted to have lunch in the park but all the benches were _____ and broken.

5 The Guardian Angels try to _____ crime by working with young people and community groups.

4 🔊 75 Listen to a story about a real-life hero and complete the notes.

TOM CRUISE THE REAL-LIFE HERO!
Year: [1] *1996*
First event: a [2] _____ and run accident
Amount Tom Cruise paid: [3] $_____
Second event took place near: [4] _____ , Italy
Third event took place in: [5] _____
Tom saved: [6] _____

Pronunciation

5 🔊 76 Look at the sentences from the radio programme in Exercises 1 and 2. Pay attention to the underlined words which contain the /r/ sound. Listen and repeat the individual words.

1 The (Guardian) Angels are a <u>crime</u> fighting <u>group</u>.

2 Some of your members have actually <u>broken</u> the law at some point in the past. Isn't that a bit <u>strange</u>?

3 The first is, well, obviously, to <u>prevent</u> <u>crime</u>.

4 This can be <u>dangerous</u> for us because we never <u>carry</u> weapons.

5 Just the fact that we are <u>patrolling</u> in an <u>area</u> is usually enough to stop people …

6 When the first Guardian Angels appeared on platforms and in <u>train</u> <u>carriages</u> <u>dressed</u> in their <u>red</u> hats and jackets …

ACTIVE PRONUNCIATION | The letter *r*

The letter r is pronounced
- after a consonant and before a vowel sound (e.g. c*r*ime).
- between two vowels (e.g. a*r*ea).
- at the beginning of a word, when it is followed by a vowel (e.g. *r*ed).

The letter r is not pronounced
- before a consonant (e.g. bu*r*glar).
- after a vowel sound at the end of a word (e.g. ca*r*).

6 Look at the sentences in Exercise 5 again. Find examples of words with the letter *r* which is not pronounced.

7 🔊 77 Listen to another sentence from the radio programme. What do you notice about the underlined words?

I think of us <u>more as</u> school prefects. You know – the older pupils in school who are responsible for keeping <u>order at</u> break times and so on.

ACTIVE PRONUNCIATION | Linking /r/ sound

The letter *r* is pronounced when it comes after a vowel sound at the end of a word and the next word starts with a vowel sound (e.g. ca*r* accident).

8 🔊 78 Try saying the underlined words from Exercise 7. Listen and repeat the individual words and the phrases.

9 🔊 79 Tick the phrases that link together with an /r/ sound. Listen and practise saying the phrases.

1 ☑ more arrests
2 ☐ for a change
3 ☐ wear a skirt
4 ☐ their work
5 ☐ your aunt
6 ☐ they are armed

10D GRAMMAR

The second conditional

1 ⭐ **Read the sentences and choose the correct forms.**

1 If I had a lot of money, I would buy a house in the Caribbean.
The speaker *has got / hasn't got* a lot of money.

2 If the weather was better, we would go swimming.
The weather *is / isn't* good for swimming.

3 I'd go to the beach today if I wasn't at school.
The speaker *is / isn't* at school today.

4 If I had my phone here, I'd take some photos.
The speaker *is / isn't* going to take some photos.

5 If this mountain wasn't so dangerous, more people would climb it.
The mountain *is / isn't* dangerous.

6 What would you do if the police arrested you?
The speaker thinks it *is / isn't* likely that the police will arrest the other person.

2 ⭐ **Choose the correct forms to complete the sentences. Both words may be correct.**

1 If I were you, I *will / would* change the locks.

2 What *you would / would you* do if someone broke in while you were in bed?

3 If Tom *were / was* a better student, he would get better marks.

4 The police officer wouldn't arrest her if he *didn't / wouldn't* think she was guilty.

5 Would you visit me if I *were / was* in prison?

6 Would you be worried if you *lose / lost* your phone?

7 I wouldn't use the subway if I *was / would* be in New York.

8 If the weather *was / were* better, we would go swimming.

3 ⭐⭐ **Complete the conversation with the correct forms of the verbs in brackets.**

Josh I'm having problems with my email. I get some very strange messages. What **1** *would you do* (you/do) if you **2** _____ (be) me? **3** _____ (you/change) your email address?

Hattie Maybe. First, I **4** _____ (make) sure that I **5** _____ (have) a good anti-virus programme on my computer. If you **6** _____ (open) an email, but **7** _____ (not have) an anti-virus, you could be in real trouble.

Josh Can you check that the anti-virus is OK? It was free.

Hattie OK, but later. I **8** _____ (help) you now if I **9** _____ (not have) so much work to do. Just be careful and don't click on any attachments. There are a lot of cyber criminals who are trying to trick people.

4 ⭐⭐⭐ **Use the prompts to write questions and answers.**

1 What / you / do / your neighbours / have / a loud party late at night?
What would you do if your neighbours had a loud party late at night?

2 I / ask / them to stop / but / if / they / not / I / call / the police
_____

3 you / steal / from a shop / if / you / have / no money?
_____

4 No, / not. I / try / to get money in some other way
_____

5 Who / you / phone / if / the police / arrest / you?
_____

6 I / phone / my mum because I know she / help / me
_____

5 ⭐⭐⭐ **Complete the second sentence so that it means the same as the first one.**

1 The only reason I'm here is that I've got nothing better to do.
If I *had something better to do, I wouldn't* be here.

2 The reason there's a lot of crime here is that there aren't any CCTV cameras.
If there _____ so much crime.

3 You get burgled so often because you never lock your back door.
If you _____ so often.

4 There aren't enough police. That's why criminals get away with their crimes.
If there _____ with their crimes.

5 Crime films are exciting because they are unrealistic.
If crime films _____ exciting.

6 ON A HIGH NOTE **Imagine that you found a wallet/purse on the bus. Write a few sentences explaining what you would do.**

10E SPEAKING

1  🔊 **80** Listen and repeat the phrases. How do you say them in your language?

> ## SPEAKING | Asking for and giving advice
>
> ### ASKING FOR ADVICE
>
> **What should I do?**
>
> **Could you give me some advice?**
>
> **Have you any ideas on how to** install this anti-virus?
>
> **Have you any tips on what I could do** to feel safer?
>
> ### GIVING ADVICE
>
> **If I were you, I'd** go to the police.
>
> **I (don't) think you should** leave your bag there.
>
> **You should/shouldn't** complain about it.
>
> **(I don't think) it's a good idea to** leave your phone here.
>
> **It's better (not) to** take the underground.
>
> **Why don't you** get an alarm put in?

2 Put the words in order to make questions and responses.

1 about / should / pickpockets / do / we / what?
What should we do about pickpockets?

2 we / on buses / warning signs / think / put / should / I

3 how to / you / on / safe / any ideas / my computer / keep / have / ?

4 well / it's / to / wi-fi / don't think / a good idea / in public / I / use

5 about bike locks / you / give / advice / could / me / ?

6 a very strong / were / buy / I'd / one / if / you / I

7 could do / safe / I / to keep / any tips / what / you / my money / on / have / ?

8 keep / in the bank / don't / why / it / you / ?

3 Complete the mini-conversations with one word in each gap.

Amy I think someone took some money from my purse during P.E. What ¹s*hould* I do?

Bil If I ²w_____ you, I'd talk to the teacher.

Jack Could you give me some ³a_____ about burglar alarms?

Leo ⁴W_____ don't you ask at electrical shop? They're really helpful there.

Luca Have you any ⁵i_____ on how to carry money safely while on holiday?

Ryan Well, I know it's ⁶b_____ not to carry it in your back pocket.

Sam Have you any ⁷t_____ on what I could do to keep my online bank account safe?

Paul Well, I don't think it's a good ⁸i_____ to check it here at school. Wait until you get home and can use your Internet connection.

4 Complete the conversation with the phrases from the box.

> better not to   don't think you   ~~give me some~~
> I were you   it's a good   on how to   should I do
> what I should   why don't you   you shouldn't worry

Elaine Could you ¹*give me some* advice? I'm going to London soon and I want to make the most of it.

Harry Well, if ²_____, I'd get a good guide book and find out what there is to see.

Elaine Have you any tips on ³_____ do to stay safe?

Harry Well, first of all, ⁴_____. The touristy parts of the city are very safe. I mean, it's ⁵_____ walk home in the middle of the night alone, but I don't think ⁶_____ idea to do that anywhere.

Elaine Have you any ideas ⁷_____ get round at night?

Harry Well, first of all, ⁸_____ stay in a hostel and meet up with other young people who you can go out with? It's always safer in a group.

Elaine That's a good idea. I can look for a room when I get there.

Harry No, I ⁹_____ should wait until then. It's a popular place and rooms get booked up quickly.

Elaine Oh. What ¹⁰_____? How can I find out the best place to stay?

Harry Go online and check out reviews of hostels written by other young people. I would stay near Oxford Circus but I'm not an expert and I'm sure other people will know more than I do.

Elaine Great, thanks. I feel much better now.

5 🔊 **81** Now listen and check your answers.

10F **READING AND VOCABULARY**

1 Complete the sentences with the words from the box. Then write which of these acts you think is the worst and which is the least bad?

bank certificates cheating credit ~~pretending~~ uniform

1 *Pretending* to be a doctor and working in a hospital.
2 Using a parent's _____ card to get money.
3 Getting a place at university by _____ in exams.
4 Stealing a pilot's _____ and pretending to work for an airline to get free flights.
5 Making fake _____ to pretend that you're a lawyer.
6 Cashing cheques that aren't yours in a _____.

The worst act: _____
The least bad act: _____

2 Read the text quickly. Which of the acts in Exercise 1 did Frank Abagnale NOT commit?

_____

3 Read the text again and choose the correct answers.

1 From the first paragraph we can say that
   a fewer criminals reoffend in Norway than in any other country in the world.
   b reoffending rates amongst ex-prisoners in the USA are increasing.
   c more than half of prisoners in the USA reoffend after they leave prison.
2 Frank Abagnale
   a stole money from banks.
   b used cheques to pay for plane tickets.
   c travelled a lot without paying anything.
3 While pretending to be a doctor, Frank
   a avoided situations in which medical skills were required.
   b almost caused someone to die because of his lack of medical knowledge.
   c learned medical techniques from staff in the hospital.
4 To become a lawyer, Frank
   a actually studied for an exam and passed it.
   b forged a state law exam certificate.
   c studied at Harvard University.
5 Frank was caught because
   a he committed crimes in France.
   b someone told the police who he was.
   c the police in France knew who he was.
6 After he was released from prison, Frank
   a used his knowledge of bank security to steal money.
   b helped the FBI and got a job.
   c received money from the FBI.

Vocabulary extension

4 Replace the underlined parts in the sentences below with the words from the box.

go straight life-threatening rehabilitation ~~released~~ reoffend sentenced to

1 The prisoners were <u>freed</u> from prison after four years.
   released
2 If you <u>commit another crime</u>, you will go to prison.
   _____
3 Will was <u>given a punishment of</u> six months in prison.
   _____
4 This disease is so dangerous it can be <u>deadly</u>.
   _____
5 Henry is determined to <u>become an honest, non-criminal person</u> from now on.
   _____
6 The process of <u>turning criminals into useful members of society</u> is vital if we want to reduce crime levels.
   _____

ACTIVE VOCABULARY | Word family

For each new word, learn all the parts of speech (noun, verb, adjective, adverb). Then you will learn three or four words instead of just one.

5 Look at these two words and the related words. Then complete the sentences with the correct words.

- **forged** (adjective/past participle) – copied, fake
  forge (verb), **forger** (noun/person), **forgery** (noun/act)
- **fraudster** – a person who steals money by cheating
  defraud (verb), **fraud** (noun/act)

1 I'm a victim of *fraud*. I paid for a holiday and then found out that the hotel doesn't exist.
2 The collector paid $200 million for a Van Gogh painting, but it was a _____. The real painting was in an art gallery in France.
3 The criminals were sentenced to five years in prison for trying to _____ the government.
4 I think these bank notes have been _____ – they feel strange.
5 The old man worked as a _____. He could copy any document and make it look perfect.
6 I knew the email was from a _____ because they had spelt the name of my bank wrongly.

6 ON A HIGH NOTE Write a few questions you would ask if you met Frank Abagnale for an interview.

The rehabilitation of
Frank Abagnale

The number of prisoners who return to a life of crime after they are released from prison varies from country to country. In Norway, where rehabilitation of prisoners is seen as important, about 20 percent reoffend after they are released. However, in the USA, where no special efforts are made to help newly-released prisoners, about 66 percent go on to commit more crimes.

Rehabilitation isn't just of benefit to the ex-criminals, but to society as a whole. One of the most interesting examples is that of Frank Abagnale. It's an amazing story and, not surprisingly, it has been made into a film: *Catch Me If You Can* starring Leonardo DiCaprio as Frank.

Frank first got into trouble when he used his father's credit card to run up a bill of $3,400 – he was just fifteen years old at the time. Soon after this, Frank left home and made money by cashing cheques in banks, but his name soon became known to the banks. That's when he started using disguises. He stole a pilot's uniform and created a fake employee ID card. Then he started to travel around the world. He didn't actually fly the planes, of course, but pilots are able to use empty seats on planes free of charge. That went on until the airline, Pan Am, became suspicious.

Frank then decided to play the role of a doctor and he was invited to work in a local hospital. Fortunately, Frank didn't actually have to do any medical work and managed to find other staff in the hospital to do it for him. However, he has said that he felt worried that there would be a time when he might put someone in a life-threatening situation, so after eleven months, he left.

Another job he took was as a lawyer. He used forged certificates to pretend that he was a graduate of Harvard University. He still had to pass the state law exams, but amazingly, after two attempts, he actually passed. Unfortunately for Frank, a real Harvard graduate was working in the same law office. He chatted to Frank about the university, but Frank obviously knew nothing of Harvard and the man became suspicious and Frank moved on again.

In the end, Frank decided to go straight and he settled down in France. However, an ex-girlfriend recognised his face on a wanted poster and he was arrested. After some time in a French prison, he returned to the USA and was sentenced to twelve years in prison. After almost five years, he was offered a chance of rehabilitation.

He was freed on condition that he helped the FBI to catch other fraudsters. Although Frank was happy to do this, it was unpaid work, so Frank also approached a large bank, told them how poor their security was, and offered to help them improve it. If the bank had rejected his idea, he might have returned to a life of crime, but, because they gave him a chance to become a useful member of society, he has spent the last forty years using his skills for the good of society.

Frank Abagnale already had the skills he needed in order to find employment when he left prison. Other criminals aren't as lucky. Shouldn't we make sure that, while in prison, all prisoners are given the training and skills they need to succeed in life 'on the outside' and to have the chance of building a normal life? It would benefit us all.

10G **WRITING** | A story

Say when and where the story happened; give some background information.

Say what happened. Use the Past Simple.

Use direct speech.

Say how people felt.

Use reported speech.

GRANDMOTHER IS AN EVERYDAY HERO!

In recent years, there has been an increase in the number of teenagers in London looking for mopeds and motorbikes to steal.

In February 2018, eighty-year-old Rosemary Bodger was walking home in Crouch End, North London **¹when** she saw two young men trying to steal a moped and threatening the owner who they **²_____** . Without thinking, she **³_____** grabbed the moped that the teenagers were trying to steal.

'I started shouting "police" as loud as I could,' she **⁴_____** . She didn't feel at all frightened, just really angry.

⁵_____ , Rosemary was alone, but soon others joined in to help. A smartly-dressed businessman ran across the street and two builders who were working nearby also arrived and chased after the thieves as they escaped. Rosemary said that she didn't think she was a hero, **⁶_____** others, including the owner of the moped disagree.

---

1 Complete the story with the words from the box.

> at first   but   had stopped   immediately   said   ~~when~~

2 Now complete the report about the owner of the moped with one word in each gap.

18th February, Crouch End, North London. Stefan Cooper, a moped rider, **¹w<u>as</u>** riding to the centre of London **²w_____** he noticed another motorbike following him. At **³f_____** , he wasn't worried but suddenly, the riders started shouting at him and demanding his keys. Stefan tried to drive towards a police station, **⁴b_____** he got stuck in traffic. When he stopped, the teenagers managed to grab his keys. He **⁵s_____** that he felt very upset by the experience. Mr Cooper would like to thank everyone who helped him and stayed with him **⁶u_____** the police arrived. The police are still investigating the incident, but have not yet made any **⁷a_____** .

3 Choose the correct words to complete the sentences.

1 The attack *happened / had happened* yesterday.
2 I was *painting / painted* the front of a shop *when / while* I saw two mopeds driving past.
3 *At first, / Before*, I didn't take much notice, *but / and* then I heard somebody shouting.
4 When I crossed the road, I realised that some boys *stole / had stolen* a man's moped.
5 *While / Later* we were waiting for the police, we looked after the victim.
6 When the police arrived, I *interviewed / was interviewed*, but I couldn't help much.
7 I *said / told* that everything had happened *before / while* I got there.
8 *Suddenly, / Eventually,* the police left and I went back to work.

4 WRITING TASK Imagine that you were a witness to the incident above. Write your story.

ACTIVE WRITING | A story

1 Plan your story.
- Say what you were doing when the incident happened.
- Think about what you saw and did.
- Make a note of what other people said and felt.
- Say how you felt while the incident was happening and afterwards.

2 Write the story.
- Use a range of past tenses to give some background and say what happened.
- Use both direct and reported speech.
- Use adverbs and adjectives to make your story more interesting.
- Say how you and other people felt.
- Connect your sentences using linking words.

3 Check that ...
- you have included all the relevant information.
- there are no spelling or grammar mistakes.
- you have used a good range of vocabulary and structures to make your story interesting.

UNIT VOCABULARY PRACTICE

1 10A GRAMMAR AND VOCABULARY **Choose the correct words to complete the sentences.**

1 Which detective series did Martin Freeman star ___?
a on **b** in **c** at

2 The police are hoping to ___ the criminals soon.
a arrest **b** suspect **c** prevent

3 How did you manage to ___ the crime so quickly?
a find **b** make **c** solve

4 If we look carefully, we should be able to ___ the clue.
a view **b** find **c** create

5 The police are asking members of the public to ___ crimes online, not by phone.
a commit **b** solve **c** report

6 I don't think real detectives ___ deductions like Sherlock Holmes.
a solve **b** find **c** make

7 The man didn't actually ___ a crime because the police stopped him before he broke in.
a commit **b** report **c** solve

8 You have ___ the law and will now be punished.
a committed **b** broken **c** stolen

2 10B VOCABULARY **Match the crimes from the box with the sentences.**

assault burglary hacking murder pickpocketing
~~shoplifting~~

1 May took three tins of meat from the supermarket.
shoplifting

2 Clyde travelled on crowded buses and stole wallets.
_____

3 Andy attacked Jack in the street, but the police never caught him. _____

4 Alice killed a man, Barry, who she used to know.
_____

5 Simon broke into a house and stole a laptop.
_____

6 Beth stole money from online bank accounts using her computer. _____

3 **Complete the sentences with the correct words formed from the crimes in Exercise 2.**

1 Alice is a *murderer*.
2 Beth is a _____.
3 Simon is a _____.
4 Jack was the _____ of crime.
5 May is a _____.
6 Clyde is a _____.

4 10C LISTENING AND VOCABULARY **Complete the sentences with one word in each gap.**

1 Directors shouldn't make *villains* in films likeable – young children may think they are heroes.

2 He should be sent to p_____ for ten years for the things he's done.

3 We need to reorganise every aspect of the j_____ system from the police to courts, judges and prisons.

4 Why have you arrested him? He's not guilty – he's i_____!

5 What happens if v_____ break the law while they are trying to stop people who have broken the law?

6 The only c_____ f_____ on our streets should be the police. It's their job to fight crime.

7 Some of the football fans at the match became v_____ when the other team scored a goal and there were fights in the crowd.

5 10F READING AND VOCABULARY **Choose the correct words to complete the sentences.**

1 The police want to *suspect / arrest / question* everybody about where they were last night.

2 The police have *arrested / found out / suspected* three people in connection with the robbery at the post office.

3 I knew I couldn't trust him because he *stole / cheated / robbed* my sandwich while I wasn't looking.

4 I've got an *alibi / alarm / assault* for the night of the robbery; I was with my friends at a party.

5 For some reason the *burgle / burglar / burglary* alarm didn't work.

6 The police arrested the *thief / robbery / victim* when he told all his friends about his crimes on social media.

7 The jewels were *robbed / stolen / caught* in the middle of the night when everyone was asleep.

6 ON A HIGH NOTE **Write about a crime you have read about or seen in a book, film, newspaper or news report (TV or online). Explain what happened and whether the criminal was arrested or not and, if they were, what their punishment was.**

1   For each learning objective, write 1–5 to assess your ability.

1 = I don't feel confident. 5 = I feel confident.

	Learning objective	Course material	How confident I am (1–5)
10A	I can use the passive.	Student's Book pp. 138–139	
10B	I can talk about crime and criminals.	Student's Book p. 140	
10C	I can identify the speaker's point of view and understand the key points in a radio programme and talk about superheroes.	Student's Book p. 141	
10D	I can use the second conditional to talk about hypothetical situations.	Student's Book p. 142	
10E	I can ask for and give advice about crime prevention.	Student's Book p. 143	
10F	I can find specific details in a short story and talk about crime.	Student's Book pp. 144–145	
10G	I can write a true or invented story.	Student's Book pp. 146–147	

2   Which of the skills above would you like to improve in? How?

Skill I want to improve in	How I can improve

3   What can you remember from this unit?

New words I learned and most want to remember	Expressions and phrases I liked	English I heard or read outside class

Self-check

GRAMMAR AND VOCABULARY

1 Complete the conversation with the words from the box. There are three extra words.

burgle clue honestly inform robbed ~~stole~~ suspicious victim vigilante wallet

Tourist I told you. Someone ¹stole my passport. I was ²_____ while I was walking back to my hotel. Why don't you believe me? I'm the ³_____ here, not the criminal!

Officer And they didn't take your money or your ⁴_____?

Tourist No.

Officer And you didn't notice anyone ⁵_____?

Tourist No.

Officer ⁶_____, there isn't much we can do, I'm afraid, but if we hear anything, we'll ⁷_____ you.

/ 6

2 Match the two parts of the sentences. There are two extra endings.

1 ☐ The robbers told the bank workers to hand
2 ☐ Sherlock Holmes was very good at making
3 ☐ The detective managed to find
4 ☐ Sometimes people break
5 ☐ In crowds, you should keep

a the law without being aware of it.
b away with their crime.
c over the money.
d an eye on your valuables at all times.
e deductions.
f for help but nobody came.
g an important clue.

/ 5

3 Complete the sentences with the correct forms of the verbs in brackets.

1 The part of the young Sherlock Holmes in the 1988 film _was played_ (play) by Michael Caine.
2 If you watched one of these old detective films, I'm sure you _____ (enjoy) it.
3 Drivers _____ (often/stop) on this road for driving too fast.
4 If I _____ (be) you, I'd put the money in the bank.
5 What _____ (you/do) if your wallet was stolen?

/ 4

4 Complete the text with the correct forms of the verbs from the box.

can earn have to ~~influence~~ make often/set only/read

/ 6

USE OF ENGLISH

5 Complete the text with one word in each gap.

Hackers? They're thieves!

Some people seem to think that hacking is less of a crime ¹than burglary or robbery. It's true that hackers don't physically attack their victims but, apart from that, there isn't much difference between them and other criminals. They break ²_____ people's homes, using a computer rather than an open window, and, once inside, they ³_____ people's money. If your house has ⁴_____ burgled, you feel nervous every time you leave it or go to bed at night. When hackers get into your computer, you feel the same way every time you go online.

Millions of pounds ⁵_____ stolen every year in online fraud. If the banks and the government took the problem more seriously, the police ⁶_____ have the resources to deal with the problem. Until then, more and more of us can expect to lose our savings to these thieves.

/ 5

6 Complete the second sentence using the word in bold so that it means the same as the first one. Use no more than three words, including the word in bold.

1 You aren't a detective so you don't see the clues.
If you were a _detective, you would_ see the clues. **WOULD**
2 They based this film on a Sherlock Holmes story. **WAS**
This _____ on a Sherlock Holmes story.
3 The new prison has been built a long way from anywhere. **MIDDLE**
The new prison has been built _____ of nowhere.
4 We have arrested three men in connection with the robbery. **BEEN**
Three men _____ in connection with the robbery.
5 Pickpockets make money because people don't take care of their valuables. **LOOKED**
Pickpockets wouldn't make money if _____ their valuables.

/ 4
/ 30

One of the most surprising success stories in crime literature has been the rise of Scandinavian detective stories. According to Gunnar Bolin, a Swedish TV producer, the Scandinavian writers ¹_are influenced_ by British crime novels. He also admits that money is an important factor. The authors knew that if they ²_____ get their books translated into English, they ³_____ much more than for books that ⁴_____ by Scandinavian fans.

Why are they so popular? The Scandinavian scenery makes a nice change from typical crime novels which ⁵_____ in Los Angeles, New York or London. They also often contain a social message as well as an exciting crime story.

If I ⁶_____ recommend one series of books, I would choose the Kurt Wallander books by Henning Mankell. These ⁷_____ into a BBC TV series.

PHRASAL VERBS

be into sth: I'm really into music.

be together: Ian's parents aren't together any more.

be with: Good friends are fun to be with, but they're hard to find.

beat up: The bully threatened to beat up the school boys.

believe in sth: It's never too late to believe in your dreams.

break into: A burglar breaks into your home and steals your things.

break up: Break up your work into smaller units.

build up: Eddie's going to build up his muscles.

burn off: You can burn off calories with aerobics.

call up: One day, his father called him up.

carry on: I carry on until I finish what I'm doing.

carry out: Scientists are carrying out experiments to get more data.

check in: After all the problems and delays I was exhausted when we finally checked in.

check out: Please check out the London to Hereford bus times.

clear up: If something is untidy, I prefer to clear it up immediately.

come from: He comes from New York.

come out: The rain stopped and the sun came out.

come round: Stan's coming round at seven.

come together: Neighbours, friends and family come together often.

come up: The sun was coming up when Adam saw the rainbows.

end up: If you break the law, you might end up in prison.

fall down: They're falling down.

find out: Let's look online to find out when the museum opening times are.

get away with: They didn't get away with it. The police caught them.

get in: The bus gets in at 15.40.

get into: How did David Garrett get into the music business?

get off: He got off the bus and ran to the station.

get on: Be careful you don't get on the wrong bus.

get on: How are you getting on with your History project?

get on (well) with sb: We get on with people who share the same background.

get out: I got out my History book.

get up: I'm going to get up early tomorrow.

give away: Do you give clothes away?

give up: We had to give up our plans for a camping trip because of the bad weather.

give sth back: He borrowed my T-shirt and never gave it back.

go ahead: 'Is it alright if I change the channel?' 'Sure, go ahead.'

go on: Something strange is going on, but I don't know what it is exactly.

go out: It's his birthday, so we're going out for a meal.

go without: You could go without food on one day a week.

grow up: The children of happy parents tend to grow up to be optimistic.

hand in: They didn't hand in their homework on time.

hand out: I handed out a worksheet to my students.

hand over: If an armed thief tried to rob me, I would hand over my money.

heat up: You use a microwave to heat up food.

hold onto: You shouldn't hold onto things for sentimental reasons.

join in: Our class started a project and then all the other classes joined in.

keep on: Keep on trying until you succeed.

keep up with: Technology helps us study, contact friends and keep up with the news.

let sb down: You can't help everyone, but I never let my friends down.

lie around: You mustn't leave things lying around on surfaces.

look after: Many of them believe that a 'higher power' is looking after them.

look at: He looks at himself in the mirror when he's driving!

look for sth: I'm looking for something to give to Mum on her birthday.

look forward to: We're really looking forward to meeting you.

miss out: She doesn't want to miss out on all the latest gossip.

mix up: Do you ever mix up languages?

move in: She's going to move in to a new flat with a group of friends.

move out: Is it hard for young people to move out of their family home?

pick sb up: Do you want to pick me up or shall I get a taxi?

pick up: I picked up a textbook and tried to hit the fly.

put off: I wonder why I always put off important things until the last moment.

put on: He still doesn't know how to put on a tie.

put up: The students put their hands up to ask questions.

put up: I wanted to put the posters up on the wall.

put up: It took us five minutes to put up the tent.

run away: He stole my money and then ran away.

set out: He was setting out on an incredible solo journey.

set up: Today Sarah will explain how to set up a home gym.

settle down: He's thirty-five but he doesn't want to settle down.

show sb round: I'll show you round the house.

sleep over: He's sleeping over at your house.

stand for: What do the letters UK stand for?

stay away from: I'll definitely stay away from the High Street tomorrow morning.

switch off: Does your phone ever switch itself off?

switch on: I switched on my computer and started playing Warplans.

take off: We boarded the plane on time but there was a delay before we took off.

take on: They have taken on three new workers.

take up: They're going to take up a new sport.

take up: Firstly, housework and travel take up less time.

throw out: You don't have to throw out those old comics in the bin.

tidy up: How often do you tidy up your room?

try sth on: You can try on the clothes in the changing rooms.

turn down: Turn that music down – it's 4 a.m.!

turn down: Why did she turn down his invitation? Doesn't she like him?

turn into: I was turning into my parents.

turn into: It started as a discussion but quickly turned into a big argument.

turn up: My friend often turns up late for class because she checks her phone at break time.

warm up: Do you always warm up before you exercise?

wash up: Please wash up the dishes after dinner.

work on sth: I'm working on an art project at the moment.

work out: I go to a gym to work out.

PREPOSITIONS

PREPOSITIONS IN PHRASES

AT
at home: We speak Italian at home.
at night: Does she work at night?
at the bottom/top: There are some flowers at the bottom of the photo.
at the last minute: Don't revise for your test at the last minute.
at the moment: At the moment I'm revising for my exams.
at university: I'd like to study at university.

BY
by heart: Don't try to learn your presentation by heart.
by train/bus/boat/etc.: Did you travel by plane or train?

FROM
from nine to five: He works in the office from nine to five.

IN
in a hurry: I was in a hurry because I had woken up late.
in a panic: I'm in a panic because I haven't revised for my exams.
in common: My best friend and I have a lot in common.
in danger: Your computer is in danger from viruses.
in front of: Practise in front of a mirror .
in pairs/groups: Check your work in pairs.
in public: He doesn't like speaking in public.
in shape: Do more exercise to get in shape.
in shock: She was in shock after the accident.
in the foreground/background: Can you see those people in the background?
in the middle of nowhere: He owned a lovely house in Devon in the middle of nowhere.
in trouble: You can tell who your real friends are when you're in trouble.
in your twenties: My sister is in her early twenties.

ON
on holiday: Did you see the sights when you went on holiday?
on the left/right: There's some countryside on the left of the photo.
on time: I didn't hand in the project on time.
on your own: What are the advantages of working on your own?

PREPOSITIONS AFTER NOUNS

advantage/disadvantage of: The advantage of working as a waiter is that you can eat for free.
bottle/can/packet/etc. of: Can I have a bottle of water, please?
campaign for: Start a campaign for tolerance on social media.
centre of: We live in the centre of Varese.
compensation for: You should send me a refund as compensation for the inconvenience.
cure for: The challenge will help find a cure for motor neurone disease.
degree in: She has a degree in Physics from Oxford University.
discount on: There's a discount on all the fruit – it's really cheap now.
fan of: I'm a big fan of memes.
invitation to: Most couple send written invitations to their wedding.
love from: Lots of love from Katy.
manager of: Who is the manager of your favourite team?
premiere of: She didn't go to the premiere of her first major film.
price of: What's the price of this book?
queue for: Was there a big queue for the checkout?
reason for: What reasons are there for a visitor to come to your town?
reduction in: Was there any reduction in the price?
relationship between: What's the relationship between Lorenzo and Martin?
rivalry between: The rivalry between Oxford and Cambridge is serious.
role model for: Which celebrities are the best role models for young people?
sense of: There's a wonderful sense of camaraderie.
victim of: I was the victim of a violent attack.
visa for: Where did he get the visa for Mauritania?

PREPOSITIONS AFTER ADJECTIVES

about to: I can't talk now – I'm about to leave the house.
appropriate for: Those clothes are not appropriate for the occasion.
based on: The film is based on a novel.
close to: He's very close to his cousins.
delighted to: I'm delighted to accept your invitation.
dependent on: Our society is too dependent on technology.
dissatisfied with: She feels dissatisfied with her life.
excited about: I'm excited about something that's going to happen in my life.
famous for: Which city is famous for the Beatles?
fascinated by: Are you fascinated by detective stories?
fed up with: I'm fed up with all this work.
full up: You should stop eating when you feel full up.
good/bad at: Are you good at solving problems?
good/bad for: Crisps aren't good for you.
good with: She's very good with animals and wants to be a vet.
interested in: I'm interested in Russian history.
keen on: I'm not keen on Mexican food.
low in: This product is low in sugar.
perfect for: This hat is just perfect for you.
scared of: Is he scared of older children?
set in: The novel is set in nineteenth century London.
similar to: She's very similar to her sister.
sorry for: She felt sorry for him.
suitable for: Which qualities are most suitable for this job?
thrilled to: I was thrilled to get your invitation.

PREPOSITIONS AFTER VERBS

adapt sth for: The series has been adapted for both radio and television.
agree with sb/sth: Which ideas do you agree with?
apply for sth: You should apply for a job.
apologise for sth: You should apologise for what you've done.
apologise to sb: Did you apologise to Katy?
apply to: Apply to Ms Diane Richard at latableronde@gmail.co.
argue about sth: Sara and Dad often argue about little things.
arrive at/in: I was glad when we arrived at the campsite.
base sth on: The movie was based on a novel and set in California.
belong to: Perhaps this dress once belonged to Jennifer Lawrence!
call for: It was an emergency so we called for an ambulance.
click on: Click on the link to open the webpage.
collect (money) for: He wanted to collect money for the charity WaterAid.
compete against: To get a full blue, you have to compete against Cambridge or Oxford.
compete in: The two ancient universities compete in many sports and games.
complain about: I am writing to complain about my stay at your hotel.
complete with: Complete the text with the words from the box.
concentrate on: You can't concentrate on your work.
copy from sb: What should I do if a friend copies from me in an exam?
count up: Count up how many questions you answered 'yes' to.
depend on sth/sb: Our personalities depend completely on our life experiences.
describe sth to sb: Can you describe the photos to me?
disagree with sth/sb: I'm sorry, but I disagree with what you said.
divide into: Please divide the cake into five pieces.
dream of sth: When she was younger, actress Kate Beckinsale dreamed of being a writer.
glance at sth/sb: I glanced at my reflection in the window.
go along: We were going along a very quiet road.
go by (a means of transport): We went by coach to Wales.
go for a drive/a swim/a walk/etc.: One morning we went for a drive.
introduce sb to sb else: When is he going to introduce you to his family?

PREPOSITIONS

invite sb to sth: Thanks so much for inviting me to your party.

know about sth: A friend is someone who knows all about you and still loves you.

laugh at sth/sb: Do you laugh at the same things?

learn about: You help others and learn about yourself.

learn from: What can we learn from this experience?

leave for: We left for the airport at eight o'clock.

leave from: Which platform does the London train leave from?

listen to: Do you listen to the same kind of music?

live on: Mystery shopping is a good way to earn extra money, but it's not enough to live on.

live without: Minimalism means living without unnecessary things.

move away from: Susie is moving away from home.

pay for: Every penny he earned went to pay for the violin.

plan on: He was planning on staying there for three months.

play for: Does he play for an English team?

protect from: The emergency services protect us from crime and save us from danger.

provide sb with sth: WaterAid provides people around the world with clean water.

refer to: Who and that refer to people.

rely on: Can you rely on your friends?

reply to: It's rude not to reply to an invitation.

report on: Millie reported on what she saw at the company.

revise for: I'm really busy because I'm revising for my exams.

roll up: When you finish, you just roll up your mat and put it away.

sail across: On January 1, Graham sailed across the River Plate on a ferry.

search for: It's easy to search for information on the Internet.

share sth with sb: How do you share photos with your friends and family?

shop for: The girls went shopping for clothes.

sit down: After a while I asked them to do some pair work and I sat down.

sit up: Sit up straight, please, children!

speak to sb: Anna speaks to her father in English.

start with: I'm going to start with a joke.

stay with: My brother Liam is staying with us at the moment.

steal from: A thief is a person who steals money from shops and homes.

study for: We're studying for our exams at the moment.

suspect of: He works for the police so nobody suspects him of the murder.

take care of: He's going to take care of his skin.

take part in: You can take part in American football or windsurfing.

take place in: The first boat race between Oxford and Cambridge took place in 1829.

talk about: Use the words to talk about people you know.

talk to sb: Who were you talking to on the phone?

thank for: Thanks for your lovely email.

wait for: I'm still waiting for someone special in my life.

walk into: Just then the head teacher walked into the room.

watch out for: Watch out for 'false friends'.

work as: I'm not sure but I'd like to work as a teacher.

work for: My dad worked for the same company for forty-five years.

work in: Do you work in an office?

work towards: We're working as a group towards a common goal.

work with: I work with some lovely people at the office.

worry about: We're worried about our exam results.

write about: We asked you to write about people whose lives inspire you.

write back: I expect you to write back to me soon.

WORD BUILDING

Prefix	Examples
co- (= with, together)	coordination, co-worker
inter- (= between)	international, internet
multi- (= many)	multiplayer, multinational
re- (= again)	redo

Prefixes that give an opposite meaning

Prefix	Examples
dis-	disappointing, disagree
im-	impossible, impatient
in-	innocent, insecure
ir-	irrelevant, irregular
non-	non-governmental
un-	unpaid, unsophisticated

SUFFIXES

Noun suffixes

Suffix	Examples
-ment	government, arrangement
-tion/-sion	emotion, permission
-ation/-ition	communication, tradition
-ence/-ance	reference, tolerance
-ty/-ity	charity, quality
-ness	illness, weakness
-ing	hacking, shoplifting
-al	criminal
-age	language, image
-sis	hypothesis, analysis
-ure	adventure, future
-hood	neighbourhood
-dom	freedom
-er/-or	murderer, author
-ist	physicist, naturalist
-ant/-ent	assistant, newsagent
-cian/-ian	mathematician, comedian
-ee	employee

Adjective suffixes

Suffix	Examples
-al	fictional, social
-ic	realistic, pathetic
-ive	impressive, imaginative
-ful	awful, colourful
-less	priceless, homeless
-ous	ridiculous, hilarious
-y	guilty, scary
-ly	deadly, likely
-able/-ible	comfortable, terrible
-ed	armed, fascinated
-ing	terrifying, surprising

Adverb suffixes

Suffix	Examples
-ly	unfortunately, clearly

Verb suffixes

Suffix	Examples
-ate	create, nominate
-ise/-ize	advise, summarize
-ify	justify, modify

PRONUNCIATION TABLE

Consonants

p	perfect, helpful, happen
b	bossy, hobby, job
t	tennis, actor, attend
d	degree, middle, word
k	kiss, school, ask, coach
g	get, luggage, ghost
tʃ	check, match, future
dʒ	bridge, page, soldier
f	false, difficult, laugh, physical
v	verb, nervous, move
θ	third, author, bath
d	this, father, with
s	saw, notice, sister
z	zone, amazing, choose, quiz
ʃ	ship, sure, station, ocean
ʒ	pleasure, occasion
h	had, whole, chocoholic
m	melon, common, sum
n	neat, know, channel, sun
ŋ	cooking, long, thanks, sung
l	lifestyle, magically, kettle
r	respect, correct, arrival
j	year, use, beautiful
w	window, one, where

Vowels

ɪ	gift, invite
e	gentle, bed
a	bad, matchbox, plan
ɒ	lot, optimistic, wash
ʌ	love, but, luck
ʊ	foot, good, put
iː	reading, three, magazine
eɪ	race, pay, break
aɪ	twice, bright, try
ɔɪ	enjoy, disappointed
uː	two, blue, school
əʊ	boat, below, no
aʊ	shout, now
ɪə	year, here, serious
eə	chair, various, square
ɑː	mark, father
ɔː	bought, draw, author
ʊə	picture, floor
ɜː	hurt, third
i	happy, pronunciation, serious
ə	apprentice, actor
u	situation, visual, influence

SELF-CHECK ANSWER KEY

Unit 1
Exercise 1
1 close 2 gifts 3 generous 4 bride 5 reception
Exercise 2
1a 2c 3b 4a 5b
Exercise 3
1 anybody 2 somewhere 3 does 4 knows 5 is
Exercise 4
1 Does 2 something 3 isn't 4 Do 5 anything
Exercise 5
1 c 2 a 3 b 4 c 5 b
Exercise 6
1 spend all their 2 isn't anywhere to 3 do it myself 4 are enjoying themselves 5 make mistakes when

Unit 2
Exercise 1
1 good 2 revise 3 pass 4 marks 5 heart 6 subject 7 Open 8 did 9 check 10 put
Exercise 2
1 manager 2 beat 3 break 4 makes 5 fans 6 champions 7 draw 8 prize 9 versus cheat
Exercise 3
1 happened 2 Did she say 3 sat 4 didn't work 5 fell
Exercise 4
1b 2a, b 3a 4a, b 5a, b
Exercise 5
1A 2C 3C 4D 5D
Exercise 6
1 prize 2 to buy 3 good 4 Did Richard use 5 isn't

Unit 3
Exercise 1
1 break 2 stay 3 airline 4 hand 5 check
Exercise 2
1 in 2 off 3 for 4 at 5 off
Exercise 3
1 saw 2 While 3 which 4 was packing 5 when
Exercise 4
1 were 2 who 3 where 4 when 5 was
Exercise 5
1a 2b 3c 4b 5c
Exercise 6
1 were 2 which 3 put 4 package 5 lying

Unit 4
Exercise 1
1b 2a 3a 4c 5b
Exercise 2
1 department 2 honey 3 croissants 4 purchase 5 fit
Exercise 3
1 much 2 most 3 enough time 4 tasty 5 less
Exercise 4
1 Is there enough 2 more annoyed 3 least dry 4 is too little 5 a couple of
Exercise 5
1 as 2 rooms 3 much 4 The 5 for
Exercise 6
1 aren't many 2 is the spiciest 3 are not as big 4 a little 5 is too small

Unit 5
Exercise 1
1e 2a 3f 4c 5d
Exercise 2
1 on 2 prepare 3 do 4 room 5 sleep

Exercise 3
1 should 2 mustn't 3 could 4 didn't have to 5 shouldn't
Exercise 4
1 couldn't 2 has 3 mustn't 4 had 5 could
Exercise 5
1b 2a 3b 4a 5d
Exercise 6
1 doesn't have 2 should get 3 get rid of 4 had to wear 5 (to) do the dishes

Unit 6
Exercise 1
1 cautious 2 vote 3 settle 4 find 5 celebrate
Exercise 2
1 give 2 take 3 get 4 build 5 lose
Exercise 3
1 am going to try 2 is getting 3 will retire 4 we will be 5 Are you going to work 6 are you meeting
Exercise 4
1 It's going to hit the bridge!
2 I'm working until nine.
3 I'm going to grow my hair long this year.
4 Will it be sunny in Greece in February?
Exercise 5
1 twenties 2 appearance 3 relaxed 4 optimistic 5 confession
Exercise 6
1 going 2 off 3 with 4 shape 5 will

Unit 7
Exercise 1
1 make 2 working 3 take 4 work 5 on
Exercise 2
1 earn 2 co-workers 3 out 4 rise 5 serve
Exercise 3
1 ever 2 have 3 long 4 for 5 since
Exercise 4
1 We have/We've just finished our dinner.
2 Rachel has already written three books.
3 Have you ever done any voluntary work?
4 They have/They've never had a summer job.
5 How long has Sandra been a nurse?
Exercise 5
1 have been in Spain for 2 have never been 3 have just had 4 think of myself as 5 has not/hasn't started
Exercise 6
1 receptionist 2 education 3 creative 4 enthusiastic 5 criticism

Unit 8
Exercise 1
1 scientist 2 laboratory 3 experiment 4 data 5 analyse
Exercise 2
1 copy 2 paste 3 drag 4 Tap 5 swipe
Exercise 3
1 to leave 2 joking 3 to block 4 joining 5 trying
Exercise 4
1 tries 2 won't try 3 to try 4 will try 5 don't try
Exercise 5
1 If 2 on 3 to 4 will 5 are
Exercise 6
1a 2c 3b 4b 5a

Unit 9
Exercise 1
1 portraits 2 brush 3 on 4 in 5 place

Exercise 2
1 curtain 2 audience 3 stage 4 tripod 5 rehearse
Exercise 3
1 had changed 2 had started 3 had walked 4 had it been 5 had killed
Exercise 4
1 he would just have 2 he would be with 3 he hadn't got time 4 they had to film 5 he wasn't starting
Exercise 5
1 the film had finished 2 she was waiting for me 3 not good at singing 4 I hadn't practised them 5 the ending hadn't been
Exercise 6
1a 2c 3d 4b 5d

Unit 10
Exercise 1
1 stole 2 robbed 3 victim 4 wallet 5 suspicious
Exercise 2
1c 2e 3g 4a 5d
Exercise 3
1 was played 2 you would enjoy 3 are often stopped 4 were 5 would you do
Exercise 4
1 were/have been influenced 2 could 3 would earn 4 are often set 5 had to
Exercise 5
1 into 2 steal 3 been 4 are 5 would
Exercise 6
1 were a detective, you would 2 this film was based on 3 in the middle of 4 have been arrested 5 if people looked after